Commonly Used Edi

MN01054792

vi

To enter the vi screen editor, type vi. If you want to work on a specific file, type vi *filename*. You can use the following commands after you access the editor. The ^ represents the Control key; for example, ^C means press the Control key while you press C. For a complete list of vi commands, see Appendix C of *Absolute Beginner's Guide to UNIX*.

^C	Interrupt a search or global command.
^G	File status.
^L	Redraw screen.
^V	Input a literal character.
^W	Move to next screen.
^Z	Suspend editor.
^^	Switch to previous file.
$	Move to last column.
%	Move to match.
&	Repeat substitution.
'	Move to mark (to first nonblank).
(	Move back a sentence.
)	Move forward a sentence.
+	Move down by lines (to first nonblank).
,	Reverse last F, f, T, or t search.
-	Move up by lines (to first nonblank).
.	Repeat the last command.
/	Search forward.
0	Move to a space, move right by columns.
;	Repeat last F, f, T, or t search.
?	Search backward.
@	Execute buffer.
A	Append to the line.
F	Character in line backward search.
H	Move to count lines from screen top.
I	Insert at line beginning.
L	Move to screen bottom.
M	Move to screen middle.
N	Search.
Q	Switch to ex mode.
R	Replace characters.
U	Restore the current line.
Y	Copy line.
ZZ	Save file and exit.
a	Append after cursor.
b	Move back a word.
i	Insert before cursor.
j	Move down by lines.
k	Move up by lines.
m	Set mark.
n	Repeat last search.
o	Append after line.
p	Insert from buffer.
r	Replace character.
s	Substitute character.
u	Undo last change.
x	Delete character.
z	Redraw window.
{	Move back a paragraph.
}	Move forward a paragraph.
~	Reverse case.

The En

If you want to work on a specific file, type emacs *filename*. After you access the editor, you can use the following commands. For a complete list of Emacs commands, see Appendix C of *Absolute Beginner's Guide to UNIX*.

Basic Cursor and Screen Control Commands

Control+l	Clear screen and redisplay everything.
Control+f	Move forward a character.
Control+b	Move backward a character.
Control+n	Move to next line.
Control+p	Move to previous line.
Esc+a	Move back to beginning of sentence.
Esc+e	Move forward to end of sentence.
Esc+<	Go to beginning of file.
Esc+>	Go to end of file.
Esc+r	Move cursor to the line in the middle of window.
Esc+f	Move cursor forward one word.
Esc+b	Move backward one word.
Control+g	Stop an active operation or erase a numeric argument or the beginning of a command.
Control+x 1	Retain one window (kill all other windows).
Control+x Control+c	Exit Emacs editor.
Control+z	Temporarily exit to shell.
Control+x <n>	Split screen into *n* windows.
Control+X o	Switch between the windows.
Control+h a	Access the apropos help system.
Control+x k	Remove help text.

Major Mode Commands

Esc+x fundamental	Activates fundamental mode.
Esc+x text-mode	Activates text mode.
Control+h m	Access help on current major mode.

Minor Mode Commands

Esc+x auto-fill-mode	Toggle autofill on or off.
Esc+x auto-save-mode	Toggle autosave on or off.
Esc+x	Toggle overwrite mode on or off.

Editing Commands

Control+d	Delete the character to the right of the point.
Delete key	Erase the character to the left of the point.
Control+x u	Undo the most recent change.
Control+y	Yank back killed text.
Control+x s	Save some buffers.
Control+x Control+s	Save file.

Search and Replace Commands

Control+s+Esc+Control+w	Search for text in the forward direction.
Control+r Esc Control+w	Search for text in the backward direction.
Esc+%	Search for text and prompt for replace.
Esc	Exits without replacing any more text.
Control+x Control+f	Find a file.

sed

The sed editor is a stream editor; sed commands are entered at the shell prompt to process one or more lines in one or more files.
SYNOPSIS
sed [-an] *command* [file ...]
sed [-an] [-e *command*] [-f *command_file*] [file ...]
The following command options are available:

- -a   The files listed as parameters for the "w" functions are created or truncated before any processing begins, by default. The -a option causes sed to delay opening each file until a command containing the related "w" function is applied to a line of input.

- -e *command*   Append the editing commands specified by the command argument to the list of commands.
- -f *command file*   Append the editing commands found in the file *command file* to the list of commands. The editing commands should each be listed on a separate line.
- -n   By default, each line of input is echoed to the standard output after all of the commands have been applied to it. The -n option suppresses this behavior.

The form of a sed command is as follows:
[*address*[,*address*]]*function*[*arguments*]

NINE UNIX COMMANDS YOU'LL USE A LOT

cd
Change working directory.

cp [-ip] *file1 file2*
cp [-ipr] *file ... directory*
  Copy files.
- -i   Inquire whether a file will be overwritten by the copy.
- -p   Preserve modes (ignore umask) and modification times.
- -r   Recursively copy directories.

grep [-bchilnosvw][-f *file*][-e] *expr* [*files*]
  Search a file for a pattern.
- -b   Block number is printed before each line.
- -c   Count of matches is printed instead of actual lines.
- -h   Headers are not printed before each line.
- -i   Ignore case in comparisons.
- -l   List only the filenames that contain a match, once each.
- -n   Number each line with its line number.
- -o   Output headers on every line.
- -s   Silent mode. Only a status is returned.
- -v   All lines except those that match.
- -w   Word mode. Expression is searched for as a word.
- -e *expr*   Expression to use is *expr*.
- *files*   Files to search in.

lp
  Print text files.

ls [-acdfgilqrstu1CFLMR] *name* ...
  List contents of directory.
- -a   List all entries; in the absence of this option, entries whose names begin with a period (.) are not listed.
- -c   Use time when file status was last changed.
- -d   If argument is a directory, list only its name.
- -f   Force each argument to be interpreted as a directory and list the name found in each slot. This option turns off -l, -t, -s, and -r, and turns on -a.
- -g   Include the group ownership of the file.
- -i   Print the *i*-number in the first column of the report.
- -l   List in long format.
- -r   Reverse the order of sort.
- -s   Give size in kilobytes of each file.
- -t   Sort by time modified (latest first).
- -u   Use time of last access instead of last modification.
- -C   Force multicolumn output; this is the default when output is to a terminal.

- -F   Cause directories to be marked with a trailing /, sockets with a trailing =, symbolic links with a trailing @, and executable files with a trailing *.
- -L   If argument is a symbolic link, list the file or directory of the link references rather than the link itself.
- -M   List in Macintosh format.
- -R   Recursively list subdirectories encountered.
- -1   Force one-entry-per-line output format.

man -k [-M path] [-m path] keyword ...
man [-acw] [-M path] [-m path] [section] name ...
  Find and display reference manual pages.
- -a   All of the manual pages are displayed instead of only the first one.
- -c   Copy the manual page to standard out instead of using more.
- -w   Which manual pages would display are listed.
- -k   Keyword lookup of description lines (same as apropos command).
- -M *path*   Search *path* instead of $MANPATH.
- -m *path*   Search *path* in addition to $MANPATH.

mkdir *dirname* ...
  Make directories.
  dirname   Name of the directories to create.

more [-cdflMsu] [-#] [+#] [+/pat] [name ...]
  Browse or page through a text file.
- -c   Clear the screen before displaying each page.
- -d   Display user-friendly messages.
- -f   Folding is not done on lines.
- -l   ^L (form-feed) is not treated as an end of screen.
- -s   Squeeze multiple blank lines into one blank line.
- -u   Underlining is suppressed.
- -#   Number of lines per page.
- +#   Start displaying # lines into the file.
- +/*pat*   Start displaying two lines before the pattern *pat* is found.
- *name*   Name of the file to display.

mv [-if] *file1 file2*
mv [-if] *file ... directory*
  Moves (renames) *file1* to *file2* and removes any pre-existing *file2*. The second form moves multiple files into a directory.
- -i   Inquire whether *file2* should be removed if one already exists.
- -f   Force the move without question.
- *file1*   Name of the file to rename.
- *file2*   Name of the new file.

Absolute Beginner's Guide to UNIX®

Lisa Stapleton

Contributing Editors:
Jonathan Leer
Scott Parker

A Division of Macmillan Computer Publishing, A Prentice Hall Macmillan Company 201 West 103rd Street, Indianapolis, Indiana 46290

SAMS
PUBLISHING

This book is dedicated to my husband and best friend,
Loren L. Hart,
who helped and encouraged me during the writing of this book

International Standard Book Number: 0-672-30460-0

Library of Congress Catalog Card Number: 94-65312

97   96   95   94   4   3   2   1

Interpretation of the printing code: the rightmost double-digit number is the year of the book's printing; the rightmost single-digit, the number of the book's printing. For example, a printing code of 94-1 shows that the first printing of the book occurred in 1994.

Composed in AGaramond and MCPdigital by Macmillan Computer Publishing

Printed in the United States of America

Overview

Contents

Acknowledgments

I would like to thank my husband, Loren L. Hart. A true UNIX wizard, he helped with some examples and with the discussion of environment variables. My thanks also go to all who participated in bringing this book together, especially to Jonathan Leer and Scott Parker, who on short notice provided additional material for the book; to Mark Sims, who checked code examples and supplied more; and to Rosemarie Graham, Dean Miller, Deborah Frisby, and Mitzi Foster Gianakos at Sams Publishing for making this book happen.

About the Author

Lisa Stapleton is a computer journalist and a former programmer and engineer. A C programmer at Allergan-Humphrey in the mid-1980s, she began her journalism career in 1986, when she became the West Coast Editor of *Information Week*. She has also served as the Reviews Editor at *Computer Language Magazine* (now *Software Development Magazine*) and *AI Expert* magazines, and as the Silicon Valley correspondent for *Supercomputing Review*. She has written for *VARBusiness*, *Upside* magazine, and *Computer Graphics World*.

Recently, she spent a year as a consulting project manager at Apple Computer, Inc., before accepting her current position as the Products Editor at *UnixWorld's Open Computing*, a magazine dedicated to the use of open systems and products in mainstream business and at technical firms.

Introduction

UNIX is rapidly becoming the most popular operating system for companies and institutions who have exhausted the capabilities of their PCs or who are retiring their expensive, tired old mainframes. Making the change to UNIX is great for companies, because they get better productivity and a wide range of hardware and software options. But the change is not always stress-free for workers. That's why so many millions of people find that must learn UNIX, and many look forward to that with about the same relish they give to April 15 or to certain moments of their annual physical checkups!

If you're one of these people, or if you're a PC hobbyist who wants to learn something new, this book is for you. If you've used a computer before, even just to do word processing, you'll have no problem learning to list and grep like the best of the technoids. This book is a jump-start for beginners and will show you how to do the kinds of things that you need to do to get real work done *soon*. It won't change your life or turn you into Steve Jobs or Bill Gates, but it will get you started fast and show you the most important things to learn first. If you do want to be the next Steve or Bill, you can always follow up this gentle introduction to UNIX with a more advanced text later.

Most important for beginners, though, is that this book is truly for you. The way it's written will reveal the adventurous, interesting nature of UNIX, which started as a grassroots push by programmers to create something inexpensive, accessible, open, and geared to the way professionals really work. So fire up the computer and get ready for a guided virtual roadtrip through UNIX.

Conventions Used in This Book

The following typographic conventions are used in this book:

* Code lines, commands, statements, variables, and any text you see on the screen appears in a monospace `computer` typeface.

* When input and output code lines are shown together, the commands and other input that you type are represented in a **`bold computer`** typeface.

✖ Placeholders in syntax descriptions appear in an *italic computer* typeface. Replace the placeholder with the actual filename, parameter, or whatever element it represents.

✖ *Italics* highlight technical terms and emphasize important points.

✖ Optional parameters in syntax explanations are enclosed in square brackets ([ ]). You do *not* type the brackets when you include these parameters.

In each chapter, you will see icons that bring specific items to your attention. A glance at the icon gives you an idea of the purpose of the text next to it.

WARNING

This icon points out potential problems you could face with the particular topic being discussed. This is advice that you should heed.

Clue: This icon marks a bit of information that you may find extremely helpful as you put your UNIX knowledge into practice.

NOTE

The paragraphs marked by this icon often take you on a brief detour from the topic at hand to give you a neat UNIX fact or a bit of UNIX history or culture.

SKIP THIS, IT'S TECHNICAL

If you don't want anything more than the beginning essentials of UNIX, don't read the material in this box. Actually, you probably will enjoy this material, but you can safely skip it without losing your understanding of the chapter.

Bon voyage!

Why Everyone's Desperately Seeking UNIX

The Legend and Lore

In This Chapter

- ✖ *What is UNIX and who uses it?*
- ✖ *Is UNIX hard to use?*
- ✖ *Could your kids learn UNIX?*
- ✖ *What is an operating system?*
- ✖ *Why does UNIX have such a funny name?*
- ✖ *Who invented UNIX and why?*
- ✖ *Why are so many companies and people moving to UNIX?*
- ✖ *Where can you get more information about UNIX and its future?*

Learning the Legend

In this chapter, I'll tell you the legend of UNIX: its history, purpose, features, and probable future. After you've read this chapter, you'll know all you need to know to talk and think about UNIX intelligently. You'll know enough, in essence, to understand why people use UNIX and what it's good for. You'll also understand why businesspeople are moving in droves to use UNIX for more and more of their business operations. Perhaps most importantly from your perspective, you'll be able to bluff your way through conversations about UNIX, keeping up even with rocket scientists about general topics in the UNIX community.

Who Uses UNIX?

UNIX is one of the computing world's best-kept secrets. It's like the air: most people, both in and outside of the computer industry, take it for granted. A huge and growing number of American businesses use the computer system, yet few of the customers of these companies (and indeed, many of the people who work at them) have any idea that such an odd-sounding thing is processing their flight reservations (Northwest Airlines), running the retail outlets that they frequent (Wal-Mart and Burlington Coat Factory), and designing the airplanes in which they fly (Boeing, Hughes).

> **NOTE**
>
> UNIX-based computer systems create the special effects for many of the world's most popular movies (Disney Studios, Lucas Films, Pixar, Silicon Graphics). Also, at the nation's biggest supercomputer facilities, UNIX is the system that rocket scientists and geneticists use in their daily work, creating the world's next generation of miracles. From analyzing the effects of world population and famine on the environment to understanding how chromosomes work, UNIX is the world's computer workhorse.

Is UNIX Hard to Learn?

UNIX is much friendlier than its name may make it sound. *UNIXWorld*, a popular magazine for UNIX users, recently did a feature on UNIX in the home—it was a real eye-opener for me. Because UNIX is so easy to learn and to use, an increasing number of families are adopting UNIX as their home operating system. Mom, Dad, and the kids are all hooked into the same UNIX network, which runs on heavy-duty cabling throughout the house. The kids grow up thinking everybody uses UNIX, and they don't find it difficult or complicated. These children are surprised when they discover that some people use computer systems called DOS and Windows.

The kids love UNIX because it has opened up the world to them, not because of any technical merits. They can use it to send electronic mail (also called *e-mail)* to their friends across the country or around the world. Using UNIX to explore the Internet, they can find other children and adults who share their interests; they also find lots of free software, such as games and educational programs. They love UNIX because it's fun.

NOTE

The Internet is a series of wires connecting computers around the world. You can think of your cable company as something like the Internet. Your cable company can connect everyone in your city by a series of wires carrying, for example, CNN or the The Weather Channel to every television on the wire (cable). Your television is essentially a one-way receiver. With UNIX, your home computer becomes both a receiver and a sender of messages on the Internet.

WARNING

If you have children, they might be out-computing you! One man told me he was sure he'd spent only a half an hour teaching his daughters UNIX; after that, they taught themselves so well that now they occasionally teach him a thing or two about UNIX. Another man told me his 9-year-old son is so good at using e-mail that he's made many friends he's never seen. The son belongs to many UNIX newsgroups, which are similar to electronic bulletin boards, and is involved in a long-standing baseball simulation with his friends. He sees nothing strange about that, even though his mother told me that because he was the first child to ever participate in the game, the adults had decided to be extra-careful about their language.

For more information about getting UNIX for a home computing system, see the resource list later in this chapter.

The ease with which UNIX can be learned and used is part of what gives it such a bright future, with uses extending from the most esoteric scientific research to the humblest of home projects. UNIX hobbyists have been known to hook up their UNIX computers to run household and outdoor lighting, sprinklers, burglar alarms, and even fish tanks. If you saw the movie *Jurassic Park*, you may have glimpsed a not-so-distant future use of UNIX: the fictional park's perimeter-fence system and security were controlled by a UNIX operating system.

How Did UNIX Get Its Funny Name?

Perhaps what holds many people back from learning about UNIX is its strange name, which is responsible for a lot of confusion. As a writer for *UNIXWorld's Open Computing*, I'm used to long pauses when I tell people the name of the magazine for which I write. Every once in a while, I forget how odd the word sounds and how easy it is for other people to confuse it with its homonym, *eunuches*.

For instance, I recently met an old friend—a bright, aware person—whom I hadn't seen for years. She asked me over lunch what I was up to, and I told her I was a writer for *UNIXWorld*. After a long pause, she finally said, "Oh my, well, I guess they need their own magazine too, but how did you get into writing about *that?*"

Actually, there's an interesting history behind the name, and it's not what you might think. In 1969, UNIX was developed by researchers at Bell Laboratories in a project headed by a computer scientist named Ken Thompson. He wanted to provide an easy-to-use alternative to an earlier operating system named Multics. To show that the new system was different from Multics, but designed to solve some of the same types of computer problems, it was named Unics. Eventually, the system's name was changed to UNIX. The name has nothing to do with harem guards; if anything, its name is a testament to the sense of humor (or lack thereof) of the programmers who designed it.

SKIP THIS, IT'S TECHNICAL

In 1957, Bell Laboratories had a need for its computer center to run many short batch jobs. Originally, an operating system called BESYS was created for this need. Shortly afterward, Bell began to use different equipment and decided to join forces with General Electric (GE) and Massachusetts Institute of Technology (MIT). Together, the three created an operating system called Multics. Multics was a general-purpose multiuser and time-sharing operating system. Later, Bell abandoned Multics to pursue yet other endeavors. Dennis Ritchie and Ken Thompson proposed to write another operating system based on Multics. They began to write the new operating system on an old, little-used computer called a Digital Equipment Corporation PDP-7. Thompson wanted many new features in this operating system, including a tree-like file structure, a command interpreter like the shell, and access to various physical devices such as modems, printers, and terminals. Thompson and Ritchie decided to name the new operating system UNIX to distinguish it from Multics. This year, 1994, is the twenty-fifth year that UNIX has been in existence. Happy birthday, UNIX!

Even soon after its creation, UNIX was extremely advanced, incorporating many capabilities that didn't become widely popular until 10–20 years later, an eternity in the computer world. E-mail, for instance, was incorporated directly into UNIX, as were some rudimentary word processing packages. Keep in mind that this was in the 1960s and 1970s, long before Microsoft Mail, cc:Mail, and Davinci were a gleam in any programmer's eye.

What Is UNIX?

Programmers will tell you that UNIX is a *multiuser, multitasking operating system*. "Great," you say, "now I need to learn three new terms, not just one."

Well, let's break them up and put them into human terms. I'll start with the words *operating system*. If people were computers, our "operating system" would include our central nervous system; the part of us that handles motor coordination, hearing, and vision; the part that processes signals from our digestive system and glands; and the part that coordinates our speech.

To continue the analogy a little further, you may have heard people talking about *programs* or *applications*. A program or application is basically a set of instructions to the computer to tell it to perform a set of duties. For instance, your nose itches. Your brain, the "operating system," picks up this annoying little sensation and runs an "application" called "scratch-your-nose" to take care of it. With the direction and assistance of the brain, the "scratch-your-nose" application tells your arm muscle to lift your hand toward your nose. Next, it tells your hand to extend one finger and move it against your nose. The operating system continues to run the "scratch-your-nose" application until it receives a signal that the irritation has stopped. The operating system manages these operations automatically, without much conscious effort, in the human body.

An application depends on an operating system in the same way that the part of you that knows how to scratch an itch or to speak French depends on the parts of your brain that interpret sounds and sensations and that coordinate your muscles to move a hand or make words. Knowledge of how to move a hand or of the meaning of French words and grammar is like the application that runs on UNIX: it performs a complex set of instructions that depends on some basic functions being handled at a much lower level.

In other words, an application or *application program* does some sophisticated, specialized, high-level activity, whereas an operating system handles the general, low-level activities that all computers and computer programs must do to run properly.

> **NOTE**
> You have probably used applications without knowing it. For example, many televisions have a program that is activated by the remote control. To turn the channel, you press a button that activates the change-channel program in your television's "operating system." Some televisions have extensive programs for picture-in-picture and surround-sound decoding.

UNIX is a *multiuser* operating system. The term *multiuser* means exactly what it suggests: more than one user can use the operating system at the same time. Just as your neighborhood fast-food restaurant is built with multiple chairs and tables to serve many customers at once, UNIX is built on the assumption that many people may be using the same computing resources at the same time. For example, UNIX can have multiple terminals (keyboards with attached video monitors). Not all computer operating systems are like this. DOS—the most common operating system for personal computers—is not designed to allow several people, working on different but connected terminals, to use a single, common computer. Although you can buy products to modify DOS and give it some limited multiuser capabilities, DOS itself is not a multiuser operating system. Because UNIX is designed with the assumption that many people will use it to share their computing resources, certain features—about which you will learn more later—are universally available on UNIX systems.

Finally, UNIX is a *multitasking* operating system. Multitasking is, roughly speaking, what happens when a fast-food employee works alternately on filling two different orders at the same time, getting a drink for A while waiting for a burger for B, then wrapping the burger for B while waiting for fries for A. Likewise, UNIX manages its resources so that it handles several orders at the same time: when you're working on a UNIX system, you can run multiple programs at once. In Chapter 2, "UNIX Interfaces: Motif and Open Look," you will learn about graphical user interfaces, known as GUIs. With GUIs, you can have several views, known as *windows*, to the UNIX operating system. With these different windows, you can run a word processor in one while running a calculator in another. This multitasking capability is part of what has made UNIX so popular.

The other consequence of the multitasking capability of UNIX is that a particular computing unit need not sit idle simply because one user has left the terminal and gone home for the evening. The computer can turn greater attention, figuratively speaking, to the "orders" being submitted by other users who are working at other terminals. This feature of UNIX is important because computers are expensive; the less wasted time and more work done, the more productive a single machine can be.

Clue: Computers are so fast that, unless a machine is being used by several people, it's spending more time idling than working on problems.

Furthermore, the multitasking capability of UNIX means that it is good at harnessing the brains of many different computers. Many companies have turned to UNIX to help them run their businesses, because UNIX lets them get more bang for the buck.

From DOS to UNIX: Making the Transition

I have mentioned DOS several times. As you may already know, many people use an operating system called MS-DOS, an abbreviation of Microsoft Disk Operating System. To glimpse some of the differences between DOS and UNIX, look at the following code fragment. (If this is your first encounter with either operating system, don't worry; you can skip over this section.)

This is an example of what would appear on my screen when I start DOS, change to a new directory, list the files in that directory, look at a particular file called

ROADTRIP, copy the file into a new file called ROADTRIP.SAV, delete the old file, and, finally, look in the directory again to see that the new file has been saved. The DOS commands are shown here in bold:

```
Microsoft(R) MS-DOS(R) Version 6.22
          (C)Copyright Microsoft Corp 1981-1991.

C:\>cd tmp

C:\TMP>dir

 Volume in drive C is VOL_DSK
 Directory of C:\TMP

.              <DIR>      06-09-93    1:14a
..             <DIR>      06-09-93    1:14a
ROADTRIP            108  05-03-94    1:20p
        3 file(s)          108 bytes
                    137469952 bytes free

C:\TMP>type roadtrip
A journey of a thousand miles begins, hopefully, with an empty
bladder and all the appliances turned off.

C:\TMP>copy roadtrip roadtrip.sav
        1 file(s) copied

C:\TMP>del roadtrip

C:\TMP>dir/w

 Volume in drive C is VOL_DSK
 Directory of C:\TMP

[.]             [..]                ROADTRIP.SAV
        3 file(s)          108 bytes
                    137469952 bytes free
```

If, however, I would use the UNIX operating system to accomplish the same tasks, I would see the following output and would enter the UNIX commands marked in bold:

```
UNIX(r) System V Release 4.0 (excelsior-bb)

login: lisas
Password:
Last login: Wed Feb  2 06:55:53 from enterprise-bb
Sun Microsystems Inc.    SunOS 5.3        Generic September 1993
you have mail
$ cd /tmp
$ ls -l
total 1
-rw-r--r--   1 lisas     vip          106 Feb 16 13:20 roadtrip
$ cat roadtrip
```

```
A journey of a thousand miles begins, hopefully, with an empty
bladder and all the appliances turned off.
$ cp roadtrip roadtrip.save
$ rm roadtrip
$ ls
roadtrip.save
```

If you are used to working with DOS, this may seem strange at first, but you'll quickly see the advantages of UNIX.

The Economics of UNIX

The most important reason UNIX has become so popular is its universality. For years, AT&T was forbidden by law from profiting from the sale of UNIX, so it licensed the operating system to many computer companies who put the operating system on their computers and, in turn, sold the computers to companies and individuals. Over the years, UNIX has been licensed for use on many kinds computers, and therefore many features of UNIX are much alike on many different brands of computers. This means that people who make their livings working with computers can learn UNIX, and they don't have to relearn everything later when they have to work on a different brand of computer.

It may seem obvious that people shouldn't have to be retrained every time their company buys a new computer. Throughout the years, many computer manufacturers—such as IBM and Digital Equipment Corporation (DEC)—deliberately put their own proprietary operating systems on their products so that, once companies had decided to buy computers from one of these vendors, those companies would be afraid to ever buy computers made by anyone else, given the difficulty and expense of retraining employees for a new operating system. They would also have to rewrite all of their computer programs if they changed operating systems. Once a company committed to a particular operating system—from IBM, for example—that company was stuck with buying computers from IBM for years and paying monopoly prices for the privilege.

Moreover, the manufacturers often came out with newer, faster machines that would run only a newer, proprietary operating system put out by the same manufacturer. This meant massive disruption for many companies who had to rewrite their computer programs and retrain all of their people every few years. It was as if every time companies wanted to buy new computers, they first had to decide whether they wanted to learn a new computer operating system that was as different from their old one as Latin is from Russian.

NOTE

Businesspeople often had to say that they were an IBM shop or a DEC shop, because once they had bought computers from these companies, they had essentially committed to one of these computer manufacturers forever. (IBM and DEC weren't the only companies who tried to lock customers in, but they were by far the most successful.) Computer buyers, therefore, used to joke about having sold their souls to IBM and DEC.

With UNIX, the situation was different. People could buy computers that ran UNIX from many different manufacturers, so they weren't locked into buying one brand of computer. That made UNIX increasingly popular with people who didn't want to pay monopoly prices for their hardware. Most of these people felt empowered by UNIX, because it meant they had a choice of which hardware to buy.

Because UNIX was judged by so many to lead to lower computing costs, the U.S. government mandated that all of the computers it bought should be capable of running UNIX. Thus, all of the government bids in the 1990s and the late 1980s have had to discuss the UNIX capabilities of the computers to be bought.

NOTE

At many colleges and universities, the departments of computer science and mathematics have adopted UNIX as their operating system. AT&T was generous in providing to universities the source code for UNIX. This has given universities two benefits. First, they had an operating system that could be modified for their purposes. Secondly, they could give UNIX to students to learn how to write and modify operating systems.

The Evolution of Different Types of UNIX

Although UNIX systems today remain remarkably similar, almost every hardware manufacturer made at least a few changes to the basic UNIX they licensed from AT&T. They changed it, in most cases, to run faster on their computers (so they could sell more computers) or to do something unique that was important to their own customers. As a result, each UNIX is a little different from all of the others, even though there is a lot of commonality among them. In essence, it's as if each UNIX were a different dialect of the same language. If you stick to the central core of the language, you'll probably understand everything just fine. If you want to use all of the slang of each dialect, you'll have a lot more to learn every time you switch dialects.

AT&T's original UNIX has gone through a number of revisions over the years. Perhaps the most popular version is called System V, Release 4. This is often abbreviated *SVR4*, pronounced "Ess Vee Arr Four." Many of today's most popular UNIX computers claim this version as their heritage: Hewlett-Packard Company's HP-UX, IBM's AIX, the Santa Cruz Operation's Xenix and UNIX, and Silicon Graphics's IRIX.

Another company, Berkeley Software Distribution (BSD), has made some major changes and improvements to UNIX, and some very successful computer companies have used versions of BSD's UNIX on their computers and workstations. In particular, Sun Microsystems Computer Corporation, the first successful UNIX workstation vendor, used BSD as the basis for its popular SunOS. More recently, Sun has introduced a new version of UNIX—Solaris 2.3, which complies with the SVR4 standard while retaining many of the BSD extensions.

In 1989, concerned over an increasingly chummy relationship between Sun and AT&T, several computer companies banded together to create their own UNIX consortium, the Open Software Foundation (OSF), and their own variety of UNIX. The resulting UNIX, called OSF/1, is chiefly used by DEC in its Alpha line of workstations.

In early 1993, Novell, a Utah-based computer communications company, bought UNIX and the part of AT&T that was responsible for updating and selling it, UNIX Systems Laboratories, for hundreds of millions. In autumn of 1993, less than a year later, the company announced that it would be giving the source code to X\Open, a non-profit company that would be responsible for improving UNIX and licensing it to others.

Also in the 1990s, Microsoft Corporation, the huge software seller and operating system vendor, developed an operating system based on UNIX. This operating system, called Windows New Technology (Windows NT for short), combines many features that are similar to UNIX with compatibility with Microsoft's popular Windows software. Many people who already have Windows software are very interested in the UNIX-like operating system.

As of this writing, rumors also abound in the user community that some vendors—notably Sun—may come out with yet another version of UNIX that would have another name and would therefore be free from licensing fees. We will have to wait and see.

> **NOTE**
>
> This book covers the basics common to every version of UNIX. Don't worry about whether your system is the right one for this book.

The Future of UNIX

Although nobody is sure what will eventually happen to UNIX, some trends seem to be contributing to its growing popularity. (There are at least 2,000,000 installed computers running UNIX, and many of these computers are used in networked environments, where many people use one computer.)

First, the large workhorse computers that big companies use—called *mainframes*—are wearing out or are otherwise needing to be replaced. For one thing, running mainframes has become increasingly expensive. Mainframe software maintenance, combined with the special room requirements and hardware maintenance, can be very costly. Many companies have decided that small UNIX systems with applications running on several personal computers or workstations are a cost-cutting alternative.

> **SKIP THIS, IT'S TECHNICAL**
>
> The combination of small UNIX systems with applications running on several personal computers has been called *client/server* technology. This means that the personal computer is used to process information and the server is used to hold the data (a *server* is a centralized repository for information, such as e-mail and data). The process of making the adjustment to client/server or UNIX technology from the mainframe environment has been termed *rightsizing*.

UNIX is ideal for managing such networks because UNIX has many advanced communications features built right in—most notably a communications facility called TCP/IP. More and more companies are deciding they need to upgrade their networks to UNIX, making the UNIX operating system increasingly popular.

Finally, there has been growing unwillingness on the part of the people who buy computer systems for corporations (often called Management Information Systems managers, or MIS managers) to stick with the computers of any one computer company. Today's computer networks are increasingly a hodgepodge of computers from IBM, Hewlett-Packard, DEC, Data General, and others. It is common for UNIX to be the glue that holds these networks together. These are called *heterogeneous networks*.

Where Can You Learn More?

In addition to this book, which will tutor and counsel you as you find your way, there are many other sources of help. Many of these are online, computerized resources; they are covered in later chapters because you must first learn how to access such online sources. There are also many more traditional sources, such as magazines and clubs.

For instance, many magazines can help you understand the general UNIX landscape, as well as give you tutorials in up-to-the-minute, hot topics on the use of UNIX and the Internet. The following sources can help you with this:

UNIXWorld's Open Computing
McGraw Hill, Inc.
1900 O'Farrell St.
San Mateo, CA 94403
415-513-6800

Open Computing is aimed at businesspeople and at explaining UNIX and *open systems*—a term that loosely means the interconnection of different sorts of computers. The articles are generally written so that people of all levels—from beginner to expert—can follow them and learn something. Often, the articles take a light-hearted approach to UNIX. Particularly interesting to beginners is a "New-to-UNIX" tutorial column and a book review section, as well as very readable sections on industry and product news. The Internet and the Information Superhighway are also covered.

Open Systems Today
CMP Publications
600 Community Dr.
Manhasset, NY 11030-3875

Open Systems Today follows the UNIX industry and the computer business. The tabloid covers product information and industry news. It also contains personality profiles and business stories about prominent people and companies in the UNIX field. It is available free for people who buy a lot of computer equipment.

UNIX Review
600 Harrison St.
San Francisco, CA 94107
800-829-5475

UNIX Review is aimed primarily at programmers, but does contain some interesting industry news and columns. For instance, several literary columns are often extremely enjoyable for their intriguing wordplay, particularly if you have a background in English classics or literature.

In addition to these sources, there are many clubs for people who use UNIX. These *usergroups* often hold local, regional, and national meetings to discuss UNIX and related computer issues. The largest such national usergroup is called Usenix; if you're interested, you can call the organization for the location and meeting times of your local organizations. These people are usually quite sociable and will let you know that you're not alone in your quest to learn UNIX. The following is the usergroup's address and phone:

Usenix
2560 9th St., Ste. 215
Berkeley, CA 94710
510-528-8649

Another area of interest for many people who are learning UNIX is information about UNIX products. All of the previously mentioned magazines carry product news, but there is also a yearly book of all of the UNIX products on the market called the *Uniforum Directory*. It is put out by Uniforum Inc. and costs several hundred dollars, but if you or your company buys a lot of computing equipment or software, it's probably worth it. To order the book (or look for it in a library), you'll need the following information:

Uniforum Directory
Uniforum
2901 Tasman Dr., Ste. 201
Santa Clara, CA 94054
800-255-5620 / 408-986-8840

NOTE

Besides the journals mentioned here, several manufacturers—Sun and IBM (AIX), for example—have magazines dedicated to their particular kind of UNIX. Also, several journals are produced by usergroups that specialize in particular kinds of UNIX.

UNIX and You

The increasing popularity of UNIX is why so many people are learning UNIX for the first time. These novices, like you, are generally unimpressed by many of the more esoteric technical features that intrigued UNIX's earlier audience of programmers, systems analysts, and system administrators. Rather, they are intelligent, creative professionals who want to learn enough to do their work, which usually doesn't include C programming or writing operating systems.

Clue: Remember the section on applications and programs earlier in this chapter? Well, applications are made of commands that in detail tell the computer what to do. The commands together form what is called a *computer programming language.* There are many computer programming languages, just as there are many spoken languages—English, Spanish, and German, for example. Each language looks and sounds different, but each can convey the same meaning. Whether I say "Go fetch a pail of water" in English, or "Traiga un balde de agua" in Spanish, or "Gehe einen eimer wasser holen" in German, the meaning is the same. In computer terms, languages such as C, BASIC, and Pascal look different, but each can tell the computer to perform the same task. Dennis Ritchie and Brian Kernighan invented the C language to help finish the UNIX operating system.

As You Move On

This book is for people like you. It is a guide for those who wish to learn enough about UNIX to be productive in their own specialty—management, technical writing, accounting, manufacturing, or drafting—but who don't want an operating system to take over their lives. They also want to know how to use computers effectively for business research and communication, so they need to know how to use the Internet and e-mail to get the information they need from all over the world. Use this book as a roadmap to guide you through the territory. The book can illuminate rough terrain, point out traps and pitfalls, and show you how to triumph and conquer in the Information Age. It will help on your way as you begin your new adventure.

Rewards

* ✖ UNIX is not hard to learn or to use. Small children can learn it, and in many places, whole families use UNIX to send each other e-mail, run household electronics and lighting, and even manage their farms.

* ✖ UNIX got its name from programmers who wanted to compare and contrast its capabilities with Multics, which was a popular operating system when UNIX was created.

* ✖ UNIX was created by Ken Thompson and Dennis Ritchie in the late 1960s.

* ✖ UNIX is a multiuser, multitasking operating system, which means many people can use the operating system at the same time, and all of them can be doing several different things at once.

* ✖ An operating system is the brains and central nervous system of a computer. It handles communications, manages the way software programs give instructions to computer hardware, and handles such things as interactions with peripherals.

* ✖ UNIX has become popular because it is common to many different types of computer hardware and because programs written to use UNIX are fairly portable.

* ✖ Computer buyers like UNIX because they aren't locked in to any particular brand of computer.

* ✖ Companies are turning to UNIX to downsize their old mainframes and to upsize their networks of PCs.

* ✖ There are many different versions of UNIX, but they are as alike as different dialects of the same language. People who use UNIX don't have to relearn everything when they move from one UNIX-based computer to another.

* ✖ Several different magazines and organizations cater to beginners, including *UNIXWorld's Open Computing, UNIX Review, Open Systems Today,* and Usenix.

Pitfalls

* ✖ UNIX is not for every home. It requires a powerful personal computer or workstation to run properly. If you have an IBM XT, AT, or 286, you might find that you must upgrade to run UNIX.

* ✖ UNIX has many abbreviations that you must memorize, for example `rm` for "remove a file." Don't fear, however; with this book and practice, you'll learn them quickly.

✖ If you tell your family and friends that you're learning all about UNIX, they might react with embarrassment or raised eyebrows until you explain that you're not talking about *eunuches*.

UNIX Interfaces

2

Motif and Open Look

In This Chapter

- ✖ *What is multitasking, and what does it have to do with UNIX?*
- ✖ *What is a character interface?*
- ✖ *What is a graphical user interface?*
- ✖ *What is an Open Look interface, and what does it look like?*
- ✖ *What is a Motif interface, and what does it look like?*
- ✖ *How can I use the Motif interface to move and resize windows?*

Why Are We Talking About This?

When you first stare at a computer screen, it can look intimidating if you don't know what to expect. In this chapter, you'll learn about what you might see, and, I hope, you'll feel more confident.

UNIX environments have been around so long that you could be using any of a variety of *interfaces* to the computer. These interfaces can look very different from one another, but they all do the same kinds of things. They take the input that you give the computer through the keyboard or by using the mouse, and they show you the results of what you've asked the computer to do. User interfaces determine both how your computer display looks and how it reacts when you press certain keys or manipulate the mouse buttons a certain way.

User interfaces started as a plain and simple keyboard-and-monitor combination (known as a *terminal*) using a character interface. Early terminals allowed only one program to display output on the screen, and they didn't allow display of graphics. With later terminals, you were allowed to switch from one program to another, but the screen would "jump" from one application to another. If you wanted to look at your word-processing screen at the same time as your spreadsheet, you were out of luck. As terminal technology advanced and began to have capabilities for graphics, developers thought of putting a "window" on the screen to hold the output of an application. In another window, they put the output from another application. Thus, the windowing system was born. The user could see output from both applications and could toggle between them at the touch of a key.

Windowing systems are useful because they are a way to represent the multitasking nature of UNIX. What does that mean? As you know, UNIX is a multitasking operating system. This means that you can do several things at the same time. For instance, in the following chapters, you'll learn how to use UNIX commands. With a windowing interface, you'll be able to enter a command in one window, then go to another window and enter another command; then UNIX will work on processing both commands at the same time.

UNIX can process several commands at the same time, while you sit back and relax. Alternatively, you can tell UNIX to process some commands in "background mode" while you continue to use your terminal to do other things. While you are still entering new commands at your terminal for one task, UNIX can work on your earlier commands for a different task.

━━ ━━ ━━ ━━ ━━ ━━ ━━ ━━ ━━ ━━ ━━ ━━ ━━ ━━ ━━ ━━ ━━ ━━

Clue: You can do the same thing if you have a character interface. You enter an ampersand before whatever commands you want to run in the background. UNIX takes care of those commands, but you can still type new commands. You won't be slowed down if it takes UNIX a while to complete its work.

UNIX was the first popular operating system to have this capability, but now others have this capability also, such as IBM's OS/2 and Microsoft's New Technology (NT) operating systems.

In the Beginning

At first, people always talked to UNIX by way of character interfaces. A *character interface* is one in which you type commands at the UNIX command line, and it types back responses. It isn't visually appealing, and many people have found it difficult to use. Such interfaces are typical of older UNIX computers.

If this is the type of interface you have, then almost everything you see on the screen looks like typing on a sheet of paper. You don't see any pictures or shapes that look like windows.

Then There Was Light…Er, Sun

As UNIX became more common, people figured out that character interfaces weren't very friendly, especially to new users. In the late 1980s, several standards for graphical-user interfaces were developed. These graphical-user interfaces—commonly abbreviated GUIs and pronounced *gooeys*—became very popular. Companies began producing interfaces that looked as if they had small windows in which you would type or insert some kind of input. For instance, in the second half of the 1980s, Sun Microsystems Computer Corporation began shipping an interface called Open Look.

A typical Open Look interface (in this case, for a program called File Manager) is shown in Figure 2.1. Notice the part that looks like a triangle in the upper-left corner. If your interface looks like this, you're using the Open Look Interface.

NOTE

If you're using a Sun computer made before 1993, you probably have an Open Look interface. After that, Sun changed to a different windowing system, one explained later in this chapter.

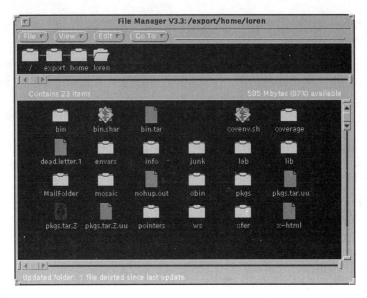

FIGURE 2.1.
A typical Open Look interface.

The drawings that you see in the figure are called *icons.* They can represent programs, files, or directories.

By double-clicking on these icons with your left mouse button, you can activate these programs. Most programs will then provide you either with written instructions on what to do next or with visual clues to indicate that you're supposed to, for example, click another icon. All you have to do is follow the directions, or the pictures, so to speak.

Also, notice the menu buttons at the top. They are File, View, Edit, and Go To. Each of these does exactly what you'd think. If you click the right mouse button on the little item called File, you'll see all of the things that you can do with a file. Similarly, if you do the same thing on the View menu button, you'll see all of the options for viewing things on your screen. To do any of these operations, click the right mouse button and follow the directions.

In the Open Look interface in Figure 2.2, there are many icons: one for a mail program called `mailtool`, one for a calendar program (the one that says 15 May on it), a wastebasket where you can dispose of files that you don't want, and a clock, as well as several others representing programs that the user, Loren, is running.

FIGURE 2.2.
Some of the many icons you could encounter in your Open Look journey.

Starting Open Look

Now, you should know that you probably won't see the windowing system when you first sit down at your terminal. You will probably see a regular screen or maybe a small, plain window within the screen, saying something like login:. This is a UNIX invitation to get started. When you log in—in the next chapter, I tell you all about logging in—the Open Look interface appears, either immediately or after you enter the following:

```
/usr/openwin/bin/openwin
```

The Mouse Buttons

Each of the mouse buttons has a different function, regardless of where you are in the Open Look interface. To use the mouse button, remember these points:

✖ The first, leftmost mouse button selects things. If you click this one, you select something or position your cursor for typing in a window.

✖ The second mouse button, which you'll use far less often, is used by some programmers to give users more options available by the mouse.

✖ The third mouse button, on the far right, calls up a menu when you press it. Which menu it brings up depends on where the pointer is when you press the button.

What Can You Do with Windowing Systems?

Windowing systems are not very difficult to use, for they involve only a few basic operations. You can close a window, make a window larger or smaller, move a window, type things into a window, or get help. The following examples show you how to do these things in this windowing system.

✖ To type something into a window, position the pointer (which usually looks like an arrow and moves when you move the mouse) in the window at the place where you want to type something. Then press the first mouse button. Now type ls -l. You'll see something similar to Figure 2.3, a list of the files that the user Loren has on his system.

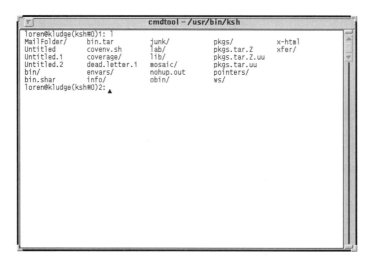

FIGURE 2.3.
Using a single window.

✖ On the upper-left corner of the window, you'll see a small square with something resembling a triangle or arrow in it. If you click on this by pressing the third mouse button, a menu pops up. This is the menu that enables you to close a window (in that case, the window becomes an icon, but you can still get the window back by clicking on its icon). You can also quit from the window by using this menu; in this case, the window (or icon) disappears completely and is gone for good.

✖ Notice that the corners are outlined in shapes that look like boomerangs. You can use these corners to resize windows. If you have the Open Look interface, read the next chapter about logging in, then come back to this section and follow these instructions to practice resizing windows. You can use your clock window for this exercise:

1. Position the arrow over the lower-left corner.

2. Press the mouse button down and keep holding it down.

3. Move the pointer to the right. The arrow will change so that it looks like a white circle. The window will expand in that direction. The same is true of the other corners; if you tug at them using the mouse, you'll expand the window in the direction in which you pull.

4. Now do the reverse. Follow steps 1 and 2, but when you get to step 3, move to the left. The window will shrink.

5. Now make the clock look more like a rectangle than a square by tugging to the right on the bottom corner. It should look similar to Figure 2.4.

6. Now do the same thing with the other corners to expand it until it looks huge (see Figure 2.5).

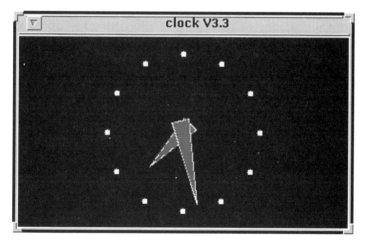

FIGURE 2.4.
For those who like wide clocks.

✖ You can move your Open Look window around. If you put the pointer on the title of the document or window, which is located at the top, and hold down the first mouse button, you actually move the entire window. (The bar that contains the title is called, creatively, a *title bar*.) Do this with the clock:

1. Position the pointer on the title of the document.

2. Hold down the first mouse button.

3. Move the mouse around. The window will move around, too.

4. When you're ready to "put the clock down," let go of the mouse button. The clock will "stick" wherever you "dropped" it.

✖ You'll also see a vertical bar, with arrows pointing up and down, on the right edge of the window, and a horizontal bar on the upper-left side. This is called a scroll bar, because if you put the pointer on the up and down arrows, you can scroll backward and forward through whatever is displayed in the window. If you put the pointer on the horizontal arrows, you can move the stuff that's in the window back and forth.

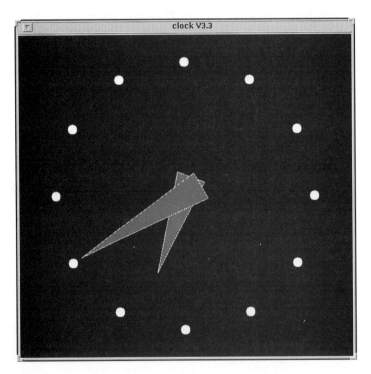

FIGURE 2.5.
It might be hard to work if there's a giant clock covering your workstation.

Moving Between Windows

Moving between windows can be a bit different from system to system, depending on how your system is set up. On some systems, you can move between windows by putting the pointer into one and starting to type where the cursor is. On others, you must actually click in a window before you can type in the window or change to it.

Adjusting Your Open Look Environment

You can customize your Open Look environment in several different ways. Using the Workspace Properties menu, you can pick which properties you want to change, including the font used in your windows, the mouse button order, and whether pressing the left mouse button displays a menu or selects whatever item you're on. You can also change miscellaneous properties, if you want. To change these properties, you go to the Workspace Menu and select the Properties menu item. You'll be presented with a list of things that you can change. Then you select the Fonts menu item, shown in Figure 2.6. Here, you can choose which font you want to see in your menus. Choose a typeface, then hold down the left mouse button and drag the mouse until your choice is highlighted, then let go. You've made a choice. To finalize it, click on the Apply button at the bottom of the display. (Until you apply a change, you can always change your mind and click on the close box in the far-left corner to close the window and forget about changing anything.)

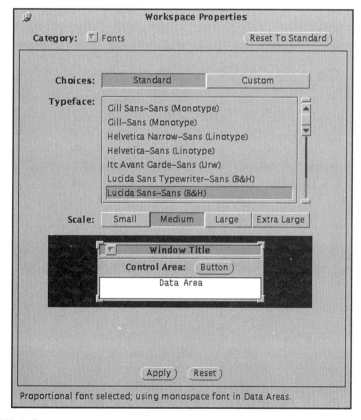

FIGURE 2.6.
Choosing from the available list of fonts.

You can also change whether pressing the left mouse displays a menu or just selects whatever item the pointer is currently on. If you want to change it, you can. If you decide you want to be like everybody else in your environment, you can click Reset To Standard, then the Reset button on the bottom of the menu (see Figure 2.7).

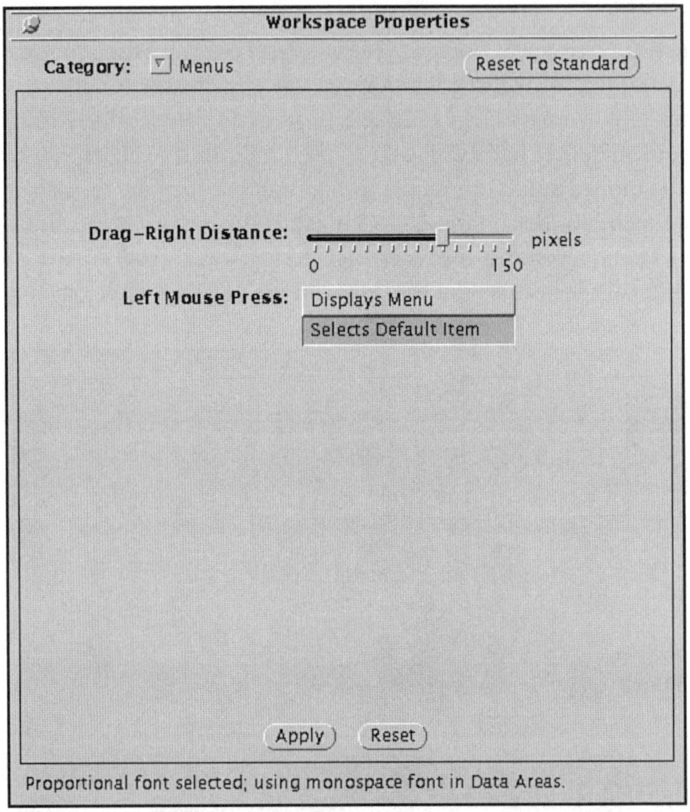

```
┌─────────────────────────────────────────────────────────────┐
│  ⌐              Workspace Properties                         │
├─────────────────────────────────────────────────────────────┤
│   Category:  ▽ Menus              ( Reset To Standard )      │
│  ┌───────────────────────────────────────────────────────┐  │
│  │                                                        │  │
│  │                                                        │  │
│  │   Drag-Right Distance:  ▬▬▬▬▬▬▭▬▬▬  pixels             │  │
│  │                         0          150                 │  │
│  │   Left Mouse Press:  ┌──────────────────┐              │  │
│  │                      │ Displays Menu      │            │  │
│  │                      │ Selects Default Item│           │  │
│  │                      └──────────────────┘              │  │
│  │                                                        │  │
│  │                                                        │  │
│  │                    ( Apply )  ( Reset )                │  │
│  └───────────────────────────────────────────────────────┘  │
│  Proportional font selected; using monospace font in Data Areas. │
└─────────────────────────────────────────────────────────────┘
```

FIGURE 2.7.
Setting the Workspace properties.

Another thing that users often want to change is the order of the mouse buttons. Some people want to have the first mouse button select things (which is what we've assumed here), and some would rather have the first mouse button pull up a menu. To change this, go to the Mouse selection from the Workspace Properties menu (see Figure 2.8).

Choose which alternative you want from the choices labeled Mouse Button Order. Then apply the change, or if you change your mind, just click on the Reset To Standard button in the upper-right corner.

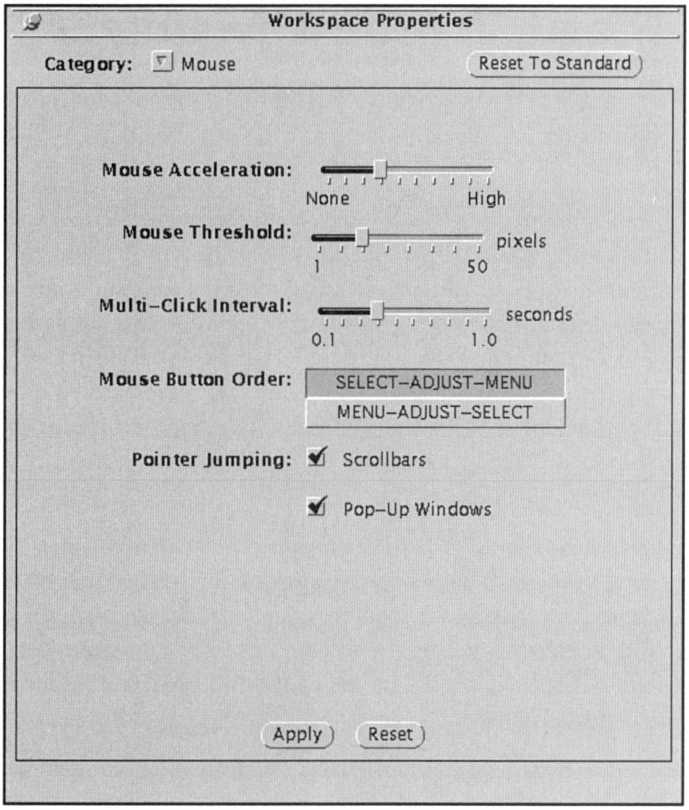

FIGURE 2.8.
Setting the mouse properties.

Who Could Ask for Anything More?

These are the main things that you can do with an Open Look interface, and these instructions will help you if you have an old Sun machine. But today, Open Look interfaces are becoming extinct. So many companies had standardized on a rival window system called Motif (pronounced *mo-teef*) that Sun was really the last holdout. Reluctantly, in 1993, Sun announced that it, too, would adopt the standard of its rivals, the Motif standard.

The Motif Window Manager

Almost all computer companies (other than those whose products run on PCs) that use a graphical-user interface (other than Microsoft Windows or SCO UNIX) use the Motif Window Manager.

If you're not working on an IBM PC, and you're not on an old Sun workstation, you're probably using a Motif interface, probably the Motif Window Manager. There are many Motif environments because so many companies have incorporated Motif into their computer systems. But they basically work similarly (although not identically), or their manufacturers couldn't claim to be Motif environments. So just as it's true that if you learn UNIX on one system, relearning it on another system means mastering at most another five to ten percent—minor differences, in other words—so moving from one Motif system to another is a matter of learning a few details.

Most people who work in Motif environments don't pay much attention to the windowing environment. That's because most of the time, you'll be using programs that conform to the Motif specifications, but add so much on top of the environment that most of the time, you won't even be conscious of it. Instead, you'll just follow the directions given for your word processor or compiler, and that's all you need to do.

What does the Motif environment look like? The following pictures are examples of objects that you might see in Motif environments, which are designed to be easily understood (see Figures 2.9, 2.10, and 2.11).

Clue: Look familiar? You might notice that these Motif icons look very much like the ones in the Open Look interface. Why is that? Both are based on something called X Windows, a way of representing communications between users and UNIX.

X Windows systems have become increasingly common in the UNIX world. Once, they were confined to UNIX systems that ran on very high-powered, complex computers. These computers had "brains" that were based on a type of computer chip that used an extremely fast kind of computer instructions called Reduced Instruction Set Computer, or RISC for short. These machines used lots of very short instructions, rather than complicated longer ones that did many things in each instruction, the type of instructions used before the introduction of RISC. These older systems were dubbed CISC, for Complex Instruction Set Computer.

FIGURE 2.9.
A clock in Motif.

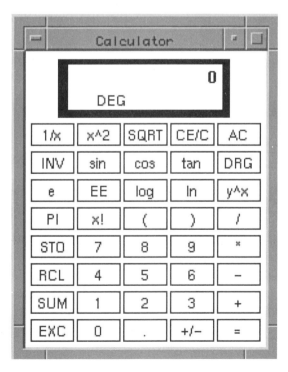

FIGURE 2.10.
Motif's built-in calculator.

33

FIGURE 2.11.
A mailbox icon in Motif.

At first, RISC systems seemed strange and unwieldy to people who were used to CISC. When the first RISC computers emerged in the mid 1980s, many people felt that they could never compete with the older, bigger computers that took up entire rooms in many big corporations, or with what were then the still-new IBM PCs and Macintoshes. But now, RISC machines have become quite popular. Today, almost all of the different popular computers are based on RISC. IBM and Apple Computer have announced plans to start making computers based on a RISC chip called the PowerPC. Sun, Hewlett-Packard, and IBM have all had UNIX machines based on RISC.

The popularity of these systems has, in turn, popularized X Windows. These days, thanks to sophisticated software, you can even get X Windows interfaces on many IBM PCs and compatible machines (such as those made by Compaq). For instance, Hummingbird Communications and several other manufacturers now make software that lets PCs run X Windows.

The Elements of Motif

The clock-like icon, called `xclock`, is exactly what you might think: a representation of an electronic clock.

- If you double-click the first mouse button on the box on the left, which looks like it has a minus sign, you'll get out of the window, and the little icon will disappear. You'll be out of the clock application entirely. To get it back, you'll have to enter `xclock` in some other window all over again.
- If you click on the middle box, which has a dot in it, the window will be iconified, and you can keep it around as a little picture until you need it. The work you've already done is still there; it's just shrunk.
- If you click on the rightmost box, which has a small square in it, the window will expand to fill the entire screen.

✖ You can also see bars around the right side and the bottom of the icons. If you click on these areas, you'll see arrows appear on the sides and bottom. If you're in a UNIX session, as the user Loren is in the following figure, you can hold down the first mouse button on the arrows, and what's in the windows will appear to "scroll" like parchment on a roll or, for you modern types, like paper towels on a roll, except that you can scroll in either direction. The same is true of the arrows across the bottom, which move what's inside the window to the left and to the right (see Figure 2.12).

```
                                  xterm
 editres*     mkfontdir*    xedit*        xmkmf*        xwd*
 fsinfo*      mwm*          xev*          xmodmap*      xwininfo*
 fslsfonts*   resize*       xfontsel*     xon*          xwud*
 fstobdf*     showfont*     xhost*        xpr*
 imake*       twm*          xkill*        xprop*
 listres*     xbiff*        xlogo*        xrdb*
 bin/X11:loren@searcher 3% cp README /tmp/README
 bin/X11:loren@searcher 4% ls
 README       lndir         xcalc         xlsatoms      xset
 appres       makedepend    xclock        xlsclients    xsetroot
 bdftopcf     mkdirhier     xdpr          xlsfonts      xterm
 editres      mkfontdir     xedit         xmkmf         xwd
 fsinfo       mwm           xev           xmodmap       xwininfo
 fslsfonts    resize        xfontsel      xon           xwud
 fstobdf      showfont      xhost         xpr
 imake        twm           xkill         xprop
 listres      xbiff         xlogo         xrdb
 bin/X11:loren@searcher 5% xbiff& xcalc& xedit /tmp/README&
 [1] 809
 [2] 810
 [3] 811
 bin/X11:loren@searcher 6% xclock&
 [4] 812
 bin/X11:loren@searcher 7% []
```

FIGURE 2.12.
A typical window in Motif.

✖ If you hold down the first mouse button on the bar containing the title (which is called, astonishingly, the *title bar*) and move the mouse around, you'll move the window around, too.

✖ To type in such a window, move the pointer to the inside of the window, put it where you want to type, and press the first mouse button. Then start typing.

✖ To quit using the Motif Window Manager, look for the menu item that says Quit or Exit. This will take you out of the window manager, and you'll see a standard UNIX character interface. You're still in UNIX, but your windowing environment is gone. To get it back, on most systems you enter `mwm` or `xinit`.

There! That wasn't so bad, was it? Now you know what the funny little things on the screen mean, and you've probably gathered that these are graphical, intuitive, and easy because they were designed that way.

What You've Learned

* In the past, most people used UNIX by typing in lines at a computer screen, and their computers answered them in words, line by line. This is called a character-based interface, or "character interface" for short.

* You now know that nobody is currently shipping computers with Open Look interfaces. However, until Sun gave up the standard in 1993, Open Look was the standard Sun workstation interface.

* You learned that the main visual difference between an Open Look interface and a Motif interface is the telltale triangle in the upper-left corner.

* Today, every major computer platform—other than PCs—uses the Motif interface. For the most part, the only computers that use the Open Look interface are those that Sun sold before 1993.

* The major window operations are opening, closing, moving, and resizing windows.

Rewards

* Windowing systems enable you to see output from multiple applications.

* In most windowing systems, you can transfer information from one window to another.

* Windowing systems give the programmer more options to communicate with you. As you use windowing systems, you will notice that error messages are elaborate and informative. Some programs even open more windows to accept information. You benefit because the applications are more attractive and are easier to use.

Pitfalls

* One of the biggest drawbacks of windowing systems is the amount of resources—such as memory and, therefore, money—they require to run. Your terminal or workstation must be capable of displaying graphics: this uses up both memory and processor time. You must also have a mouse connected to your workstation.

✖ You can be overzealous about windows. Opening window after window with application after application running can be convenient and fun—that is, until your machine runs out of memory and the processor is slowed to a snail's pace. Be frugal with your windows and applications.

A Guerrilla Guide to Getting Started

3

In This Chapter

✖ *How do you get into the UNIX system and get out of it?*

✖ *How do you type in a simple file and save it?*

✖ *How do you know where you are in the UNIX file system?*

✖ *How do you navigate through the UNIX file system?*

✖ *How do you create your own files and directories?*

✖ *How do you escape from failed commands and weird states?*

✖ *Who else is using your UNIX computer or UNIX network?*

✖ *Where and how can you find other people to help you when you get stuck and need help?*

✖ *What can you do when you get lost?*

Look, Bunky, It's Not So Bad

So you have to learn UNIX. Cheer up, Bunky, it's not so bad. At its best, learning UNIX is an exhilarating adventure, like a road trip. At its worst, it's not any worse than losing your luggage in Outer Mongolia. You're going to learn how to survive and even triumph.

As with any trip, you need to know where to start, how to read the roadmap, how to navigate through the UNIX landscape, who might be able to help you, and how to contact these allies.

Soon, you'll know enough about UNIX to be dangerous. In other words, you'll know the most important commands, and this will be enough for you to do much of the work you need to do. For example, you'll learn the most common uses of the following commands and procedures:

- ✖ `cat` (concatenate)
- ✖ `cd` (change directory)
- ✖ `cp` (copy)
- ✖ `login` (get into the system)
- ✖ `logout` (get out of the system)
- ✖ `passwd` (change password)
- ✖ `lpr` and `lp` (line printer, or print command)
- ✖ `ls` (list)
- ✖ `man` (manual or man pages)
- ✖ `mv` (move or rename)
- ✖ `pwd` (path of the current directory)
- ✖ `rm` (remove a file)
- ✖ `mkdir` (make a directory)
- ✖ `rmdir` (remove a directory)

Even more important, you'll know how to learn what you don't already know. You'll have some tricks up your sleeve when you get stuck, need to punt, or need to learn something new. This is the most important thing to know when you learn any new subject.

Your Greatest Advantage

In all great stories and in role-playing games such as "Dungeons and Dragons," heroes and heroines have their strengths and advantages as they pursue their Holy Grails. Listen to your sage, offbeat old advisor (me, of course), because here is your advantage: learning UNIX is a lot like learning how to drive a car; you have to learn how only *once*. After you've learned the basics, all UNIX systems will be about as similar as cars, and you'll only have to get used to a different feature here or there. Consistency in commands from one kind of UNIX to another is one of the UNIX operating system's greatest strengths, and it makes your task somewhat easier.

This aspect of UNIX was popularized in the movie *Jurassic Park*. Remember the scene where the velociraptors are trying to get into the secured control center where the heroes are holed up? While the adults are desperately trying to close the door on the menacing dinosaur claws, the little girl wanders over to the computer, types in a few words, and exclaims, "Oh, this is *UNIX*. I can do *this*." Seconds later, she enters the magic words, the doors slam shut, and the heroes live to fight again in the next scene.

She could do that because she knew the basics of the UNIX command set. (It also helped that half of the companies that contributed computer equipment to the movie sell UNIX products, but who am I to be so cynical?) UNIX knowledge is a very transferable skill, and people who have it can easily take their expertise from machine to machine and from job to job (and from reptile to reptile, for that matter). Remember that the next time you get frustrated or face a "meat-o-saurus." UNIX gets easier, almost automatic, the more you use it.

Your Greatest Strength

It's very important that you know that when it comes to computers you're the boss, even if you don't feel like the boss sometimes. Keep in mind that everyone, from the casual computer user to the world's experts, remembers the First Time At The Computer. It's intimidating for most people, but remember that a computer is nothing more than glass, plastic, and circuitry that has been designed to mimic human thought. You, on the other hand, have the power to think, and the character to persevere and to triumph. Computers have no character and no will. As the announcer used to say on the old "Outer Limits" series, "We (humans) control the horizontal, we control the vertical…" We humans do control computers. We just have to phrase our instructions in a way that computers can understand. Remember this if you ever feel that the computer is getting the better of you.

> **WARNING**
>
> If you remember the television show *Police Squad*, then you remember that some of the silly antics of the characters were the result of literalism. In one classic line, Lt. Drummer would tell his partner, "Cover me, I'm going in," and a blanket or coat would be thrown over him; you and I know that what he really wanted was cover fire.
>
> Computers are much like the characters in the show; they take every command literally. This means that if you tell UNIX to remove all your files, the files are gone forever!

Your Computing Environment

You will probably be talking about your *computing environment*. This term has nothing to do with ecology, but refers to the general setup of your computers and peripherals. (Peripherals are what attach to computers, such as printers, detachable disk drives, and display monitors.) Your environment consists of both a hardware and a software environment.

A hardware environment includes all of the computers and physical devices that are hooked to them. Depending on your computing environment, your hardware setup can be one of several different kinds:

* ✖ A stand-alone workstation
* ✖ A diskless workstation
* ✖ A terminal hooked into a UNIX host

Stand-Alone Workstation Users

If you're at a stand-alone workstation, you aren't relying on other systems for your operating system. A stand-alone workstation usually has its own processor and memory. A stand-alone workstation can be attached to other systems on a network, but it doesn't rely on these computer for resources. Remember the Internet I told you about in Chapter 1, "Why Everyone's Desperately Seeking UNIX"? The Internet is a network. A network allows computers to send e-mail and to share printers.

> **SKIP THIS, IT'S TECHNICAL**
>
> The *processor*, also called the *central processing unit* or *CPU*, is the heart of every computer. It is similar to your brain; it is the "thinking" part of your computer. If you give the processor a math equation such as 1+1, the processor adds the two numerals together and returns the answer, 2.

If this is your situation, you need to start or *boot* your UNIX work sessions by making sure that your computer is turned on. Because there are so many different kinds of computers, you'll need to find out where the ON/OFF switch is by asking someone, by looking at the instructions that came with the computer, or by looking for the ON switch.

Clue: Sometimes called the *power switch*, the ON switch or button is sometimes labeled with 0 on one side and 1 on the other (1 is ON for these models).

> **WARNING**
>
> Don't be trigger-happy with that ON/OFF button. UNIX prefers to be left on. While UNIX is running, it is actively managing its resources. If you turn UNIX off "cold turkey," you can damage the UNIX file system. The UNIX file system holds your files and possibly the files of many other users.

Some workstations are designed to stay on forever, and some have a sleep mode that dims the screen but lets you immediately start working at the same place you left off. If you're unsure about whether or not to turn off your computer, you could ask a knowledgeable person at your workplace. If it's your home computer, then you'll probably want to turn it off when you're done to save on power costs, unless you get direct electronic mail feeds from the Internet. (You probably don't.) There is no harm in doing so, as long as you always follow the proper procedures before you turn off the power.

Clue: If you really must turn off the workstation that UNIX is operating on, you might be interested in this—most UNIX operating systems have a command called shutdown. The shutdown command syntax varies from one UNIX type to the next. Later in this chapter, I'll tell you how to use the man command to display instructions on shutdown and various other UNIX commands and procedures.

Diskless Workstation Users

If you're working on a diskless workstation, your computer relies on a host server for its operating system. A *host server* is a stand-alone computer with a large amount of disk storage and memory to allow the diskless workstation to boot off its operating system. Your system administrator will have set up the host and the workstation to make this little bit of magic happen. Diskless workstations usually have a processor and some memory, but as the name implies, it is diskless. This means that you can save and retrieve your files only to and from the host.

Clue: If you try to boot your diskless workstation and it doesn't start, there might be several causes. The following are two of the more obvious ones:

- ✖ Your workstation might not be connected tightly to the network.
- ✖ The host computer may have a problem. Call your system administrator and ask if the host computer is OK. If it is, tell your system administrator that your workstation is having problems.

Diskless workstations can do all the things that stand-alone workstations can do. If you compare the two, however, you might notice a little difference in performance, such as slowness in the diskless workstation when the host computer is swamped. Diskless workstations do require a network.

WARNING

If you're on a network, check with your system administrator before you turn off your workstation.

Some businesses hook their computers together in such a way that, at night, when not many people are working, the brains of the computers all work together on big problems, such as processing all of the day's business transactions. This is known as *distributed processing*. If you're on a network, you should never turn off your computer unless you've been told that it's OK to do so. Otherwise, you could cause others to lose hours of work if they get kicked off the computer unexpectedly, without having a chance to save all of their work. That, in turn, might make you a very unpopular character in your workplace.

I found this out the hard way when I first made the transition from working on a single, stand-alone workstation to a network. I thought that I was being conscientious by shutting down and turning off my computer when I left work. The next day, there was strongly worded e-mail from an irate programmer who, unbeknownst to me, regularly worked from home by logging into several machines, including mine. When I turned off my computer, he'd been in the middle of something, and he'd immediately been disconnected and lost all of his work for that session. It took a lot of sweet talk, a lot of crow-eating, and a huge box of chocolate-chip cookies before I managed to get back on his good side.

Clue: Programmers seem to be responsive to food. Remember this if you ever need a programmer to help you. A Snickers bar can take you a long way.

Terminals Hooked to a UNIX Host

You might be working in the third type of environment: terminals connected to a central computer. Terminals are primarily input-and-output devices, a keyboard and monitor with a small amount of intelligence. Terminals don't have the brains to do all the processing that a full computer can handle. Tied to a central computer, terminals are a great solution for many businesses. Each terminal is much cheaper than a full workstation would be, and many people can type commands at their terminals at the same time. This is because the central computer is so much smarter and faster than all of the terminals connected to it; it can keep up with all of the terminals and people who are asking it to do things. The computer takes only a tiny fraction of a second to process a request for information, and it takes people far longer than that to type their requests.

You'll be able to communicate with other users on the computer through e-mail, because you're all hooked into the same place. You may even be able to talk to people worldwide using the Internet.

Clue: In this environment—terminals connected to a central computer—it's OK to turn off your terminal when you quit using it. Just make sure you remember to turn it back on before you start working again! In many places, you'll need to tell the computer you're ready to leave by typing something such as `bye`, `exit`, or `quit`. More on that later.

Making Friends in High Places: Your Most Powerful Allies

At most UNIX installations, you'll meet a person called a *system administrator* (or the *SA,* in UNIXspeak). Take it from me, it is worth getting to know this person. System administrators control access to all the computers, keep them in good working order, handle all hardware and software changes to the network, and make sure that all the communications which tie the computers together are working correctly.

First, You Need the Magic Words

Before you get started, you need to be authorized to use UNIX. This means you need to get an account or account name, often called a *login name*—a loose term meaning a name by which the computer knows you—and permission to use UNIX. In networked UNIX systems, only system administrators have the magic words to create an account for you. After the SA has done that, you'll get your own magic words: a login name and a password.

The login name (sometimes called the *account name*) usually looks something like your personal name, and it gives you an electronic workspace of your own. In this workspace, you can create your own documents and store your own information, and you can deny access to these documents and information to others, if you wish. UNIX users often refer to this as your home directory. When you log in, you are automatically put into your home directory. I'll go into the concept of directories later, but the important thing is that each user on the system has one; you have yours, and you can do what you want in your home directory without affecting the documents and information in the home directories of other people.

The *password* you'll get is a security precaution so that unwanted visitors can't pretend they're you. It can be composed of letters and numbers. In many computer systems, it must have a combination of uppercase and lowercase letters as well. This is because UNIX distinguishes between uppercase and lowercase letters, and using a combination of the two decreases the probability that someone could guess your password.

> **NOTE**
> Many SAs require you to use at least six alphabetical characters and two non-letters. This is to make it difficult for "spies" to figure out your password.

Clue: When selecting a password, you should observe the following rules:

✖ Don't use derivations of your name. Passwords based on names are far too easy to figure out, because the name helps limit the number of letter combinations a code-breaker must try.

✖ Don't use the name of your kids, spouse or significant other, parents, dog, or cat.

✖ Don't use important dates, such as birthdays and anniversaries.

✖ Don't use your telephone number.

✖ Don't end your password with a number or increment the number every time you change your password.

✖ Do use a combination of upper- and lowercase letters with numbers and punctuation marks (!@#$%&). UNIX is a case-sensitive operating system. This means that uppercase *M* and lowercase *m* are treated as different characters.

✖ Do use passwords that sound like phrases, such as `MyHeadHurts`, `Yikes!`, `Im4Utwo`, and `End2End`.

The first time you log in to UNIX, you should change your password. Most system administrators will make the system prompt you for a new password. I'll tell you how to change your password later in this chapter.

Clue: Some companies have either shortcuts or additional procedures for logging in. Therefore, it's a good idea to ask the system administrator if the standard login procedures are enough, and if not, what else you need to do.

WARNING

As soon as you can, memorize your password and destroy the paper copy of it. Until you destroy it, make sure you don't keep the copy anywhere near your computer, because if you're on a network, unscrupulous people can gain entry by using your password and can do a tremendous amount of damage in your name. Above all, the worst thing you can do is to put a stick-on note on your computer with your account name and password on it. This may seem an obvious point, even insulting to your intelligence, but an operator for my bank once told me that about 25 percent of the people who use automated teller cards actually write the number on the card, so I figured I'd better warn you.

Logging In and Out

When you sit down at a UNIX computer, workstation, or terminal, you should see a login line and perhaps a welcome, something like this:

```
Welcome to SAMS Publishing (Solaris 2.3)

login:_
```

The cursor should appear next to login: (indicated by the underline in this example). Type your login name, then press the Enter key.

NOTE

On some keyboards, the Enter key is called the Return key. From now on, unless otherwise stated, you should press the Enter key after all of the commands you type. That's how UNIX knows that you're done typing a line.

You should see something like the following:

```
password:
```

Type your password. Don't be alarmed if the letters don't show up as you type them. This is a security precaution so that nobody can look over your shoulder while you're typing and learn your password. After you have typed in your password, press the Enter key. You may see some important messages or information that you should read. These messages tell you when the system will go down, news of the day, and other special information.

Let's go over an example. When I log in, the sequence looks like this:

```
UNIX(r) System V Release 4.0 (sams)

login: lisas
password: <what I type here is not displayed>
Last login: Wed Feb  2 06:55:53 from enterprise-bb
Sun Microsystems Inc.    SunOS 5.3        Generic September 1993

   .
   . (Some informative system messages appear here.)
   .
$ _
```

Clue: In this book, whatever you type into the system is marked in bold when shown with the system's response, as in the preceding example. Remember that after you type the bold characters, you should press the Enter key.

Clue: If your first login wasn't successful, try again. You might have mistyped your password. Also, make sure that you type your password and login name in the correct case. Type uppercase and lowercase letters exactly as they were given to you. UNIX considers the passwords hero, HERO, and heRO to be three different passwords, not one.

Also, if you mistype something when you're typing in your login name or password, many UNIX systems make you start over, rather than let you backspace or delete.

Sometimes, a system administrator will give you a password and then tell you to change it as soon as you get on. Very often, they'll make your first password the same as your name, but of course, it's easy for a dishonest person to guess that your password could be your name.

To change your password, you must be logged in. Then you enter the `passwd` command, and you'll be prompted to change your password, as in the following example:

```
$ passwd
Changing password for lisas.
Old password: End2End
New password: Yikes!
Retype new password: Yikes!
```

For the sake of this example, I'm showing you here the old and new passwords. Normally, when changing passwords, you will not see anything you type after the colon.

Keep in mind what makes a good password, and choose one carefully. Worrying about your password may seem a little bit paranoid—after all, your files won't exactly contain state secrets—but once a hacker gets into a UNIX system in a networked environment, the intruder can easily get to the other computers on the network. Then the intruder can change or obliterate expensive data and programs, wreaking havoc on businesses or individuals. Better safe than sorry!

> **WARNING**
>
> When your system administrator gives you an account name and a password, you have a responsibility—to your colleagues and to yourself—to keep your password secure. If, for example, I break your password and enter your network with malicious intentions, I can remove files, make changes to data through applications that you have access to, and send messages to your boss, saying that his mama wears army boots. Who will get blamed? Not me, but you! So be paranoid about your password security.

UNIX and Shells

After you have entered the system, you should see a shell prompt character, such as the dollar sign in the last line of this example:

```
UNIX(r) System V Release 4.0 (sams)

login: lisas
Password: <what you type here is not displayed>
```

```
Last login: Wed Feb  2 06:55:53 from enterprise-bb
Sun Microsystems Inc.   SunOS 5.3    Generic September 1993
you have mail
$ _
```

This is called the *shell prompt* because it prompts you to do something. It is your clue that UNIX is ready to process your next command. For this reason, the line on which you type your commands is called the *command line*. You used the command line when you changed your password with the `passwd` command.

The part of UNIX that handles your interaction with UNIX is called the *command interpreter* or *shell*. There are several common shells, and you could be using any one of them. If you see the $ prompt, you are probably using the Bourne shell or the Korn shell. If you see the % prompt, you're probably using the C shell.

There are some differences in these shells and in the way some commands work in these shells. Most of these differences are only important when you're doing serious programming at the more advanced levels. In this book, in the few places where there are big differences that you might notice, I'll note them and warn you about them. Your job is to not get too excited when there are minor differences in the way your screen looks when you execute commands.

Later in this book, I'll cover some of these differences in greater detail, and I'll show you how to pick the best shell for the kind of work you do. Changing back and forth between the shells will also be covered, but for now, it's enough for you to know what a shell prompt looks like and the basic definition of a shell: the part of UNIX that handles the processing of your commands.

Looking Around for Your Buddies

What can you do, now that you've successfully logged in?

The first thing you can do is enter a simple command. The `who` command tells you who else is logged on the system, which can be useful if you need help. (If your computer isn't connected to anybody else's computer, you'll see just your own name.)

```
$ who
lisas     ttyp9   Jan 10 09:09
loren     ttyp10  Jan 10 08:32
marks     ttyp2   Jan 10 07:06
zacharyp  ttyp3   Jan 10 07:01
carolynp  ttyp4   Jan 10 07:20
deborahf  ttyp5   Jan 10 07:28
scottp    ttyp6   Jan 10 07:31
$ _
```

The login names of the current users are on the left. The entry immediately to the right of the name tells you what machine, window, or device they're using. The date is next, and the time at the far right tells you when other users logged in. If you see other such names, you're not alone on the UNIX system.

Exploration: Getting to Know the Natives

If you're on a network, you can send e-mail to anyone who is logged in. If not, you can send e-mail to yourself.

Let's try the easy stuff first. To send e-mail, enter the `mail` command, followed by the login name of the person to whom you're sending e-mail. Then type your message and press Enter. To finish entering your message, press the period key (dot), then press Enter. This will send your message and put you back at your shell prompt. Try it by sending e-mail to yourself, as I have done here:

```
$ mail lisas
This is just a test. It's my very first UNIX e-mail.
. <Press Enter>
$ _
```

The name after the `mail` command is called the *address* of the mail message you're about to send. Most of the time, this is your login name or the login name of the people to whom you want to send e-mail.

Clue: If you type the dot, followed by the Enter key, and you don't see the shell prompt, hold down the Control key and press *d* (that is, press Control+d), and see if that works. If it does, then you should end all of your e-mail this way.

To read your e-mail, use the `mail` command again. You will find that many UNIX commands have multiple uses. The `mail` command both sends and reads messages. Look at this e-mail, the message I just sent to myself:

```
$ mail
From lisas Wed May  4 06:48:35 1994
Return-Path: <lisas>
Received: by sams.mcpnet (4.1/SMI-4.1)
        id AA16560; Wed, 4 May 94 06:48:35 EST
Date: Wed, 4 May 94 06:48:35 EST
From: lisas
```

```
Message-Id: <9405041148.AA16560@sams.mcpnet>
To: lisas
Subject:
This is just a test, but it's my very first UNIX e-mail.
```

Pressing the Enter key the first time shows you your message and the header information, which is the part that has the `From:` and `To:` information, as well as the date and time sent and received. UNIX adds these parts automatically. Pressing Enter a second time shows you the contents of the message. If there had been more than one message, you would have kept pressing Enter to read each one, and when you had read the last one, pressing Enter would have returned you to the shell prompt.

SKIP THIS, IT'S TECHNICAL

The e-mail header shows how your e-mail got to you. If you look at the preceding example, you'll notice various lines with strange combinations of characters. The line beginning with `From` is who sent you the message and when. In this case, I sent myself a message. The line beginning with `Return-Path:` is the address of the person who sent the message. It is used by the sender of e-mail when he or she wants a reply to a message.

The `Received:` line demonstrates how e-mail is somewhat like the U.S. Postal Service. Your postal mail is dropped off in a box in your hometown. A mail carrier goes to the box and puts it into the truck to be sent to the address on the envelope. When it arrives at its destination, it is taken to the address. In the case of UNIX e-mail, every time the mail message is passed from "mailbox" to "mailbox," a record is kept of who touched it. If your e-mail message has to go a long way on the Internet, this header will be huge.

The `Date:`, `From:`, `To:` information is the part of the header that you'll be most concerned about. You'll notice that these lines have more readable information. The `Message-ID:` line is basically a unique identifier for the message—you can ignore it most of the time.

To send e-mail to someone else, you should get that person's login name from the `who` command. (If you're sending e-mail to yourself, this step is unnecessary.) Remember, the login name will probably be the entry that looks most like a name, and in most UNIX systems, it will be on the far left, as in the following example:

```
$ who
lisas     ttyp9    Jan 10 09:09
loren     ttyp10   Jan 10 08:32
marks     ttyp2    Jan 10 07:06
```

```
zacharyp ttyp3   Jan 10 07:01
carolynp ttyp4   Jan 10 07:20
deborahf ttyp5   Jan 10 07:28
scottp   ttyp6   Jan 10 07:31
$ _
```

To address the e-mail, type the following command,

```
mail otherloginname, yourloginname
```

where `otherloginname` is the account where you want to send e-mail, and `yourloginname` is the name you used when you logged in (not your password, but the one you typed at the login prompt). This command will send e-mail to the person using `otherloginname`, and it will send a copy to you at `youraccount`. (If you're sending e-mail to yourself, you'll get two copies of the same message.)

Now type a simple message, like the following:

```
Hi, I'm just getting started using UNIX. This
is my first mail message. Could you let me know
if you get it? <Enter>
.<Enter>
$ _
```

> **NOTE**
>
> In the preceding example, the word *Enter* in angled brackets is merely to remind you that you should press the Enter key.

You've just "reached out and touched someone." Congratulations! You've sent e-mail, your first useful work on a UNIX system.

You can send copies of e-mail to any number of people. You just need to separate their names with commas. In the last example, instead of entering `mail otherloginname, yourloginname`, you could have also sent e-mail to users Jane and Jim by starting with the following command and doing everything else exactly as before:

```
$ mail otherloginname, yourloginname, jim, jane <Enter>
```

Later, you may want to see if you've received a response to your e-mail. To do this, make sure you're logged in (you'll be logged in if you haven't logged out or if you haven't left your computer unattended for so long that the computer gave up on you and automatically logged you out). Enter the `mail` command at the prompt (remember to press Enter). When I did this recently, I got a listing that looked like this:

```
1 loren@sams.com Wed Jan 1 8:40 1644 Raratongan getaway
```

Of course, yours will look a little bit different, because you'll either have a listing of your own messages from your own friends, or you'll have no e-mail at all. My e-mail listing told me that

- ✖ I had one message.
- ✖ It was from loren@sams.com (his e-mail address).
- ✖ It was sent on Wednesday, January 1 at 8:40 a.m.
- ✖ It was about our upcoming adventure to Raratonga, in the South Seas.

To read the e-mail, I press Enter again. The message is displayed:

```
Let's really take our vacation someplace exotic this year. Let's
go back to Raratonga. South Seas, rainforest interior, jungle
expeditions, archaeological expeditions! It will be great! When
can you get away?
<Enter>
$ _
```

Clue: If you're ever typing commands and the prompt disappears, the computer may still be executing the last command that you typed. You're not at the UNIX command line, but within that command, so your results will be unpredictable. Try to figure out what was the last command you typed. If it was the mail command, you can press Enter until you see the prompt; or press Control+d; or type a period (dot) on a blank line, followed by Enter. This should get you out of the mail command.

> **NOTE**
> You'll learn more about electronic mail later in this book, but now you know how to do the two most important e-mail operations: sending and receiving.

What Are Files?

Like any adventurer, you have to have a place for your secrets, so you need to learn about files, specifically the electronic kind. Like top-secret file folders, electronic files are containers for information. They can contain any kind of information. They can hold text, such as a letter. They can hold a computer program (a binary or executable file), such as the electronic version of "Dungeons and Dragons."

Your files can be named almost anything, but you must observe certain conventions. Luckily, these conventions are very permissive.

❌ All UNIX systems have a limit on how long a filename can be. This limit varies. Most modern systems accept at least 14 characters, but all UNIX systems accept filenames of seven characters or fewer.

❌ Also, many UNIX systems don't accept different types of punctuation for filenames, so you should avoid any punctuation other than perhaps the underscore (_) or a period (.). No UNIX system will let you use a slash in a filename, and you'll see why shortly.

❌ You can't have a space between two different parts of a filename. For example, `my file` would be illegal, but `my_file` would be OK. If you stay within these limitations, the computer doesn't care whether you call your file `grail`, `treasur`, or `heyyou`.

Also, as I pointed out earlier, UNIX is literal-minded and fussy. It interprets the filenames `Glargon` and `glargon` as different files. If your system ever acts as if it doesn't recognize your filename, check the capitalization.

How to Make a File

If you use a word-processing program such as FrameMaker or WordPerfect for UNIX, you're already using a program to create files. If you want, you can look at these files using just the commands UNIX provides, but they'll look kind of funny, because word-processing programs usually put many strange-looking symbols into the files they create, in addition to normal letters, punctuation, and numbers. You're a clever and resourceful adventurer, so you can create simple text files using the `cat` command.

SKIP THIS, IT'S TECHNICAL

The `cat` command is called the *concatenate* command. The `cat` command writes information to the standard output—the screen—unless told to redirect information somewhere else. If you don't give `cat` a filename, it will read standard input (the keyboard).

Before you create a file with `cat`, let's see some of things it can do. Have you ever been to the Grand Canyon? Canyons are great for echoing what you yell into them. The `cat` command can echo in a similar way:

```
$ cat <Enter>
$ Hello <Enter>
```

```
<control+d>
Hello
$ _
```

In the preceding example, I typed `cat` and pressed Enter. The cursor moved to the next line and waited for me to type something. You can tell whether the system is waiting for you by the presence of the shell prompt. Next, I typed `Hello` and pressed Enter. After I pressed Enter, I held down the Control key and pressed d. You will notice that `Hello` was then displayed on the screen. Basically, the `cat` command concatenated `Hello` to the display.

To save to a file whatever I type, I would need to redirect the output from the screen to a file. For example, to create a file named `roadtrip`, I would enter the `cat` command, followed by a right-angle bracket (>)—also called the redirection symbol—and then the name I want to give the file. You try it:

```
$ cat > roadtrip
_
```

Notice that the shell prompt disappears, and the cursor is sitting on a blank line. You are now in the `cat` command's insert mode, where you can type the contents of the file as you would on a piece of paper. Enter the text shown in bold in the following example, and press Control+d when you are finished to exit the insert mode and return to the shell prompt.

```
$cat > roadtrip <You've already typed this line.>
A journey of a thousand miles begins, hopefully, with an empty
bladder and all the appliances turned off.
<Control+d>
$
```

You've created a file called `roadtrip`. In this example, the `cat` command told the computer to run the `cat` command.

The redirection symbol (>) told the computer to put the words that were displayed on the screen into a file called `roadtrip`. The words *redirection symbol* may sound a little bit intimidating, but if you think "put it here" every time you see it—where "here" is the thing the arrow points to—it's easy to understand. Entering Control+d returned you to the UNIX command line.

Looking at Your Files

Now that you've created the file, you can look at it by entering `cat roadtrip`:

```
$ cat roadtrip
A journey of a thousand miles begins, hopefully, with an empty
bladder and all the appliances turned off.
$ _
```

In this example, you've used `cat` to simply display the contents of the file you just created. When you use `cat` to display a file, it displays the entire file to the screen immediately, even if the file is many pages long.

You can also print your file onto paper by typing `lpr` (or `lp`, if `lpr` doesn't work for you), then the filename. These command names stand for "line printer." Some UNIX systems use `lp`, whereas others use `lpr`. It's best to ask your system administrator which of these to use. You'll also need to ask your system administrator which printer you're hooked to, so you know where to pick up your output.

Clue: To exit the `cat` command normally, enter Control+d. To abort the command without letting it finish its work, enter Control+c. It's usually best to try Control+d first, because it's the least drastic form of escape. These *escape sequences*, as they're called in UNIXland, work on most commands.

One caution, though, about Control+d. If you type it when you're at the UNIX command line, at the prompt, you could be logged out of UNIX. If this happens, you need to repeat the login procedures to get back into UNIX.

Where Do Your Files Live?

Your files are kept in *directories*. Just as files contain information, directories hold files. Think of them as an electronic filing cabinet for electronic files; each directory can hold many files. In theory, a directory could hold an almost unlimited number of files, up to the size of the storage medium (disk size).

Unfortunately, my beautiful analogy only goes so far. The difference between physical filing cabinets and directories is that directories can contain directories, but it is exceedingly rare to find filing cabinets inside filing cabinets. In this sense, directories are like Russian Marioshka dolls, or those little Russian novelty boxes, in which a big black lacquer box contains a smaller box that contains a smaller box that contains a smaller box. Each box has enough room for someone to put something in addition to a box in the box. Similarly, a UNIX directory can contain any combination of directories and files, which would be like someone putting jewelry in some of these little boxes, so that any box could hold, say, a precious necklace, a pirate treasure, and a smaller box.

How to Find Your Files Using the *ls* Command

You know that you have at least one file in your main directory, or *home directory*, which is the directory you're automatically put into when you log in. You should have at least one, roadtrip, because you've already created it. If not, go back to the section in this chapter that explains how to make a file. Now you're going to learn how to list your files.

The command to do this is, not surprisingly, the ls command, short for "list." Try it:

```
$ ls
letter1    letter2    memo6.10   memo7.5    roadtrip
$ _
```

You should see a list of all of your files, which may only include the file roadtrip unless you've created others or inherited them from someone else, so don't worry if your display doesn't look exactly like mine. As long as you have a list of filenames, including at least roadtrip, don't sweat it.

Getting the Low-Down on Your Files

Often, it's important to know more about the files than you can discover using the simple ls command. For instance, you may want to know when a file was last changed. To do this, you take the basic list command and add a switch, or option, to it. A *switch* provides extra instructions to the computer that tell it exactly how you want it to execute the basic command. Switches are therefore very important to UNIX users, because they make every command like an order at Burger King: You can "have it your way." You'll learn a lot more about switches later, after you've gotten the basics down. For now, use the ls command with the -l switch after it:

```
$ ls -l
total 5
-rw-r--r--   1 lisas     vip          1010 Feb 16 13:58 letter1
-rw-r--r--   1 lisas     vip          3868 Feb 16 13:58 letter2
-rw-r--r--   1 lisas     vip           499 Feb 16 13:59 memo6.10
-rw-r--r--   1 lisas     vip           218 Feb 16 13:59 memo7.5
-rw-r--r--   1 lisas     vip           106 Feb 16 13:36 roadtrip
$ _
```

You should see a listing of your files, complete with a lot more information than you saw before. The important thing to notice now is the date and time your files were last changed. This can be useful if you forget the name of the file you last worked on. (Of course, I've *never* had this happen to me, but I can imagine being in this situation.)

Copying and Removing Files

Now that you know how to make and list your files, you need to learn how to copy your files using the `cp` command. To copy the file `roadtrip` into a new file called `roadtrip2`, enter the following command:

```
$ cp roadtrip roadtrip2
$ _
```

That's all there is to it.

To make sure you've really copied it, use the `ls` command:

```
$ ls
letter1    letter2    memo6.10   memo7.5   roadtrip    roadtrip2
$ _
```

If your directory contains other files, they'll show up when you do the `ls` command. That's OK. Just make sure both of the listed files are there.

Now make another copy of `roadtrip` and put the copy into `roadtrip3`. Can you guess how? If not, here is the command:

```
$ cp roadtrip roadtrip3
$ ls
letter1    letter2    memo6.10   memo7.5   roadtrip    roadtrip2   roadtrip3
$ _
```

After you enter the `ls` command, you'll see the addition of your third `roadtrip` file, `roadtrip3`.

Getting Rid of Files

Now that you've copied the file several times, you can delete the old one. That's easy, too. The command for removing files is called `rm`, short for "remove." In general, you enter `rm` followed by the filename and—poof!—your file is history. To remove your `roadtrip` file, for example, enter the following:

```
$ rm roadtrip
$ ls
letter1    letter2    memo6.10   memo7.5   roadtrip2   roadtrip3
$ _
```

You can see that the `roadtrip` file is no longer listed by `ls`.

Some UNIX installations have a version of the `rm` command that attempts to save users from themselves. On these systems, when users try the `rm` command, they're asked whether they really want to remove their files. If they don't respond with either a y or a yes, the system won't remove the file. If your system doesn't do this, you can accomplish the same thing by typing rm -i, and you'll be prompted to answer y or n for each file for which you use rm -i, as shown here:

```
$ rm -i *
remove letter1 ? y
remove letter2 ? y
remove memo6.10 ? y
remove memo7.5 ? y
remove roadtrip2 ? n
remove roadtrip3 ? n
$ ls
roadtrip2  roadtrip3
$ _
```

Now you can get a fresh copy of roadtrip by using the cp command to copy roadtrip3 into roadtrip:

```
$ cp roadtrip3 roadtrip
$ _
```

You have now copied the contents of roadtrip3, which are the same as the original copy of roadtrip, back into roadtrip.

Files and Directories Revisited

You already know what a directory is. Now you're going to learn how to make one. It's easy. The command is cleverly called mkdir, short for "make directory." (Those UNIX types are so original.) To make a directory called adventure, for example, you would enter mkdir adventure at the prompt. Then to make sure that the new directory is there, you can use the ls -l command:

```
$ mkdir adventure
$ ls -l
total 3
drwxrwxrwx   1 lisas     vip           37 Feb 16 15:15 adventure
-rw-r--r--   1 lisas     vip          106 Feb 16 13:36 roadtrip
-rw-r--r--   1 lisas     vip          106 Feb 16 14:22 roadtrip2
-rw-r--r--   1 lisas     vip          106 Feb 16 14:19 roadtrip3
$ _
```

You now have a new directory called adventure. The d at the far left of the line (that is, the first character in the permissions string) indicates that adventure is a directory.

Now try making up a directory name and using mkdir to create the directory. Then use the ls command and you'll not only see your files, but the two new directories you just made. If you'll look at the listing, you'll see the small d indicating you've made a directory. Here's what I would see when I make another new directory, this one called mydir:

```
$ mkdir mydir
$ ls -l
total 4
drwxrwxrwx    1 lisas      vip              37 Feb 16 15:15 adventure
drwxrwxrwx    1 lisas      vip              37 Feb 16 15:15 mydir
-rw-r--r--    1 lisas      vip             106 Feb 16 13:36 roadtrip
-rw-r--r--    1 lisas      vip             106 Feb 16 14:22 roadtrip2
-rw-r--r--    1 lisas      vip             106 Feb 16 14:19 roadtrip3
$ _
```

Moving and Renaming Files

Now that you know how to make directories, you can move files into directories
with mv, the "move" command. To move the file roadtrip2 into the directory called
adventure, enter the following commands:

```
$ mv roadtrip2 adventure
$ ls
adventure    mydir    roadtrip    roadtrip3
$ cd adventure
$ ls
roadtrip2
$ _
```

On the first line, you move the roadtrip2 file to the adventure directory. Next,
you list the directory and see that the roadtrip2 file is missing. When you change
directories to adventure and list that directory, you see the file. The mv command
actually copies the file to the desired location and removes the old copy. The mv
command will also rename the file either in the current directory or when you
move the file to a new directory.

How to Change Directories

Now you're going to move to one of your new directories. To do that, you'll use
the cd (for "change directory") command, as introduced in the preceding example.
To change from your home directory to the adventure directory, enter the following command:

```
$ cd adventure
$ ls -al
drwxrwxrwx    1 lisas      vip              37 Dec 31  1979 .
drwxrwxrwx    1 lisas      vip             323 Dec 31  1979 ..
$ _
```

SKIP THIS, IT'S TECHNICAL

The -a option on the ls command shows *all* files, including hidden ones such as the dot (.) and dot dot (..). The . is UNIX's name for the current directory, and .. is the UNIX name for the parent—or preceding—directory in the hierarchy.

To get back to your home directory, type cd, then a space, then two periods:

```
$ cd ..
$ _
```

Alternatively, you can enter simply cd:

```
$ cd
$ _
```

You should now be back in your home directory. The home directory is the directory that your system administrator has given you as your own personal area. You've essentially jumped down one level in the directory structure, and then back up one level, so you're in the same place where you started.

Finding the Shining Path: UNIX File and Directory Structures

Remember that I explained how directories could contain files, but directories could also contain other directories? Well, UNIX has an interesting way of expressing the concept of containment.

To show that a file is contained in a directory, UNIX uses a slash (/) after the directory name. A file named children that is contained in a directory called family would be called family/children. A file called expenses contained in a directory called accounting would be called accounting/expenses.

To show that a directory is contained in a directory, use the same technique. A directory called employees contained in a directory called personnel would be written personnel/employees. This means that employees is a subdirectory of the personnel directory. If the directory of employees contained a file called jssmith, for an employee of the company, we might write personnel/employees/jssmith. The hierarchy of files and directories is shown in Figure 3.1.

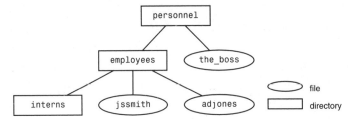

FIGURE 3.1.
Directories can contain files and other directories.

When you think about it, these hierarchical descriptions are like an inclined path that tells you where to go to find a file or a directory. You can walk up the path, or you can walk down it. That's why they're called *pathnames*.

How Do You Know What Directory You're In?

Funny you should ask. Early UNIX pioneers doubtlessly got tired of always knowing the path to a file or directory, but never having a big red X on the map that said, "You are here."

Well, luckily they did something about it. They created the pwd command, which tells you where you are. Try typing in the pwd command, and you should see the directory with your login name on it (at the end of the path, at the far right). When I do this, I get the following listing:

```
$ pwd
/home/lisas
$ _
```

This tells me what I already knew: I'm in my own home directory.

> **SKIP THIS, IT'S TECHNICAL**
> The pwd command can be remembered as the "print working directory" command. It displays on the screen where you are in the UNIX file system.

Absolute and Relative Pathnames: Wherever You Go, There You Are

Now we get to an important distinction. Remember the saying, "Everything is relative"? Not in UNIX. As a matter of fact, there are two types of paths in UNIX: *absolute* and *relative*. What you learned in the preceding section was how to use relative pathnames.

To understand this difference, remember that the UNIX directory system is a hierarchy. There are directories above that contain yours, and your directory now contains at least one directory, called adventure. Because your adventure directory is contained in your directory, it is also contained in the directories that contain yours. (Think Russian Marioshka dolls and little nested boxes now.)

Relative pathnames are always defined relative to where you are in this directory hierarchy. It's as if a friend asked you where the bathroom was, and you said, "It's down the hall and to the right." Your friend would know that you meant to go down *your* hall and turn right from there. It was understood that you didn't mean to go down someone else's hall, because you were describing how to get to the bathroom from the house where you and your friend already were. That's the way it is in UNIX; relative pathnames are defined from where you are.

If you're in your home directory (the one with your name on it), and you type cd adventure, UNIX starts with your directory, and looks for the directory called adventure. It doesn't look for adventure anywhere else. A very important consequence of this is that you can use relative pathnames only to refer to files and directories that are "beneath" the directory you're in at the moment, because they're the only ones that can be defined starting with the directory you're already in. Because UNIX starts looking for files and directories in the directory you're already in, then goes looking in the directories contained in those directories, then in the directories contained in those directories, UNIX won't know what you're talking about (and will tell you so) if you try to look for files or directories "above" yours or "next to" yours. You'll get a message that says something like file not found or directory not found.

What if your friend had flown in from Outer Mongolia, was calling from the airport, and wanted to know where you lived? You couldn't assume he knew which house was yours; that's the whole reason he called you. You would have to define where your house was from the airport, which is the central point that you two have implicitly agreed to use as your reference point. You might tell him to get on the freeway, take the exit, and make a right on Archaeology Drive. If it were a

UNIX path and the airport were the central directory, we might write the instructions as /freeway/exit/archaeology.

Absolute pathnames always start with a slash (/). They are always defined from the highest point in the UNIX directory hierarchy—a central, absolute point, if you will—which is called the *root*. When you type a slash and your login name (for me, that's /lisas), UNIX knows you're referring to your own home directory.

NOTE

UNIX natives often speak of "logging in as root" or of getting the *root password*.

This *root* is a highly privileged, powerful place to be, so a person who was either destructive or didn't know what he or she was doing could cause a tremendous amount of damage, such as erasing other people's files or changing passwords. Therefore, the root password, which is the password you need to log in to the root account, is usually a very guarded secret, restricted to a few people. Therefore, asking your system administrator for the root password will make you as popular as asking a teetotaling host for a great big bottle of Jack Daniels. It is not, in short, a good idea. Yet system administrators say it's a very common request, and it drives them nuts to have to explain why users can't have the root password.

Wildcards and Filenames

Sometimes you want to have a way to specify files that have similar names, start or end with the same letters, or contain certain combinations of letters. UNIX has some neat tricks to help you do this.

Suppose you want to list all of the files in your directory that start with *r*. (That may include all of them, if you just have the roadtrip series of files.) UNIX file systems have a tool called *wildcard* characters. They work very much like a wildcard does in most card games; they can stand for any other card you want to have.

In UNIX, the most commonly found wildcard character is the asterisk (*), often called "star." It stands for any number of other characters. If you want to list all of the files that start with the letter *r*, but you don't care how many characters come after the *r*, you could do it like this:

```
$ ls r*
```

roadtrip   roadtrip2   roadtrip3$ _

Right now, the star might not seem like a big deal, because you only have a few files in your directory; but if you have many files, this is a useful trick.

You could also use the * at the beginning or in the middle of filenames or, for that matter, directory names. For instance, to list files ending in 3, enter the following ls command:

```
$ ls *3
roadtrip3
$ _
```

In this example, you told the computer to look for all of the files that ended in the numeral 3, no matter how many letters or numbers came before the 3.

Another common wildcard character is the question mark (?), which can stand for one character at a time. For instance, if you wanted to list all of the files in your directory that started with the word roadtrip and had just one more character (a character is a letter, number, or legal punctuation symbol) after it, you'd enter the following command:

```
$ ls roadtrip?
roadtrip2    roadtrip3
$ _
```

Note that you listed roadtrip2 and roadtrip3, but not roadtrip, because you told the system that it was supposed to list the file only if it had at least one more character after it.

One more trick, and you'll be done with this topic. To illustrate this next trick, you'll need use the cp command to create roadtrip4, roadtrip5, roadtripA, roadtripB, roadtrip45, and roadtripC. Enter the following code:

```
$ cp roadtrip roadtrip4
$ cp roadtrip roadtrip5
$ cp roadtrip roadtripA
$ cp roadtrip roadtripB
$ cp roadtrip roadtripC
$ cp roadtrip roadtrip45
$ _
```

The last type of wildcard you'll learn now enables you to specify a range of characters you're looking for by enclosing the range in square brackets [ ]. For example, to list all of the roadtrip files that end in a digit between 3 and 5, enter the following ls command:

```
$ ls roadtrip[3-5]
roadtrip3    roadtrip4    roadtrip5
$ _
```

Why did you get this list? You didn't get `roadtrip`, because you asked for at least one extra character after the word, and the last character in `roadtrip2` is the 2, which is outside the range of the list. Of course, the *A* and *B* at the end of `roadtripA` and `roadtripB` aren't in the range specified, either.

Letters can be used in the range, as well. Just as you would expect, *A* comes before *B*, and *a* comes before *b*. Try it:

```
$ ls roadtrip[A-C]
roadtripA    roadtripB    roadtripC
$ _
```

> **WARNING**
>
> Be very, very careful using wildcard characters with the `rm` command because you could accidentally wipe out more files than you intended. It's best to use `rm -i`, which queries you about whether you want to remove each individual file.

Removing Directories

The thing to remember about removing directories is that it's easy, but UNIX won't let you remove a directory unless there are no files in it. If you try, you'll be told that UNIX can't remove a directory with files in it. This is the most common mistake people make when trying to remove directories. (Nothing bad happens if you try. UNIX won't do it, that's all.)

To remove a directory, type `rmdir` (for "remove directory"), followed by the directory name. Use `rmdir` to remove the `adventure` directory:

```
$ rmdir adventure
$ _
```

When All Else Fails…

Read the directions. This seems like a simple principle, but to some people, it might as well be rocket science. Seriously, the good news is that UNIX has a great feature: UNIX was the first major operating system with built-in, online documentation. When you get lost, you can often figure out what to do by calling up the *manual page*, also called *man page*, which is an electronic, online copy that explains what a command does and how to use it.

The bad news, though, is that the language of manual is, well, a little dense. The other good news is that you've got an excellent, first-class guide and translator (me again), and I'll teach you how to read the native language. It's not so tough, once you know a few words, a bit of the grammar, and a few phrases. Before you can say, "The pen of my uncle is on the table" or "Which way, Sahib?" you'll be babbling away like the locals.

To use the manual page, or man command, type man and then the command name. Try this with cat. Enter the following:

```
$ man cat
```

You'll see a display like the following. (Some of the details may be a bit different on your system. Don't worry about it; we're interested in the general features of man pages now.)

```
NAME
     cat - catenate and print

SYNOPSIS
     cat [ -benstuv ] file ...

DESCRIPTION
     Cat reads each file in sequence and displays it on the standard
     output. Thus

                    cat file

     displays the file on the standard output, and

                    cat file1 file2 >file3

     concatenates the first two files and places the result on the
     third.

     If no input file is given, or if the argument '-' is encountered,
     cat reads from the standard input file. Output is buffered in the
     block size recommended by stat(2) unless the standard output is a
     terminal, when it is line buffered. The -u option makes the output
     completely unbuffered.

     The -n option displays the output lines preceded by lines numbers,
     numbered sequentially from 1. Specifying the -b option with the -n
     option omits the line numbers from blank lines.

     The -s option crushes out multiple adjacent empty lines so that the
     output is displayed single spaced.

     The -v option displays non-printing characters so that they are
     visible. Control characters print like ^X for control-x; the
     delete character (octal 0177) prints as ^?. Non-ascii characters
     (with the high bit set) are printed as M- (for meta) followed by
     the character of the low 7 bits. A -e option may be given with the
     -v option, which displays a '$' character at the end of each line.
     Specifying the -t option with the -v option displays tab characters
     as ^I.
```

```
SEE ALSO
     cp(1), ex(1), more(1), pr(1), tail(1)

BUGS
     Beware of 'cat a b >a' and 'cat a b >b', which destroy the input
     files before reading them.
```

Clue: If you can't see the whole man page, press the space bar. Press it again to see more, and it will scroll down. Unfortunately, you can only scroll forward in this way, so if you go past the part you want to look at, you'll have to type the command again and start again from the top.

When you press the space bar to read man pages, UNIX is using the more command (without telling you) to show you each screenful of text. You can also use this command explicitly to look at your files. To see each part of the file, you press the space bar every time you want to move to the next page of the file. To use more, enter the word more, then the filename. To get out of it, either press the space bar until the command finishes normally, or press q for quit. To see other options available in the more command, press h for help.

So, how do you read this thing? The name of the command and a brief description are always at the top, under the word NAME. That part is easy.

Sometimes, however, the next item—SYNOPSIS—can look a little weird, as it does in this case. What on earth could -[benstuv] mean?

The synopsis tells you the form of the command. That is, it tells you how to use it. In this case, the synopsis tells you that you have to type cat, followed by the name of the file you want to concatenate, or join.

The -[benstuv] after the command tells you which options you can use with the command. The dash means that you have to type a dash if you want to use an option; the brackets mean that using a switch is optional, and you don't have to use one at all. (Remember, a switch is a shorthand way of telling the computer you want the command to be carried out in a special way.) The benstuv part means that you can choose to type cat -b *file*, cat -e *file*, cat -s *file*, cat -t *file*, cat -u *file*, or cat -v *file*.

These *switches*, or *options*, as they are sometimes called, are detailed in the second half of the next section—titled DESCRIPTION—of the man pages. The description always lists these options and describes what each does. In this case, it says, in fairly plain language, what you already knew: you can either use cat to display a file to the screen (which in this case is *standard output*, as it's called in UNIXland), or you can use it to enter input from your keyboard (which is *standard input*, as it's called here). You can use it to stick two files together and make them go into a third by using the > sign and then the third filename, which is what the `cat file1 file2 >file3` means.

One of the most important sections—BUGS—describes problems that you many encounter with the command. It's always a good idea to read this section before you try to use a new command, because this section can tell you how to avoid many of the pitfalls involved in using it.

In this case, this section of the man page tells you to avoid one of the most common mistakes people make when they use the `cat` command. They want to put two files—let's call them A and B—together and put them into file A. They type `cat A B > A`, or concatenate files A and B, then put the result into file A. UNIX starts processing the command by clearing out the file that everything is supposed to go into. Then, when UNIX tries to read file A so it can tack file A onto file B, there is nothing in file A, because UNIX started by erasing it. That means that you've just wiped out file A by using `cat` this way, so if you'd invested a lot of time and effort in creating file A, you'd be experiencing—to use a technical term—a total bummer.

Clue: While I'm on the subject of accidentally wiping out a file, let me pass on a fanny-saving piece of the sacred UNIX wisdom handed down through many generations of klutzy-fingered UNIX hackers. Your system administrator, if you have one, may be able to resurrect the file; the only downside to this is that you'll have to eat some crow and throw yourself on the mercy of your system administrator, maybe even promise him or her your first-born child. Often, your system administrator makes backups of all of the files on your system. If you know the filename that you've wiped out and can tell the SA the approximate time and date you wiped it out, the SA can often restore an older version of the file. Depending on when the last backup was made, some of your changes to the file may be lost, and you'll have to try to remember what changes to make to the older version to bring it up to speed.

Another lifesaver in the man pages is the SEE ALSO area. This section tells you where to look for related commands. If you aren't sure whether a particular command is the one you want, you'll often find the right one under SEE ALSO.

Let's try this again with another command. Type man pwd, and you'll see something like the following man page:

```
NAME
     pwd - working directory name

SYNOPSIS
     pwd

DESCRIPTION
     Pwd prints the pathname of the working (current) directory.

SEE ALSO
     cd(1), csh(1), getwd(3)

BUGS
     In csh(1) the command dirs is always faster (although it can give a
     different answer in the rare case that the current directory or a
     containing directory was moved after the shell descended into it).
```

This documentation tells you a number of interesting things, some of which you already know. You've already seen that pwd tells you where you are in the directory structure (the pathname of the current working directory, in UNIXspeak). The man page also shows you that there's only one way to call pwd, because there are no options listed under the SYNOPSIS heading. By looking at the man page, you can see that you've already mastered the pwd command; there's not much more you can do with it.

That's not the case, however, with the list command (ls), which is in many different ways a very useful command. Type man ls, and you'll see something that looks like this:

```
NAME
     ls - list contents of directory

SYNOPSIS
     ls [ -acdfgilqrstu1MR ] name ...

DESCRIPTION
     For each directory argument, ls lists the contents of the
     directory; for each file argument, ls repeats its name and any
     other information requested. By default, the output is sorted
     alphabetically. When no argument is given, the current directory
     is listed. When several arguments are given, the arguments are
     first sorted appropriately, but file arguments are processed before
     directories and their contents.

     There are a large number of options:

     -M   List in Macintosh format, giving attributes, creator and type,
          data and resource fork sizes, and time of last modification
          for each file.

     -1   List in long format, giving mode, number of links, owner, size
          in bytes, and time of last modification for each file. (See
```

below.) If the file is a special file the size field will
instead contain the major and minor device numbers. If the
file is a symbolic link the pathname of the linked-to file is
printed preceded by "->".

-g   Include the group ownership of the file in a long output.

-t   Sort by time modified (latest first) instead of by name.

-a   List all entries; in the absence of this option, entries whose
     names begin with a period (.) are not listed.

-s   Give size in kilobytes of each file.

-d   If argument is a directory, list only its name; often used
     with -l to get the status of a directory.

-L   If argument is a symbolic link, list the file or directory the
     link references rather than the link itself.

-r   Reverse the order of sort to get reverse alphabetic or oldest
     first as appropriate.

-u   Use time of last access instead of last modification for
     sorting (with the -t option) and/or printing (with the -l
     option).

-c   Use time when file status was last changed for sorting or
     printing.

-i   For each file, print the i-number in the first column of the
     report.

-f   Force each argument to be interpreted as a directory and list
     the name found in each slot. This option turns off -l, -t,
     -s, and -r, and turns on -a; the order is the order in which
     entries appear in the directory.

-F   Cause directories to be marked with a trailing '/', sockets
     with a trailing '=', symbolic links with a trailing '@', and
     executable files with a trailing '*'.

-R   Recursively list subdirectories encountered.

-1   Force one entry per line output format; this is the default
     when output is not to a terminal.

-C   Force multi-column output; this is the default when output is
     to a terminal.

-q   Force printing of non-graphic characters in file names as the
     character '?'; this is the default when output is to a
     terminal.

The attributes printed under the -M option are the 5 characters
FDRLI which are interpreted as follows:

F if the entry is a folder (directory);
D if the entry's data fork is open;

R if the entry's resource fork is open;
L if the entry is locked;
I if the entry is marked invisible.
If the condition represented by the attribute flag is not true, a -
is shown instead.

The mode printed under the -l option contains 11 characters which
are interpreted as follows: the first character is

d if the entry is a directory;
b if the entry is a block-type special file;
c if the entry is a character-type special file;
l if the entry is a symbolic link;
s if the entry is a socket; or
- if the entry is a plain file.

The next 9 characters are interpreted as three sets of three bits
each. The first set refers to owner permissions; the next refers
to permissions to others in the same user-group; and the last to
all others. Within each set the three characters indicate
permission respectively to read, to write, or to execute the file
as a program. For a directory, 'execute' permission is interpreted
to mean permission to search the directory. The permissions are
indicated as follows:

r if the file is readable;
w if the file is writable;
x if the file is executable;
- if the indicated permission is not granted.

The group-execute permission character is given as s if the file
has the set-group-id bit set; likewise the user-execute permission
character is given as s if the file has the set-user-id bit set.
These are given as S (capitalized) if the corresponding execute
permission is NOT set.

The last character of the mode (normally 'x' or '-') is t if the
1000 bit of the mode is on. See chmod(1) for the meaning of this
mode. This is given as T (capitalized) if the corresponding
execute permission is NOT set.

When the sizes of the files in a directory are listed, a total
count of blocks, including indirect blocks is printed.

FILES
      /etc/passwd to get user id's for 'ls -l'.
      /etc/group to get group id's for 'ls -g'.

BUGS
      Newline and tab are considered printing characters in file names.

      The option setting based on whether the output is a teletype is
      undesirable as "ls -s" is much different than "ls -s ¦ lpr".
      On the other hand, not doing this setting would make old shell
      scripts which used ls almost certain losers.

SEE ALSO
      "Inside Macintosh", Volume I, p. I-105, Apple Computer Co.,
      Addison-Wesley, for a discussion of resource and data forks.

Whoa! Get a load of all the options listed on the man page for ls! (It may look a little strange and intimidating to see so much documentation, but my approach is to read what looks interesting and understandable, and ignore the rest.) Of course, you already know how to use ls -l. Some of the most interesting options include ls -t, which sorts the files by the last time they were changed. This is useful for finding the file you last worked on, when you can't remember its name. Sometimes, you want to call up the last file you looked at, even if you didn't modify it; for that, you can use ls -u. If you want a list of all of the files that are programs (*executable files*, in programmer language), you could use ls -F. If you want to list the directories contained in the directories that are in your home directory (sounds funny, but you might want to see what's "below" the immediate list of directories that ls normally produces), you could type ls -R.

You should explore your man page for any other interesting options not included here, if not now, then later when you get more experienced and feel a little adventurous. That's because some installations have extra options peculiar to their site or their particular flavor of UNIX.

Here's one more important thing: you can often use several options for a given command at the same time. You do this by typing a dash, then the letter for the option. For instance, if you want to list all of the information about your files and directories (-l for long format), but you want to sort them by the time they were last modified (-t for time sort), with files and directories that have remained unchanged the longest listed first (-r for reverse order), the command to do this is ls -ltr. The order of the options is unimportant here; the important thing is that all the options you want follow the command.

You can use the man command to tell you more about—you guessed it—the man command. Type man man, and you should see something like the following:

```
NAME
     man - display the on-line manual pages

SYNOPSIS
     man [ -acw ] [ -M path ] [ -m path ] [ section ] name ...

DESCRIPTION
     Man provides on-line access to the UNIX manual pages. The manual
     pages are also accessible via the ManTen HyperCard application.
     See MachTen User's Guide.

     Man displays the UNIX manual pages entitled name.

     The options are as follows:

     a     Display all of the manual pages for a specified section and
           name combination. (Normally, only the first manual page found
           is displayed.)
```

c   Copy the manual page to the standard output instead of using
        more(1) to paginate it. This is done by default if the
        standard output is not a terminal device.

M   Override the list of standard directories which man searches
        for manual pages. The supplied path must be a colon (":")
        separated list of directories. This search path may also be
        set using the environment variable MANPATH. The
        subdirectories to be searched as well as their search order is
        specified by the "_subdir" line in the man configuration
        file.

m   Augment the list of standard directories which man searches
        for manual pages. The supplied path must be a colon (":")
        separated list of directories. These directories will be
        searched before the standard directories or the directories
        specified using the M option or the MANPATH environment
        variable.

w   List the pathnames of the manual pages which man would display
        for the specified section and name combination.

The optional section restricts the directories that man will
search. The man configuration file (see man.conf(5)) specifies the
possible section values that are currently available. If only a
single argument is specified or if the first argument is not a
valid section, man assumes that the argument is the name of a
manual page to be displayed.

ENVIRONMENT

    MACHINE
        As some manual pages are intended only for use on certain
        architectures, man searches certain directories applicable to
        the current machine. Man's determination of the current
        machine type may be overridden by setting the environment
        variable MACHINE to the name of an architecture (see
        machine(1)). Machine specific areas are checked before
        general areas.

    MANPATH
        The standard search path used by man may be overridden by
        specifying a path in the MANPATH environment variable. The
        format of the path is a colon (":") separated list of
        directories. The subdirectories to be searched as well as
        their search order is specified by the "_subdir" line in the
        man configuration file.

    PAGER
        Any value of the environment variable PAGER will be used
        instead of the standard pagination program more(1).

FILES
    /etc/man.conf   man configuration file (see man.conf(5))

SEE ALSO
    apropos(1), machine(1), whatis(1), whereis(1), man.conf(5)

BUGS
```
     The on-line manual pages are, by necessity, forgiving toward stupid
     display devices, causing some manual pages to not be as good as
     their typeset counterparts.

     The MachTen manual page files are formatted for the ManTen
     HyperCard application. HyperCard uses carriage returns (cr) where
     UNIX applications expect newlines (nl). This is obvious using the
     -c option. In this case use tr(1) to translate characters.
```

This man page is, in many ways, like the legend to a map. It's the instructions to the instructions. Admittedly, much of this page probably looks like gobbledygook right now, but you'll revisit it later, and I guarantee it will make more sense.

The last important thing to know about man is the -k option. This option will help you get around one of the most irritating features of the man command: to get information about a command you want to use, you need to at least know the command name. What can you do when you don't even know that much? You use man -k, which will search in the NAME section of all the man pages for any word you specify. Type man -k display, and you'll call up all of the man pages that mention the word *display*. When I do this, I find several pages are written to the screen, and the first is the man page for the man command. Your results may be slightly different because man pages vary a little bit, but the principle is the same. If you don't know what command you want, think up words that might be in the description of the command you want, and use man -k to find the right one.

> **WARNING**
>
> The -k option may not work for you if your system administrator has not set up the man page for this option. You can send him or her an e-mail to make certain that the option will work.

How Do You Blow This Palace? (Logging Out)

To log out, make sure you're not in the middle of any commands. Enter logout. If that doesn't work, type bye or exit, and that should get you out of UNIX. You now have to log back in again when you want to use UNIX.

What You've Learned

You've come a long way in this chapter. You know enough to find your way around, and you can use the most important UNIX commands to get some useful work done. You've got your basic tools assembled, you know how to navigate, and your real adventure is about to begin. You're now ready to conquer whatever faces you.

Rewards

- ✖ You know how to use login to get into UNIX.
- ✖ You know how to send a simple e-mail message to get help.
- ✖ You can read e-mail.
- ✖ You've learned what files and directories are.
- ✖ You know how to create a file and look at it using cat.
- ✖ You can print a file using lp or lpr.
- ✖ You understand the hierarchy of files and directories, and you can navigate through the directory system using cd and cd ...
- ✖ You know how to use wildcard characters to specify groups of filenames and directory names.
- ✖ You can remove files and directories.
- ✖ You can figure out where you are by using pwd.
- ✖ You can read simple man pages to figure out how to use new commands.
- ✖ You can use logout to get out of UNIX.

Pitfalls

- ✖ Asking for the password to the root directory will make you unpopular with your SA.
- ✖ Unscrupulous people can do a great deal of destruction in your name if you fail to keep your password secure.

Working in UNIX Environments

4

Pipes, Permissions, Tees, and Changing Directions

In This Chapter

✖ *What are permissions on files and directories?*

✖ *How do you give permissions to other people?*

✖ *How do you take away permissions on files and directories?*

✖ *What are the redirection operators and how are they used?*

✖ *What are pipes and why are they important?*

✖ *What is a tee and how is it used?*

✖ *How do the three great utilities—*grep, sort, *and* diff*—work?*

✖ *How can you combine* grep, sort, *and* diff *with pipes, tees, and redirection operators to do interesting work?*

Permissions in Workgroup Environments

UNIX was created to help programmers work together more smoothly. Therefore, UNIX has always assumed that many users would be working—creating and changing files—at the same time. Some way had to be found to let people work on their own files and perhaps on selected files of coworkers, while at the same time protecting all files from manipulation by unauthorized users. That's why the creators of UNIX built in the concept of file and directory permissions.

Permissions specify who can use a file or directory and how. In essence, permissions determine who can do what to a file or directory. This means that you can create a file and say whether other groups of people can look at the file (*read permissions*, abbreviated as r) or change it (*write permissions*, abbreviated as w).

> **NOTE**
>
> Later, when you start learning UNIX shell programming, you'll be able to say who can use the programs that you write. This is called *execute* permission; it is abbreviated x because people who use a program are executing the program.

If someone tries to change one of your files, and you haven't given that person permission to write to the file, UNIX won't allow the change. Conversely, if someone tells you to work on a file and you find that you can't, it's probably because that person forgot to give you permission to change (that is, write to) the file.

When a file is created, its creator is automatically made the owner of the file. Only the owner of a file (and people with special authorization, such as system administrators, who can make themselves someone called the *superuser*) can specify who can use a file and how it can be used.

> **NOTE**
>
> You shouldn't bother your system administrator unnecessarily, but if you find yourself having difficulty running a particular program or creating a file, do pick up the phone and tell your system administrator. He or she will enter the *superuser* mode and fix your access to a particular program or file. The superuser is really the *root account.*

Permissions for a file are specified for the owner, the owner's group—which, in a corporate environment, generally includes the people in your immediate workgroup—and the general public, which includes all other authorized UNIX users on your network or computer.

You can look at a file or directory's permissions by using the ls -l command in your home directory. When I used the ls -l command, this is what I found:

```
$ ls -l
total 9
drwxrwxrwx  1 lisas    vip            37 Feb 16 15:22 mydir
-rw-r--r--  1 lisas    vip           106 Feb 16 13:36 roadtrip
-rw-r--r--  1 lisas    vip           106 Feb 16 14:22 roadtrip2
-rw-r--r--  1 lisas    vip           106 Feb 16 14:19 roadtrip3
-r--------  1 lisas    vip           106 Feb 16 15:57 roadtrip4
-rw-r-----  1 lisas    vip           106 Feb 16 15:57 roadtrip45
-rw-rw----  1 lisas    vip           106 Feb 16 15:57 roadtrip5
-rw----r--  1 lisas    vip           106 Feb 16 15:57 roadtripA
-rw----rw-  1 lisas    vip           106 Feb 16 15:58 roadtripB
-rw-------  1 lisas    vip           106 Feb 16 15:58 roadtripC
-rwxr-xr--  2 lisas    vip           664 Feb 16 15:58 change.it
$ _
```

The roadtrip, roadtrip2, and roadtrip3 files can be read or written by me because the permissions for the owner are rw (read, write). These files can be read but not changed by anyone else. The roadtrip4 file cannot be read or written to by anyone else and can't be changed even by me because it has r only for the owner. The roadtrip45 file can be read by anyone belonging to the vip group, whereas roadtrip5 can be read or written by those belonging to vip. All other users can read roadtripA and can read or write roadtripB, *except* those in the group vip because that group has no permissions. The file change.it is an example of a file with execution permission. It can be executed by anyone belonging to vip or by me. Others can only read it.

To understand permissions in another way, look at the file permissions on roadtrip, as shown in Figure 4.1.

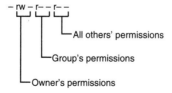

FIGURE 4.1.
Permissions for the roadtrip file.

The first character tells you whether or not you're looking at a directory; this is a file, so you see a dash (-) instead of a d. The next three characters always tell you the permissions given to the owner of the file. The first character in that set tells you whether you have read permission. If you do, you'll see an r in this position; if not, you'll see a dash (-) because a dash means that no permission is given. I have read and write permissions on the file roadtrip, but there is a dash where the execute permission would go. A dash in the execute position means that if this file were a program that could be executed (instead of being a simple text file, as it is), I would not have permission to run the program.

The next group of three characters shows the permissions given to your group. Your group, sometimes called the *workgroup*, is determined by your system administrator; your workgroup usually has to do with your function. In this case, my group can read the file, but as it now stands, no one can write to the file.

Finally, the last three characters show you the permissions given to the public at large, meaning people who aren't in your group. In this case, they can read the file, but they have no other permissions.

When you create a file on a UNIX system, certain permissions are set up by default; that is, they are created automatically. The creator, who is automatically made the owner of the file, has read and write permissions. Your workgroup gets read permissions, and normally, others outside the group have only read permissions.

You can change these permissions. Why would you want to do that? Well, perhaps you want users outside of your group to be able to write to a file that you own. You would have to give those users write permission for that file. Also, if you wanted to make sure that you didn't accidentally overwrite a file or change it, then you'd have to remove the write permission that is automatically given to you as the owner of the file.

> **WARNING**
>
> If you give one person in your workgroup a special permission in your file, then *everyone* who is in that group also gets that permission. Permissions given to a user outside your group have this drawback as well.

The command to change permissions on a file is chmod. To use it, you enter chmod, followed by a list of *permission changes* and then the filename.

A permission change has three parts. The first is a letter that indicates who the permission change affects. It can be a u for the file's owner, a g for the file's group, an o for others—meaning the rest of the UNIX-using public—and an a for everyone. The second part of a permission change is an operator that indicates whether you're adding, deleting, or setting exact permissions. These possibilities are represented by +, -, and =, respectively. Finally, the third part of a permission change has the permissions r for read, w for write, and x for execute.

Admittedly, this all sounds a little bit complicated, so some examples may help you cope. The following are some legal chmod commands and what they do:

chmod o+w crypt	Changes the write permission for the general public on the file crypt.
chmod o+r tomb	Gives the general public read permission on the file tomb.
chmod o+rw jungle	Gives the general public both read and write permissions.
chmod o-rw rainforest	Removes the read and write permissions for the general public on the file rainforest.
chmod uog-w desert	Removes the write permission on the file desert for everyone, so nobody can accidentally overwrite the file.
chmod o-r tomb2	Removes the read permission for people outside of the owner's group.
chmod uog=r aircraft	Lets everyone have only read permission on the file aircraft.

If you think about it, only certain types of chmod commands make sense. For instance, you wouldn't want to give the general public more permissions on your file than you have, so a command such as chmod u-r, o+r roadtrip wouldn't make sense, and neither would chmod u-w, u+w. It would be silly to give anyone write permission without read permission, because, of course, someone who can't look at the file won't be able to write to it. Only a few permissions make sense for files.

Try changing the permissions on your roadtrip2 file. Start by looking at the permissions with the ls -l command. (Putting the filename roadtrip2 after the command means you'll only see information for roadtrip2.) Here is the result:

```
$ ls -l roadtrip2
-rw-r--r--  1  lisas    113  Feb 1  3:44  roadtrip2
$ _
```

Use the chmod command to remove read permission for everybody except you:

```
$ chmod go-r roadtrip
$ _
```

> **WARNING**
>
> When using an option such as o-w,g+r, be careful *not* to type a space after the comma. If you do, your UNIX system may try to interpret g+r as the filename, not as a continuation of the permission changes you want, and you will see something like chmod: g+r: no such file or directory.

Now list the file roadtrip2 by using the ls -l command:

```
$ ls -l roadtrip
-rw-------   1 lisas    vip           106 Feb 16 13:36 roadtrip
$ _
```

Directories and Permissions

Permissions also apply to directories, but their meanings are slightly different. For instance, if you have read permission for a directory, you can list all of its contents—all the files and directories it contains—but you don't automatically get read permission for all of the files and directories that the directory contains. The permissions on these files and directories are all independent of the permissions on the directory that contains them.

If you have write permission for a directory, it means that you can create or put files into the directory, or delete them if you wish. You don't need to have write permission for the directory in order for you to have write permission for files already contained in the directory. In other words, you may have permission to write lines or data to an existing file in a directory, but in some cases you may not have permission to create new files in that same directory.

To change permissions on a directory, use the chmod command exactly as you did for files, keeping in mind the different meanings of the read and write permissions discussed in the preceding paragraphs. Let's explore how this works. Begin by re-creating the adventure directory:

```
$ mkdir adventure
$ _
```

Now, to change permissions on your adventure directory, start by looking at the existing permissions. Here is what I found:

```
$ ls -l a*
drwxr-----   1 lisas    vip            37 Feb  2  4:40 adventure
$ _
```

Then enter chmod u-w adventure and list the permissions on the directory, and you'll see that they have changed:

```
$ chmod u-w adventure
$ ls -l a*
dr-xr-----   1 lisas    vip          37 Feb  2  4:40 adventure
$ _
```

You can now try to move a file into the directory using the mv command:

```
$ mv roadtrip2 adventure
$
```

It doesn't work, does it? You got an error message because UNIX wouldn't let you do it. Now change the permissions back to what they were by using the chmod command again:

```
$ chmod u+w adventure
$
```

Try to move a file into the directory. It should be easy now, using the following command:

```
$ mv roadtrip2 adventure
$
```

Using *chown* and *chgrp*

The chmod command has two similar companions: chown and chgrp. The chown command changes the owner of a file. You would use this command if you were done using a file and wanted to pass it on to someone else.

Only the owner and the superuser—who has ultimate permissions—can change the ownership of a file. Consider carefully whether you want to relinquish your ownership. Once you change the ownership of a file, even if you created it, you no longer own it and you can't get it back without begging the new owner.

The chown command is used less frequently than it used to be, because now many e-mail systems provide ways for someone to mail a copy of a file from one person to another; even so, chown is still occasionally convenient. To use the command, enter chown, followed by the filename and then the login name of the person to whom you want to transfer ownership. For instance, chown lisas roadtrip3 changes ownership of the file to the user lisas.

Similarly, if you belong to a workgroup called admin, and you want to transfer ownership of a file to a group called accnting, you would use the chgrp command, followed by the filename and the new group to whom you want to transfer group permissions. The following command would change the group ownership of the file trsurchest to accnting:

87

```
$ chgrp accnting trsurchest
$ _
```

Three Useful UNIX Commands

The grep, sort, and diff commands are useful in helping you deal with files. They can help you find and sort information contained in files, and they can help you manage changes to your files.

Looking for Words and Phrases in Your Files with *grep*

When you're dealing with files on a UNIX system, one of the most useful commands is grep, which can help you find a file when you can't remember its name. If you can remember an exact phrase or word, you can use grep to search a file or directory for the phrase until you find the file you seek.

For instance, you may remember that you have a file which mentions the phrase *thousand miles,* but you can't remember what its name is. You can find all of the files containing this phrase by using the grep command, which is colloquially called "doing a grep for *thousand miles.*" To use the command, you type grep, followed by the phrase you wish to search for enclosed in single quotation marks ('), followed by the directory name. (If you already know the filename and are looking for the line where the word or phrase occurs, you can type a filename instead of a directory name.) For instance, entering the following command will find the roadtrip files in your home directory that contain the phrase *thousand miles*:

```
$ grep 'thousand miles' *
roadtrip:A journey of a thousand miles begins, hopefully, with an empty
roadtrip1:A journey of a thousand miles begins, hopefully, with an empty
roadtrip2:A journey of a thousand miles begins, hopefully, with an empty
roadtrip3:A journey of a thousand miles begins, hopefully, with an empty
roadtrip4:A journey of a thousand miles begins, hopefully, with an empty
roadtrip45:A journey of a thousand miles begins, hopefully, with an empty
roadtrip5:A journey of a thousand miles begins, hopefully, with an empty
roadtripA:A journey of a thousand miles begins, hopefully, with an empty
roadtripB:A journey of a thousand miles begins, hopefully, with an empty
roadtripC:A journey of a thousand miles begins, hopefully, with an empty
$ _
```

The grep command looked through all of the files in the directory, then picked out all of the files that contained the phrase *thousand miles,* and displayed both the filename and the line that contained the phrase. If a file contains the sought-after phrase more than once, each line will be displayed; but in this example, you know that each file contains only one occurrence of the phrase.

To "grep through a file," as UNIX-heads say, enter the grep command, followed by the expression you seek enclosed in single quotation marks, then the filename. Try using this technique to find the word *journey* in the file roadtrip2:

```
$ grep 'journey' roadtrip2
A journey of a thousand miles begins, hopefully, with an empty
$
```

The grep command is a great way to supplement your memory and to bail yourself out when you can remember some details about what was in your file, but not the filename itself. In a sense, it gives your UNIX file system one of the best features of a database: it can be searched.

Clue: I know an editor who keeps online the text of every magazine for which he writes. When he needs to do story research, he uses grep to find articles that the magazine has already done on the subject. He can find a half-dozen articles faster than anyone else on the staff can dial into online services such as Dialog and America Online, so we call him "the grep man" or "the grepster" in appreciation of his favorite command.

Actually, the power of grep lies in learning to use *regular expressions* as the search specifier—switches, also called *options*, are less powerful. Learning regular expressions is a bit beyond the scope of this book, however, so here I'll teach you some of the switches that I use frequently.

To begin, notice that for the sake of example I've modified some of the roadtrip files to capitalize some characters:

```
$ grep "thousand miles" *
roadtrip:A journey of a thousand miles begins, hopefully, with an empty
roadtrip1:A journey of a thousand miles begins, hopefully, with an empty
roadtrip45:A journey of a thousand miles begins, hopefully, with an empty
$ grep "THOUSAND MILES" *
roadtripA:A journey of a THOUSAND MILES begins, hopefully, with an empty
$ _
```

The -i option ignores the case of the search specifier. Although I type THOUSAND MILES, both lowercase and uppercase versions are returned:

```
$ grep -i "THOUSAND MILES" *
roadtrip:A journey of a thousand miles begins, hopefully, with an empty
roadtrip1:A journey of a thousand miles begins, hopefully, with an empty
roadtrip2:A journey of a Thousand Miles begins, hopefully, with an empty
roadtrip3:A journey of a Thousand miles begins, hopefully, with an empty
roadtrip4:A journey of a thousand Miles begins, hopefully, with an empty
roadtrip45:A journey of a thousand miles begins, hopefully, with an empty
roadtrip5:A journey of a thousand MILES begins, hopefully, with an empty
```

```
roadtripA:A journey of a THOUSAND MILES begins, hopefully, with an empty
roadtripB:A journey of a ThOuSaNd MiLeS begins, hopefully, with an empty
roadtripC:A journey of a THOUSAND miles begins, hopefully, with an empty
$ _
```

If I only want to know the names of the files in which the phrase "*thousand miles*" appears, regardless of case, I would enter the following:

```
$ grep -il "thousand miles" *
roadtrip
roadtrip1
roadtrip2
roadtrip3
roadtrip4
roadtrip45
roadtrip5
roadtripA
roadtripB
roadtripC
$ _
```

Clue: If you are interested in finding more options for the grep command, try entering man grep at the shell prompt.

Using *sort*

Another great little UNIX command is sort, which can sort the contents of your files. The sort command is also good for creating quick-and-dirty tables out of text files. The results of these sorts are plain ASCII text, so you can save them in files and then put them into tables or reports. There are many different switches (or options) for the sort command. Because of this variety and because the kind of sort you'll want to do will probably depend on the format of the data you have, you should check the man page for sort to see which options best fit your needs. For now, we'll look at a simple example.

To see how sort works, create a small test file:

```
$ cat > phonetest
Consuela 555-773-9944
Lee      555-415-7742
An       555-326-1365
Marie    555-437-9132
George   555-415-9807
Ctrl+d
$ _
```

Now you have a file, and you can sort it alphabetically by name:

```
$ sort phonetest
An         555-326-1365
Consuela 555-773-9944
George     555-415-9807
Lee        555-415-7742
Marie      555-437-9132
$ _
```

The sort command used your file phonetest as input and produced a sorted list. If you had wanted to save the sorted list, you would have entered something like sort phonetest > phonetest2, which would have put the contents into a file.

NOTE

It would not be a good idea to overwrite the original phonetest file, so I used phonetest2 to protect my original. Programs have been known to accidentally scramble data.

What's the Big *diff*?

The diff command compares two files and shows you which lines in each file are different from each other. To use it, you enter the command diff, followed by two filenames. UNIX responds by showing you all of the lines in the files that are different.

To see how diff works, you need to create a file called compare:

```
$ cat > compare
A journey of a thousand miles begins, hopefully, with an empty
bladder and all the appliances turned off.

It's also a good idea to pack a lunch.
Ctrl+d
$ _
```

You'll recognize the first part of this file as the sentence that's stored in the roadtrip files. You've also added a blank line and another sentence, so now you can use diff to see this difference:

```
$ diff compare roadtrip
3,4d2
<
< It's also a good idea to pack a lunch.
$ _
```

What does this output mean? The arrows (<) in the output indicate that the line displayed is in compare, but not in roadtrip. If there had been lines in roadtrip that were not in compare, the extra lines would have started with the opposing arrow, (>). UNIX does this to differentiate between the lines in the first file and those in the second. To see this, try the following:

```
$ cat > compare
A journey of a thousand miles begins, hopefully,
with an empty bladder and all the appliances turned off.

It's also a good idea to pack a lunch.
Ctrl+d
$ _
```

Now you've fixed it so that the first line of compare doesn't contain the words *with an*, but roadtrip does. Furthermore, because of this change, the second line is also different. You should expect to see these differences, then, if you use the diff command:

```
$ diff compare roadtrip
1,4c1,2
< A journey of a thousand miles begins, hopefully,
< with an empty bladder and all the appliances turned off.
<
< It's also a good idea to pack a lunch.
---
> A journey of a thousand miles begins, hopefully, with an empty
> bladder and all the appliances turned off.
$ _
```

Admittedly, the differences between these two files were predictable, but diff can be a lifesaver, especially if you have several versions of a file that you've been working on and you can't remember how you've changed each version. You can then use diff to help you remember what you've done. Maybe you asked someone to look at your file and make some changes, but you don't want to re-edit the entire file, just the changes. You can then use diff to see what the other person has changed.

There Must Be 50 Ways to Move Your Data

One of the most interesting things about UNIX is that it's easy to move the data in files from one place to another and to use the output from one command as the input to a second command. This makes it easy to link commands together to do some very useful things. That's one of the reasons why UNIX is so flexible and can be used so many ways; these building blocks can be assembled to create interesting command lines and programs.

You've already used one of the tools that re-routes data to wherever you want it to go. Do you remember what it was? If you said the redirection operator (>), you're right. Do you remember how you used the redirection operator to put the results of the cat command into a file? To refresh your memory, you did it like this:

```
$ cat roadtrip > roadtrip2
$
```

In this example, the results of using the cat command were sent—or redirected, as UNIX types would say—into a file called roadtrip2. The important thing to realize is that the redirection operator can be used with any command, not just with cat. Broadly speaking, the *output redirection operator* (>) changes the destination of data or results.

To fully understand the redirection operator, you need to understand the concepts of *standard input* and *standard output.* These are the names that UNIX aficionados have given to the standard places from which UNIX systems get their input and to which they send their output. UNIX systems usually get their input from users' terminals or workstations and usually write output to these same terminals and workstations. That's why the output of your UNIX commands is displayed to your monitor or terminal. You can change that if you wish. For example, you can redirect the output of your command to a file, as you did in the preceding example with the cat command. As you already saw, if you enter only the cat command followed by a filename, the results are displayed to your screen, but aren't saved in a file. If you redirect the output to a file, the output is saved to that file, and you can use it later.

The same principle applies to input. You can tell UNIX that you want the input to come from a place other than the screen. The operator that does this is the *input redirection symbol* (<). The most common way of using this feature is to tell UNIX to use a file as input to a command. For instance, the cat command copies the standard input (the stuff you type) to the standard output, which is on your screen. If you enter the following command, cat takes its input from the file roadtrip and displays it to the screen:

```
$ cat < roadtrip
A journey of a thousand miles begins, hopefully, with an
empty bladder and all the appliances turned off.
$ _
```

This command is, in many ways, the opposite of cat > roadtrip, which takes the input from the screen and puts it in a file. You can combine the input and output redirection operators in the same command. In the following example, the cat command takes its input from the file roadtrip, and its output is put into a file that the cat command creates for the purpose:

```
$ cat < roadtrip > Mexico
```

UNIX sees the < operator and tells the cat command to accept input from the roadtrip file. The output from cat is then redirected to a newly created file called Mexico. If you want to, you can now enter cat Mexico, and you'll see a file that's identical to roadtrip.

A variation on the theme of redirection is the >> operator, which does the same thing as > when you use it with a file, except that the redirected output is added to the end of the target file instead of wiping out what, if anything, was already in the file. If you repeat the preceding command using the *output append redirection symbol* (>>) instead of (>), you'll get a file that's twice the length of the original Mexico file:

```
$ cat < roadtrip >> Mexico
$ cat Mexico
A journey of a thousand miles begins, hopefully, with an
empty bladder and all the appliances turned off.
A journey of a thousand miles begins, hopefully, with an
empty bladder and all the appliances turned off.
$ _
```

The contents of the file roadtrip are added to the existing Mexico file, which doubles its length. To see how the result would have been different if you had used the > operator instead, try it now:

```
$ cat < roadtrip > Mexico
$ cat Mexico
A journey of a thousand miles begins, hopefully, with an
empty bladder and all the appliances turned off.
$
```

In this case, the first cat command wipes out the existing file, Mexico, and replaces it with roadtrip, which is half the length of Mexico (so to speak). In effect, you've replaced the file Mexico with a copy of roadtrip. You'll note that you've already used the same command before, but when you used it then, the file Mexico hadn't yet been created, so you didn't wipe out an existing file before filling it with the result of using the cat command on roadtrip.

The cat command isn't the only one that can be used with a redirection operator. For instance, you could put the results of the sort command into a file:

```
$ sort phonetest > magicbag
$ _
```

Pipes

By now, you've seen that you can combine commands with the redirection operator to save results to a file. There are other ways of stringing commands together. The first of these is to combine commands using pipes. Pipes do exactly what you might think they do; they can take the output of one command and use it as input to another command (see Figure 4.2). Just as water flows through pipes, data can flow through these pipes from one command to another. You can, therefore, combine commands in very interesting ways.

For instance, you could link commands as follows:

```
$ grep '415' phonetest ¦ sort > holdresults
$
```

The grep command finds the phone numbers in phonetest that have a 415 prefix, then pipes those lines into the sort command. The sort command then puts these phone numbers in alphabetical order by name. The results are then put into the file holdresults, which you can view with the cat command:

```
$ cat holdresults
George  555-415-9807
Lee 555-415-7742
$ _
```

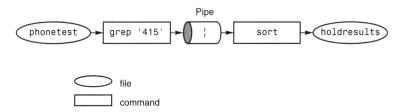

FIGURE 4.2.
The pipe makes the output of one command become the input for another command.

Suiting You to a *tee*

The last data mover you need to learn is tee. It works like a T-connector in plumbing that will send water to different places in your house: tee sends output to two different places. This makes it easy to send input to a file and send it to standard out (the screen) at the same time; or, if you use tee in conjunction with pipes, you could send output from one command to another and send it to a file so that you could look at it later. You'll use this feature more in the advanced chapters—when you learn shell programming—but for now, you need to understand how the operator works and how to read command lines that use it.

For instance, the following code displays the output of the grep command and puts this output into a file called secrets (see Figure 4.3):

```
$ grep '415' phonetest ¦ tee secrets
Lee 555-415-7742
George  555-415-9807
$ _
```

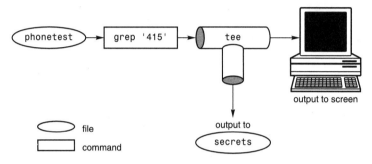

FIGURE 4.3.

The tee command creates two copies of the output of a command; you can direct the output as you wish.

You can combine pipes, tees, and redirection operators all in the same command, if you wish. You'll do a lot of that when we get to shell programming, but for now, you can pull together everything you've learned if you can figure out this command:

```
$ grep '415' phonetest ¦ tee hold ¦ sort > results
$ _
```

Looks intimidating, huh? Don't worry; just break it down into pieces. The first part is a grep command that says to look for the characters 415 in the phonetest file. The first pipe says to take the output of that command and use it as input to the next command, which is tee hold. The tee command says to stick this input into a file called hold. If you use the cat command on the file called hold, you get:

```
$ cat hold
Lee 555-415-7742
George  555-415-9807
$
```

This is what you would expect; the grep command picked out the lines containing 415 in the order in which it found them in the phonetest file. The results of this procedure were then stashed in the hold file.

The next pipe takes output from the tee command. Remember what tee does? It diverts a copy of input to a file, but the other copy of the data is still there. The pipe makes it flow into the sort command, which sorts this input into alphabetical order. The output of this sort command is then redirected into a file called results. You can view results by using the cat command on this file, and you'll see that the two names have now been put into alphabetical order:

```
$ cat results
George  555-415-9807
Lee 555-415-7742
$ _
```

Congratulations! You've learned how to use the flexibility of UNIX to assemble complex command lines. That's a big step toward attaining mastery of the power of UNIX.

What You've Learned

In this chapter, you have learned how to change permissions on files and directories. Changing permissions is useful for when you want to give file access to a friend or when you want to protect yourself from overwriting a file. You learned how to search files for data and how to sort your data. Lastly, you learned how to redirect output with redirection symbols and the tee command.

Rewards

✗ You learned what permissions on files and directories are, and how to change them using chmod, chgrp, and chown.

✗ You learned that UNIX normally gets its input from standard in—your terminal or workstation screen—and writes the output of commands to standard out.

✗ You learned how to redirect input and output from standard in and standard out.

✗ You now understand that a pipe (¦) enables you to redirect the standard output of one command to the standard input for another.

✗ You learned that the tee command enables you to copy output between standard out and another command.

✖ You understand how to use diff—the difference command—to find changes made to a file or the difference between two files.

✖ You know how to use grep to find phrases in your files.

✖ You can use the sort command to alphabetize words in a file or sort numeric data.

✖ You learned how to combine diff, grep, and sort with pipes, tees, and redirection operators.

Pitfalls

✖ Changing the ownership on your files or directories with the chown command can lead you into trouble. You could lose the rights to your own files. Be careful!

✖ File permissions should be handled with care. Always check your work. It is easy to leave access to others without knowing it.

✖ Redirection can lead to disaster if you redirect output over your original file. Always redirect to a new file.

✖ You can "freeze" your pipes with too many redirection symbols. Use several small steps for a task, instead of trying to do everything on one command line.

Scoping Out the Territory

Setting Yourself Up to Succeed in Your Quest

In This Chapter

✖ *What is a shell, and how is it used?*

✖ *What are the different shells?*

✖ *What are environment variables, and how do they interact with UNIX and with the shells?*

✖ *What are the following environment variables, how do they work, and how should you set them?*

PATH
EDITOR
VISUAL
PAGER
DISPLAY
USER
HOME
MAIL
PWD
SHELL
TERM

Should You Read This Chapter?

This chapter is designed for people either who aren't working in a corporate environment where a system administrator can help them with such things as installing new software, or who are learning to program in UNIX systems. If you are installing your own software (especially freeware, which usually requires that you be fairly self-sufficient to use it) or if you expect to do UNIX shell programming or system administration later on, you should read this chapter. If not, you can safely skip to the next chapter without worry.

Shells and a Little White Lie About UNIX

Now is the time when I tell you that I haven't been entirely honest with you in the preceding chapters. That's because you weren't quite ready to understand some of the more subtle points about the UNIX environment in which you work. However, if you've gotten this far, you're ready to learn some of the more esoteric-yet-crucial details about the UNIX operating system and operating environment.

What I've withheld from you is that UNIX isn't really executing most of your commands. There's actually something between you and the UNIX operating system, an intermediary of sorts, called a *shell*. A shell is the user's interface to the computer and executes commands for the user.

When I've written "UNIX interprets the command to mean…," or "UNIX thinks you mean…," I was actually committing jargon abuse, because I was finessing the fact that you aren't interacting with UNIX directly. You're interacting with a shell.

Why did I do that? Because when you're learning a new subject, you want to know the details that matter, when they start to matter. Until now, it probably didn't matter to you what your environment was like or why it differed from your concept of it. Now, you're at a level where you need to start to care about more subtle concepts. You need a more exact view of the UNIX world.

You're actually interacting with a shell when you type commands on the UNIX command line. Most shells will take a command line as input from the user, process that command line, and then execute the command.

A shell also enables a user to display and change the user environment described previously. If the command you type is an internal shell command, then the shell takes care of it; if, however, the command is not an internal command, the shell will look for a program and run that program. The program, when UNIX finds it, will inherit the user's environment.

SKIP THIS, IT'S TECHNICAL

Because UNIX is a multiuser operating system, it must manage the resources available to anyone who might be logged in; it must prevent one user from "stepping on the toes" of another user. For example, when I use a UNIX system, I cannot create a program that will directly access a disk drive and read or write data based upon its hardware track and sector numbers. If I could, I might write over your data, and you might write over mine if you created a similar program! Instead, a request must be made on my behalf to get or place the data. UNIX will handle how and where the data is placed on the disk. UNIX knows how to manage the disk, and users don't have to worry about the details (or about losing data because of another user).

UNIX does its management by having a central core called the *kernel* that operates in what is generally called *protected mode*. The processes and functions performed by the kernel cannot be invoked without some sort of middle man to ask it to do the desired operation. This hides the underlying hardware from the user. When you are typing commands at your workstation or terminal, the *shell* is acting as the middle man.

Two shells were available with early UNIX systems: the Bourne shell, named after its creator Stephen Bourne; and the C shell, so named because it was based on the C language. Many other shells are used in UNIX environments, but most of them are derived from one of these two, and, as a result, are very similar to one of these.

Historically, many users have used the Bourne shell to write shell programs—usually called *shell scripts*. The Bourne shell is usually referred to as the UNIX shell or simply "the shell," perhaps because it is the oldest of all the shells. Therefore, most early shell scripts were already written using the Bourne shell. On the other hand, the C shell has often been used for interactive shells because it supports more interactive capabilities than the Bourne shell.

The people who use the Bourne shell and C shell are mostly programmers who grew up with the UNIX operating system and its associated shells, so they are very familiar with them. You may find that such users frequently switch from one shell to another (although many users prefer a particular one). I do not advise today's beginners to switch back and forth between these two shells, even if both shells are available.

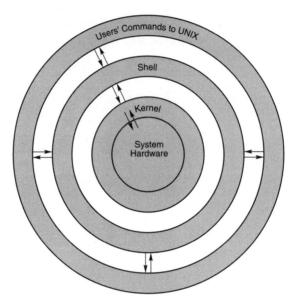

FIGURE 5.1.

The shell manages the command requests of multiple users.

That's because the shells are similar enough to cause great confusion. Learning several shells would be a lot like trying to learn French, Spanish, and Italian all at the same time; it's easy to confuse the French version of one, two, three—*un, deux, trois*—with the Spanish version—*uno, dos, tres*. If you're like most people, learning both at the same time would result in what linguists call "linguistic interference." After all, shell programming languages are just that, languages.

I suggest that you pick a shell and stick exclusively to that shell until you feel ready for the challenge of learning another. For many people, this decision will be made for them, because the system administrator may have already configured the system to use one or the other. This is your shell by default, but you are by no means restricted to using that shell. If you prefer one shell as your default over the others, simply send e-mail to your system administrator saying that you want your shell changed. By the way, you can switch from one to the other on the fly.

> **NOTE**
>
> A number of other shells have evolved since the early days of UNIX. In particular, the Korn shell supports everything the Bourne shell does, and the Korn shell has incorporated some of the C shell's most convenient features, such as the capability for users to see the last 20 or 30 commands they typed.

How do you know which shell you've been using? You can usually tell by looking at the prompt (I say "usually" because system administrators can change the prompt). The Bourne shell has a dollar ($) sign prompt or a prompt that ends with a $. The C shell usually uses a prompt that ends in a percent (%) sign. You can also find out your shell by entering a command at the shell prompt:

```
$ grep lisas /etc/passwd
lisas:2034:205:Lisa Stapleton:/bin/sh
$ _
```

The /etc/passwd is a file used by the system administrator to set up user accounts. It includes your account name, user identification number, group identification number, real name, and default shell. The default shell is of greatest concern. The grep command extracts from the /etc/passwd file the line containing lisas. The last thing on the line is /bin/sh, which is the name of the default shell. The sh indicates the Bourne shell. A /bin/csh indicates the C shell, and /bin/ksh indicates the Korn shell.

Because the Korn shell is less common than the other two, it won't be covered here in great detail. It's basically a Bourne shell with a few features of the C shell thrown in for good measure. Virtually all UNIX systems have either the Bourne or the C shell, so I'll focus on how to use these.

Pick a shell and stick to it. Read the discussion of the other shells, but don't study their commands very intently until you feel comfortable with your chosen shell. If you're using the Korn shell, read the sections on the Bourne shell and the C shell, and that should explain the high points of the Korn shell.

The Bourne Shell

As I mentioned earlier, the Bourne shell was written by Stephen Bourne and is abbreviated sh, for "shell." If you're not already in the Bourne shell but have decided to use it, you can change your shell by entering /bin/sh at the UNIX command line to start the Bourne shell. Every time you log in, special configuration files tell the operating system what shell to run for you. These configuration files can be different for each individual.

Shell Commands

You already know a few shell commands. You just didn't realize that they were shell commands when you learned them. For instance, the pwd command, which shows you the current working directory, is a shell command that happens to work in the same manner in both the Bourne and C shells.

The cd command, which changes directories, is another familiar shell command that works the same in both shells. You already know this one. For instance, if you enter cd /tmp at either the Bourne or C shell prompts, the effect is the same; you'll change your current working directory to /tmp:

```
$ pwd
/usr/home/lisas
$ cd /tmp
$ pwd
/tmp
$
```

Types of Variables in the Bourne Shell

One of the most important concepts of shells is that of variables. A *shell variable* holds one or more values, such as character strings and integers.

In the Bourne shell, there are two kinds of variables: local and environment. *Local variables*, sometimes called *shell variables*, have meaning only to the shell you're in. If you ever set these variables and suddenly change your shell, they won't remain set. *Environment variables*, on the other hand, have meaning outside the shell in which they're set. They mean something to the UNIX operating system and don't have to be interpreted by the shell. You can make local variables into environment variables by using the export command, which is explained in one of the following sections.

Environment variables, such as PATH, should remain constant for all invocations of the shell. The PATH variable is searched by the shell as it looks for programs that you invoke on the command line. If you enter the grep command at the command line, the shell uses the PATH variable to search every directory on the PATH line, looking for grep to run. You will see more on the PATH variable later in this chapter.

> **SKIP THIS, IT'S TECHNICAL**
>
> Environment variables are passed from one process (program) to another. The shell you are in is really a UNIX process. You already know that you can execute programs from your shell, but you can also execute another shell, /bin/sh. Inside the new shell, you can execute yet another copy of the shell. No matter how many times you execute the shell, the environment variables and their values are passed from one shell to the next. The local variables are not passed, however, because they are valid in only one shell at a time.

Predefined Environment Variables in the Bourne Shell

The following are some common predefined environment variables in the Bourne shell:

✖ CDPATH   This variable contains the list of places (directories, in other words) that the cd command will look for directories. For example, the following shows that when I enter the cd command, my HOME directory will be searched:

```
$ echo $CDPATH
.:..:$HOME
$ _
```

Clue: The CDPATH variable doesn't have a value by default. It must be set in your login script (such as .profile). This example shows that the system first searches the current directory for the specified directory name. If not found, it then looks in the parent directory. Lastly, it looks in your HOME directory.

✖ MAIL   This is the filename of your mail file. Shells use it to check to see if you have new e-mail so they can notify you. Mail programs use it to know where to get your incoming mail. The following is a sample value for a user named zachary:

```
$ echo $MAIL
/usr/spool/mail/zachary
$ _
```

✖ PS1   The primary prompt for command lines. This prompt is displayed when the shell is being run interactively and is waiting for the next command. The default value (if you don't change it) for PS1 is $:

```
$ echo $PS1
$
$ _
```

✖ PS2   The secondary prompt for command lines. You probably won't be using this one much until you get to the chapter on shell programming. This prompt is displayed when the shell is waiting for the rest of a command that has not been completed. The default value for PS2 is >:

```
$ echo $PS2
>
$ _
```

- **TERM** This environment variable should have the name of the type of terminal you use. This is important because almost any program that moves a cursor around a screen—such as editors or forms-based programs—needs to know your terminal type because different keys mean different things to different terminals, and not all terminals recognize all of the same keys.

  Your system administrator, if you have one, has probably already set this variable, so you probably won't have to change it. Unless your terminal sometimes does unexplained things when you press normal-looking keys, this value is probably okay. Here's an example:

  ```
  $ echo $TERM
  vt100
  $ _
  ```

- **EDITOR** This environment variable is used by many different programs, such as `mail` and `rn`. These programs execute the editor specified by this environment variable. If you want to use a different editor than the default editor, you should set this environment variable:

  ```
  $ echo $EDITOR
  /usr/ucb/vi
  $ _
  ```

- **VISUAL** This environment variable is used by many different programs in much the same way that the `EDITOR` environment variable is used:

  ```
  $ echo $VISUAL
  /usr/ucb/vi
  $ _
  ```

- **SHELL** This is the filename of the shell that many programs will run if you use a shell escape character, usually the exclamation point (more on that in the chapter on shell scripts). The default value for `SHELL` is your login shell:

  ```
  $ echo $SHELL
  /usr/bin/sh
  $ _
  ```

- **PAGER** This environment variable is used by many different programs to determine which program they should use to display files for you.

  ```
  $ echo $PAGER
  /usr/ucb/more
  $ _
  ```

✖ DISPLAY This variable is used by X-Windows to determine where your display is. This value can change to allow a program to run on one computer while it opens up graphic windows on a different computer. A common value is localhost: 0.0:

```
$ echo $DISPLAY
localhost:0.0
$ _
```

✖ USER This is your user name based on your login name:

```
$ echo $USER
zachary
$ _
```

✖ PATH The PATH variable is very important to you, even though you're a fairly new UNIX user. It tells UNIX where to look to find the commands that you type. If you type the name of a games program called rubyquest, UNIX looks for it first in its list of shell commands. UNIX then looks for the name in the list of paths in the PATH environment variable. If you're ever tried to install software and received error messages indicating that the program you're trying to run can't find a particular file or directory, you need to check the value of the PATH variable to see if that's the problem, and set it appropriately:

```
$ echo $PATH
PATH=.:$HOME/bin:/bin:/usr/sbin:/sbin; export PATH;
$ _
```

NOTE

Think of the PATH as a list of places for your computer's personality—call her Shellie—to check for a treasure. If you ask for an emerald, Shellie will first look in her pockets (internal commands), and if they come up empty, she will look in each place on the path, in order, until she finds a real emerald.

The shell will do something quite similar. If you give it a command, it will first look to see if that command is an internal command for the shell, and then it will look in each directory in the path to see if there is a file with the same name as the command that is also executable. If it finds the command, the command will be executed with the rest of the parameters as arguments.

> For instance, the following command tells the shell to look first for
> commands in the directory /bin. If the command you type isn't found
> there, the shell will go and look for it in /usr/bin. If the command isn't
> there, the shell looks for it in /usr/local/bin. Finally, if the command
> still hasn't been found, the shell looks in the home directory of the user in
> the subdirectory called bin.
>
> ```
> PATH =/bin:/usr/bin:/usr/local/bin:$HOME/bin:
> ```

✖ HOME   This variable is set when you log in UNIX. It is the pathname of
your home directory:

```
$ echo $HOME
/usr/home/lisas
$ _
```

To set the preceding or any local variables, use the name of the variable you want
to set, followed by the equals (=) sign, followed by the value you want to give to
the variable. Surround the value to the right of the = sign with quotes. It is important to have no white space on either side of the = sign.

For example, you probably didn't realize it, but you can change the symbol you
see for the UNIX command-line prompt. The variable is called PS1 (all uppercase), so to set the variable, which is local, enter the following command:

```
PS1="Awaiting Your Every Command, Master! "
```

Now press Enter a few times. Your prompt has been changed to something more
appropriate to your station in life. Now change it back to what it was. Assuming
your prompt was the dollar sign, the following command will make the change:

```
PS1= "$"
```

This change will be in effect only until you log out. When you log back in again,
any prompt you've already set in a previous session will be forgotten and replaced
with your standard prompt.

```
$ PS1="Awaiting Your Every Command, Master! "
Awaiting Your Every Command, Master! echo $PS1
Awaiting Your Every Command, Master!

Awaiting Your Every Command, Master! PS1="$ "
$ _
```

NOTE

After you learn to use vi (or some other editor or word processor that can edit ASCII text files), you can make permanent changes to variable settings. This is done by placing the changes in your login script. For the Bourne shell and the Korn shell, this is a hidden file called .profile. For the C shell, there are two hidden scripts: .login and .cshrc. The first is read only when you log in to the system. The second is read whenever a new C shell is invoked. These are discussed later. Below is an example .profile. With this setup, you would always see Awaiting Your Every Command, Master! for your prompt.

```
Awaiting Your Every Command, Master! cat .profile
PATH=.:$HOME/bin:/usr/ccs/bin:/bin:/usr/sbin:/sbin; export PATH;
MANPATH=$MANPATH:$ONLINE_BACKUP/man:/usr/man; export MANPATH;
EDITOR=vi;export EDITOR;
CDPATH=.:..:$HOME; export CDPATH;
PS1="Awaiting Your Every Command, Master! "
```

More About Bourne Shell Commands

The export command is used to make local variables into environment variables. The following command makes the PATH variable into an environment variable. All commands that are executed from the Bourne shell will have the same initial value of PATH.

```
$ export PATH
$ echo $PATH
PATH=.:/$HOME/bin:/usr/ccs/bin:/bin:/usr/sbin:/sbin
$ _
```

The cd command is used to change your current working directory. The following example shows how you would change to a temporary directory:

```
$ cd /tmp
$ _
```

The pwd command, on the other hand, displays your current working directory. This command takes no parameters. The following example shows what you would get if you executed the pwd command immediately after the preceding example:

```
$ pwd
/tmp
$ _
```

If you enter the cd command without a parameter, the cd command takes you back to the directory in the environment variable $HOME. The following shows a combination of commands to demonstrate the cd command:

```
$ echo $HOME
/usr/home/lisas
$ pwd
/tmp
$ cd
$ pwd
/usr/home/lisas
$ _
```

As you have noticed by now, the echo command outputs the parameters that are passed to it. Whatever the value of the object to the right of the command, that's what you'll see. It also echoes on the command line a string that is passed to it. The following example asks what kind of terminal I'm using, and prints the following string:

```
$ echo $TERM
vt100
$ echo 'Can we say UNIX'
Can we say UNIX
$ _
```

The exit command quits the current shell. If that shell is also the login shell (the shell you began with when you logged in), the user is automatically logged out of UNIX. You'll use this command more when you do shell programming.

```
$ exit
Hey, I'm out of here

UNIX(r) System V Release 4.0 (excelsior-bb)

login: _
```

The C Shell

The C shell, so named because of its similarity in appearance to the C language, does almost everything the Bourne shell does, but it also has an interesting feature called *history* that can save you a lot of work. Before you begin, if you aren't already in the C shell and you want to use it, enter /bin/csh at the prompt:

```
$ echo $SHELL
/sbin/sh
$ /bin/csh
% _
```

The History Feature

One of the best features of the C shell and Korn shell is the history feature, which lets you see a listing of the most recent commands you've entered. This is particularly helpful if you're trying to figure out why something seems to have gone wrong, and you don't know why UNIX is behaving strangely. Often, you didn't enter a command exactly the way you thought you did, and that is the source of the problem.

To use this feature, you must set an environment variable to activate the history list:

```
$ set history=99
$ _
```

Before going any further, you must record a few commands in the history list, so enter the following commands at the prompt:

```
% ls -l roadtrip
-rw-r--r--    1 lisas     vip             106 Feb 16 13:36 roadtrip
% cat roadtrip
A journey of a thousand miles begins, hopefully, with an empty
bladder and all the appliances turned off.
% ls -l r*
-rw-r--r--    1 lisas     vip             106 Feb 16 13:36 roadtrip
-rw-r--r--    1 lisas     vip             106 Feb 16 14:22 roadtrip2
-rw-r--r--    1 lisas     vip             106 Feb 16 14:19 roadtrip3
-r--------    1 lisas     vip             106 Feb 16 15:57 roadtrip4
-rw-r----    1 lisas     vip             106 Feb 16 15:57 roadtrip45
-rw-rw----    1 lisas     vip             106 Feb 16 15:57 roadtrip5
-rw----r--    1 lisas     vip             106 Feb 16 15:57 roadtripA
-rw----rw-    1 lisas     vip             106 Feb 16 15:58 roadtripB
-rw------    1 lisas     vip             106 Feb 16 15:58 roadtripC
% _
```

After you're done with that, enter the following command to see a history of your commands:

```
% history
    1  ls -l
    2  cat roadtrip
    3  ls -l r*
    4  history
% _
```

You see that there are four commands in the history list. The four commands listed are the only commands you have entered since the set history=99 was entered.

Clue: You can probably guess that if you reset the history variable, the list will also be reset. You should set your history variable to 20 so that all of your history will appear on one screen.

The numbers give you the order in which the commands were executed. These numbers are important, because one of the neat ways you can use the history feature is to reduce the need to retype different commands. You can execute any of the commands in your history by entering an exclamation point (!)—commonly called *bang* by UNIX users—followed by the number of the command you wish to execute again. If you enter the following shell command, you'll execute the `ls -l r*` command, which corresponds to the number 3 in the history:

```
% !3
ls -l r*
-rw-r--r--    1 lisas     vip           106 Feb 16 13:36 roadtrip
-rw-r--r--    1 lisas     vip           106 Feb 16 14:22 roadtrip2
-rw-r--r--    1 lisas     vip           106 Feb 16 14:19 roadtrip3
-r--------    1 lisas     vip           106 Feb 16 15:57 roadtrip4
-rw-r----    1 lisas     vip           106 Feb 16 15:57 roadtrip45
-rw-rw----    1 lisas     vip           106 Feb 16 15:57 roadtrip5
-rw----r--    1 lisas     vip           106 Feb 16 15:57 roadtripA
-rw----rw-    1 lisas     vip           106 Feb 16 15:58 roadtripB
-rw-------    1 lisas     vip           106 Feb 16 15:58 roadtripC
% _
```

That was easy enough. Now enter the numbers corresponding to the first two preceding commands, that is `ls -l roadtrip` and `cat roadtrip`. You'll re-execute the first two commands in the history file:

```
% !1
ls -l roadtrip
-rw-r--r--    1 lisas     vip           106 Feb 16 13:36 roadtrip
% !2
cat roadtrip
A journey of a thousand miles begins, hopefully, with an empty
bladder and all the appliances turned off.
% _
```

Finally, you should know that you don't always have to use numbers with the `history` command. You can also tell the `history` command to repeat the last command that started with certain letters. For instance, to execute the last command in the preceding list that started with the letter *c* (in other words, the `cat` command), enter the following command:

```
% !c
cat roadtrip
A journey of a thousand miles begins, hopefully, with an empty
bladder and all the appliances turned off.
% _
```

This command will execute the last command that started with the letter *c*, which in this case is the *only* one that started with *c*, the `cat` command. If you'd had several commands that started with *c*, you would need to give the history feature enough letters to specify uniquely which command you want to execute. If you had to distinguish between a `chmod` and a `cat` command, entering `!ch` would be enough to specify that you want the `chmod` command, not the `cat` command; `chmod` would be the command in the history that started with *ch*.

Entering an exclamation mark and a letter may be easier for you, because you don't have to keep entering the history command to get the right numbers to use; rather, you can enter an exclamation point and a few letters that you know you've recently typed. Be careful not to accidentally issue any commands that might alter your files in undesirable ways, unless you're sure that's the right command.

NOTE

If the history feature has to choose between two commands that haven't been uniquely described, it will choose the last one that fits the description given, and it will execute that command.

Clue: You should know about another powerful feature of history before going on. It is bang bang (!!). The !! will execute the last command in the history list.

Predefined C-Shell Variables

Many of the variables and commands that work in the Bourne shell also work in the C shell. For instance, echo, home, cdpath, term, prompt, and mail mean the same things in the C shell as they do in the Bourne shell.

Here are some new variables you need to learn now, because they are included in the C shell:

✖ nobeep   Sets your terminal so that it doesn't beep at you when you make a mistake. Setting nobeep to *on* means your colleagues never need know when you've made a mistake.

✖ noclober   Setting this variable to *on* means that UNIX won't let you accidentally overwrite your file with, for example, a bad cat command.

✖ savehistory   This variable is a number, and it determines the maximum number of commands to be kept in your history.

✖ `ignoreeof`   Remember how you learned to enter Control+d to get out
of weird states in UNIX, but you also learned that if you
entered it too many times, you'd be logged out of UNIX?
If you set this variable to *on*, you won't be logged out of
UNIX for too many Control+d commands.

How to Set Variables in the C Shell

The C shell uses many of the same concepts that were discussed in the section on
the Bourne shell. Both shells have local and environment variables, and both enable you to *export* local variables so that they become environment variables and
can be used by other programs that you might use or write.

The main difference between the use of variables in the two shells is in the format
of the command that sets variables. Instead of using an equals sign (=), as you do
in the Bourne shell, you must use the `set` command.

For instance, to set your terminal to be a VT100, you would enter the following:

```
% set term=vt100
% _
```

To get rid of annoying beeps, you'd use the following command:

```
% set nobeep
% _
```

Note that the word "on" doesn't appear in the command. That's because when
you set a C-shell variable that can only be on or off (that is, it's not to be set to a
number or a word), it's automatically turned on. All you have to do is set it, and
it's on. The same idea applies to the following example:

```
% set noclober
% _
```

Finally, to see how to set a variable to a number, look at the following example,
which sets to 20 the number of commands that the system will remember and
display when you enter the `history` command:

```
% set history=20
```

━━ ━━ ━━ ━━ ━━ ━━ ━━ ━━ ━━ ━━ ━━ ━━ ━━ ━━ ━━ ━━ ━━ ━━ ━━

Clue: To remove a variable added with the `set` command, use the `unset`
command:

```
% set noclobber
% set
argv    ()
```

```
cwd      /usr/home/lisas
home     /usr/home/lisas
noclobber
path     (. /usr/ccs/bin /bin /usr/sbin /sbin /usr/ucb  )
prompt   %
shell    /bin/csh
status   0
term     vt220
user     lisas
% unset noclobber
% set
argv     ()
cwd      /usr/home/lisas
home     /usr/home/lisas
path     (. /usr/ccs/bin /bin /usr/sbin /sbin /usr/ucb  )
prompt   %
shell    /bin/csh
status   0
term     vt220
user     lisas
% _
```

Some Common C-Shell Files

In C-shell environments, you may hear references to the following files and their contents. You don't have to do anything with them at this point, but you should know the following general definitions of what they are. You might ask your system administrator to explain to you how she has set up these files for you, so you can ask her to make any changes that could make you more efficient and comfortable in your environment:

- ✖ .login   This file is checked once every time you log in. This is the file where you would put environment variables that you want set every time you log in.

- ✖ .cshrc   This file is re-executed or, as shell programmers say, *sourced* every time you execute csh. This is commonly where you would set csh local shell variables, such as those that contain pathnames.

- ✖ .logout This file is checked for instructions each time you log off the machine. This usually is where the commands that clear the screen or display an exit message are placed.

Local Variables in the C Shell and How to Set Them

Setting local variables in the C shell is quite simple. For example, to set the history command to set variables in the C shell, do this:

```
% set history=20
% _
```

As you have learned, the variable history is set to the value 20. Local variables are created with the set command, which is built into the C shell. A local variable is valid only in this running of the shell. To see all the local variables currently in use, enter set without parameters:

```
% set
argv    ()
cwd     /usr/home/lisas
home    /usr/home/lisas
path    (. /usr/ccs/bin /bin /usr/sbin /sbin /usr/ucb  )
prompt  %
shell   /bin/csh
status  0
term    vt220
user    lisas
% _
```

Some of these variables—such as home, path, and shell—you have seen in the Bourne shell. The cwd is the current working directory, basically where you are now; cwd will be different from the home variable if you are working in a directory that is different from your home directory. The prompt is your current shell prompt (%); user is your account name; status is the result of your last command; and argv is a list of parameters passed to your shell.

SKIP THIS, IT'S TECHNICAL

The status variable is a special variable that will be set by executed commands to give you feedback on whether the command executed properly or didn't find what it expected. If you execute grep to search for journey in the roadtrip file, this is what happens:

```
% cat roadtrip
A journey of a thousand miles begins, hopefully, with an empty
 bladder and all the appliances turned off.
% grep journey roadtrip
A journey of a thousand miles begins, hopefully, with an
% echo $status
0
% grep JOURNEY roadtrip

% echo $status
1
% _
```

Now don't panic, this isn't as bad as it looks. First you use cat roadtrip to see the contents of roadtrip. Next you search for journey in roadtrip and use grep to return the line that contains the word *journey*. (See Chapter 4, "Working in UNIX Environments," for a review of grep.)

> When grep completed, it set the status variable to 0, meaning the search
> was successful. You entered echo $status to see that it is set to 0. The
> second execution of grep tries to find the uppercased JOURNEY, but it is
> unsuccessful and sets the status variable to 1 for failure. Thus, you can use
> status to help make decisions in processing.

Creating Environment Variables in the C Shell

Environment variables in the C shell are created differently from the local variables. To create an environment variable, use the setenv command, which is built into the C shell. Environment variables for the C shell are the same as they were for the Bourne shell. They are valid for every C shell that is invoked. To create an environment variable, enter setenv, followed by the variable name and value:

```
% setenv PRINTER sams_lp
% _
```

This sets the variable PRINTER to the value sams_lp. To see all the environment variables in the C shell, enter printenv at the shell prompt:

```
% printenv
HOME=/usr/home/lisas
PATH=(. /usr/ccs/bin /bin /usr/sbin /sbin /usr/ucb  )
SHELL=/bin/csh
LOGNAME=lisas
TERM=vt220
PWD=lisas
% _
```

This is very similar to the local variables, except LOGNAME replaces user and PWD replaces cwd. Did you notice that the environment variables are all in uppercase characters? This is how you tell them from the local variables. You can see individual variable values by entering printenv with the variable name:

```
% printenv HOME
/usr/home/lisas
% _
```

Aliases

One last thing about the C shell that you should know and will find very useful is aliases. An *alias* is basically another name for something, a synonym. UNIX aliases enable you to associate a very long command with one word. For example, you could print your local variables and have them sorted:

```
% set
argv    ()
home    /usr/home/lisas
```

119

```
path    (. /usr/ccs/bin /bin /usr/sbin /sbin /usr/ucb  )
prompt  %
shell   /bin/csh
status  0
cwd     /usr/home/lisas
term    vt220
user    lisas
prompt  %
% set ¦ sort
argv    ()
cwd     /usr/home/lisas
home    /usr/home/lisas
path    (. /usr/ccs/bin /bin /usr/sbin /sbin /usr/ucb  )
prompt  %
shell   /bin/csh
status  0
term    vt220
user    lisas
% _
```

First, I entered set to see the local variables not sorted. Then I entered set, piped
to sort, to see the variable sorted. Now I need to make an alias for set ¦ sort and
name it ss:

```
% alias ss set ¦ sort
% ss
argv    ()
cwd     /usr/home/lisas
home    /usr/home/lisas
path    (. /usr/ccs/bin /bin /usr/sbin /sbin /usr/ucb  )
prompt  %
shell   /bin/csh
status  0
term    vt220
user    lisas
% _
```

You can see from this example that ss is now the command for set ¦ sort. To
reverse this alias, enter unalias ss at the shell prompt:

```
% unalias ss
% _
```

To see all your aliases, enter alias without parameters at your shell prompt:

```
% alias
ss=set ¦ sort
ll=ls -l
la=ls -la
% _
```

Clue: If you're a big DOS fan or are making that step from DOS to UNIX, you might want to use some of these aliases:

```
% alias dirw ls        (same as dir/w)
% alias dir ls -l      (same as dir)
% alias type cat       (same as type)
% alias edit vi        (same as edit)
```

To Learn More

To learn more about your shell, use the man command followed by the proper abbreviation for the shell:

```
$ man csh
$ man sh
$ man ksh
```

What You've Learned

In this chapter, you have learned the basics of the Bourne shell and C shell. You can now tell the difference between local and environment variables. In the C shell, you know how to recall your commands with history, and you know how to make aliases for your favorite commands.

Rewards

✖ You understand that shells are the intermediaries, or interfaces, between you and the UNIX operating system.

✖ You know that the Bourne shell (sh), the C shell, and the Korn shell are very popular shells.

✖ You know the difference between local and environment variables, and you know how to use export to turn local variables into environment variables.

✖ You know the most common variables and how to set them from either shell.

✖ You know how to use the history command to look at your command history.

✖ You know how to use ! followed by either a history number or a few letters that identify the command you want to re-execute.

Pitfalls

✖ Don't enter the exit command too often, or you could find yourself needing to log back into UNIX again.

✖ You will spend tremendous amounts of time coming up with little acronyms to alias your favorite commands.

✖ Jumping from the Bourne shell to the C Shell can be a little confusing at first, but with practice you will make the transition.

✖ When you become proficient with variables, someone might accuse you of being a UNIX shell script programmer. Egad!

Emacs, vi, and sed, Oh My!

6

Or, Why People Invented Word Processors

In This Chapter

✖ *Why would anyone want to use an editor such as Emacs, vi, or sed?*

✖ *What are some of the free editors that are provided with almost all UNIX systems?*

✖ *How can you use vi to do such basic editing tasks as moving through a file a letter at a time, a word at a time, or a line at a time; inserting, deleting, or moving text; and making changes to text?*

✖ *How can vi users set up their vi environment so they can be their most productive?*

✖ *What is Emacs, and what is the Free Software Foundation?*

✖ *How do you use Emacs to do basic editing tasks?*

✖ *What is a stream editor?*

✖ *When is sed the most convenient editor to use?*

▶

✘ *What are the most common options and commands in the* sed *editor?*

✘ *How can you use* sed *to quickly make global changes throughout your files?*

UNIX Text Editors

In this chapter, you're going to learn about the ugly side of UNIX—its editors. These editors are definitely a trip back to the state-of-the-art circa 1976. If you have worked on a modern word processor such as Word for Windows or WordPerfect, these UNIX editors will seem positively barbaric.

In the old days, believe it or not, people used text editors for everything, not just for occasionally editing a text file. They used text editors to write reports, business letters, and presentations, as well as to write programs and UNIX scripts. Today, you'd have to be mentally deficient—one burger shy of a Happy Meal, as the kids say—to produce reports, letters, and presentations with a text editor.

That's because modern word processors can handle all kinds of things—fonts, formats, page layout—that are either horrendously complicated or just plain impossible using the old-style editors. This is, in part, because many of these newer word processors produce proprietary-formatted documents, and each has its own scheme for creating these documents, so they're not limited to text-only, the way UNIX text editors are.

> **NOTE**
>
> *Proprietary format* means that the company which produced the word processor has made its way of creating and reading files specific to its word processor. These word-processing files or documents cannot be read by a competitor's word processor without some kind of conversion program. If you have a word processor, try outputting its contents to the screen with cat, and you will see a mumbo-jumbo of gobbledygook on the screen. This file is in a binary form from the word processor and must be read and displayed by the word processor.
>
> A *text-only format* uses the plain ASCII-format characters. It has no proprietary format. It can output text to the screen. You have been doing that all along in the book. Man pages, shell scripts, and the roadtrip file are examples of plain text.

I will tell you, however, that if your word processor can save documents as text, ASCII text, or text with line breaks, you could use it to produce whatever files, scripts, or programs you'll need to create. With a little bit of work, you can avoid entirely the need to learn vi, Emacs, or any of the other editors mentioned here.

To their credit, the old-style text editors grew up with the UNIX operating system and are therefore sometimes the most efficient editors for some tasks you'll need to do when you work with UNIX. For instance, because most popular, free UNIX mail programs and newsgroup readers use vi as their editor, it is often easiest to use the vi editor to type a reply or edit your response.

This is true, for example, of the newsreader rn. When you want to reply to someone's message, you can tell the newsreader the name of a text file that you've prepared, if you've already done so. If you don't provide a filename, you're automatically put into vi to edit a reply. When you exit vi, you're prompted to send the reply, abort the reply, or return to editing the reply. If you are done with the reply, you can send it. Editing the reply with vi, you'll probably need a maximum of about a dozen commands.

That's why you need to learn enough in this chapter so that you can accomplish such tasks. Then, I'll provide you with a complete command summary, so if you're interested in learning more, you can experiment with the commands some more on your own.

One advantage of the old-style text editors is that they're free, which makes up for an awful lot of failings. This is especially true in the world of UNIX software, where the cost of a few programs can equal a down-payment on a house in New York or California. The vi and sed editors are included with almost all versions of the UNIX operating system, and the Gnu Emacs text editor is available for a song. You will have to decide whether to use one of the editors mentioned in this chapter or a different one that is capable of saving your work as text files. If you wish to exercise the latter option, you can skip to the next chapter.

The *vi* Editor

The vi editor, like all of the editors discussed in this chapter, works on text files. This old type of program is called a *line editor*, because it represents each line of the file separately. This is different than most modern word processors, which use paragraphs as their most basic unit. Thus, vi doesn't do some of the most basic things that you may have come to expect, such as automatically wrapping the text at the end of the line so that it continues onto the next line. Each line is different, and you'll have to remember to press the Enter key at the end of each line.

Starting the *vi* Editor

To start vi, enter vi, followed by the name of the file you wish to edit, at the UNIX prompt. Fire up vi with the roadtrip file:

```
$ vi roadtrip
```

The screen becomes blank, and the contents of roadtrip are written to the screen for you to edit:

```
A journey of a thousand miles begins, hopefully, with an empty
bladder and all the appliances turned off.
~
~
~
~
~
~
~
~
~
~
~
~
~
~
~
~
~
"roadtrip"
```

You are now in vi. If you hadn't given vi a filename and had instead typed vi only, vi would have automatically created a new, temporary workspace, called a *buffer*, but not a true file. You could then save your work to a file when you were ready. If you had given vi a filename that hadn't been created already, the program would have created an empty file by that name and put you into vi to edit that file.

In case you're wondering, you can ignore the tilde marks (the little squiggles). They represent lines on which nothing has been written.

Moving Through Files with *vi*

The first thing you might want to do is to move the cursor around in the file. In some systems, the up and down arrows can move the cursor around, so try this first because it's the easiest thing to remember. However, in many systems, you'll have to resort to vi commands.

> **SKIP THIS, IT'S TECHNICAL**
>
> In the early days of computing, terminals didn't have up, down, right, and left arrow keys. They normally didn't have a number pad or function keys, such as F1. The PageUp, PageDown, Home, End, Insert, and Delete keys were missing as well. To get around this problem, the developers of vi implemented keystroke sequences to manipulate the cursor. The l, j, k, and h keys were chosen to move the cursor because with them, you can move the cursor with one hand on a normal terminal. They are all on the home row of the keyboard (see Figure 6.1). You will learn all of these cursor-moving keystrokes, plus some more recent alternatives.

The main keys that you use to move through the file are all next to each other. Pressing the letter l moves the cursor to the right, one letter at a time, but not past the beginning of the line. (Isn't that easy to remember? Unfortunately, almost none of these commands are mnemonic. You just have to remember these commands or use the command summary at the end of this chapter.) Use l to move the cursor to the right a few times.

Clue: Instead of using the l key to move forward, you can use the space bar to move the cursor forward one letter at a time.

The opposite command is h. Pressing h moves the cursor to the left (of course), one letter at a time. If you're already at the beginning of the line, nothing happens. Try using this command a few times to move back to the beginning of the file, where you started.

To move down a line at a time, press j. Do this, and you'll be at the next line of the file. To get back, press k, which moves the cursor up a line at a time. Try moving back and forth through the file a few times by pressing j and k.

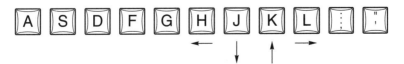

FIGURE 6.1.
The main cursor movement keys in vi are located on the home row of the keyboard.

The b key takes the cursor back through the file a word at a time, and you'll always land at the beginning of a word. Use this command to go from the end of the file back to the first word of the first line. Note that when you're at the beginning of a line, this command takes you to the last letter of the preceding line.

The w key takes the cursor forward through the file a word at a time, always landing at the beginning of each word. The vi editor considers any combination of letters, underscores, and digits with no white space—tabs or blanks—to be a word.

The $ key takes the cursor to the end of the line, and 0 takes the cursor to the beginning of the line.

Sometimes you need to go to either the top (the beginning) or the bottom (the end) of the file. To get to the bottom—the end—of the file, use the G (that is, Shift+g) command and you'll be taken to the end of the file. Similarly, to get to the top of the file, type 1G (1, followed by Shift+g). Basically, if you enter a number followed by G, you'll be taken to the line number you typed.

NOTE

UNIX is case-sensitive. The vi editor was written to take advantage of case-sensitivity. In the preceding paragraph, you entered G to go to the bottom of the file. The G command is capitalized to tell you that you must enter a capital G (Shift+g) in order for the command to work properly. Lowercase g makes the screen flash, which means that you have entered an invalid key. Try it. As you learn more about vi, you will see that the lowercase and uppercase versions of a letter do different things or complement each other in function.

Clue: If you're a little confused about where you are in your file, you can enter Control+g and vi will tell you the number of the line you're on, as well as the percent of text that is above the line you're on. For example, if there are four lines of text in your file and you are on line 3, pressing Control+g tells you that your cursor is on line 3 and that 75 percent of the text is above the cursor. Try it!

Because the roadtrip file is so short, you may not fully appreciate the usefulness of this command, but when you're dealing with hundreds or thousands of lines of text, this one is a lifesaver.

Appending and Inserting with *vi*

When you first enter vi, you're automatically put into *command mode*, which means that vi interprets every keystroke and every character you type as a command or part of a command. If you want vi to interpret your typing as letters and words to be put into your file, you must change modes. Otherwise, how would vi know whether you wanted it to interpret your typing as part of the file you're working on or as commands? You need to signal that you're changing between the two.

When you're entering text, the two most important commands are the i and a commands, which stand for *insert* and *append*. Insert mode is used to insert text where the cursor is. Append mode lets you add text after the current cursor position. To enter insert mode, enter a lowercase i. Now insert the phrase Setting Off On A Roadtrip, followed by pressing the Enter key twice:

When you're done, your file should look like the following:

```
Setting Off On A Roadtrip

A journey of a thousand miles begins, hopefully, with an empty
bladder and all the appliances turned off.
~
~
~
~
~
~
~
~
~
~
~
~
~
~
~
~
~
~
~
~
```

You're still in insert mode, which means that anything else you enter will be added to the file. Press the Esc key to get out of this mode.

Now use the forward movement keys—j and l—and go to the period at the end of the word off on the last line of the file.

```
Setting Off On A Roadtrip

A journey of a thousand miles begins, hopefully, with an empty
bladder and all the appliances turned off.
~
~
~
~
~
~
~
~
~
~
~
~
~
~
~
~
~
~
```

When you're done inserting or appending text, you'll need to get back into command mode, so that vi will quit interpreting the letters you enter as text to be entered into the file and start interpreting them as commands. To get out of insert or append mode, press the Esc key.

To get back into insert mode after you've been entering text, you need to press Esc first, then press a or i for append or insert, respectively.

> **Clue:** The single most common mistake that people make when using vi is not realizing that they're in command mode when they are attempting to insert or append text. What could happen, you ask? Well, every letter they type is interpreted as a command, not as a letter of text. By the time people discover their mistake, they may have already done several (usually bad) unintended things to their files. That's why it's important to remember whether or not you're in insert mode and to always press the Esc key when you're finished entering text.

Searching for Patterns

To find a particular word or part of a word, type the slash mark (/), followed by the text you seek, then Enter. The vi editor starts looking for the text at the current position of the cursor, continues to search for text to the bottom of the file, and then wraps around to the top and continues searching.

If you want to search the entire file for a word or pattern, you need to reposition the cursor at the top of the file to make sure vi finds the word or pattern. To do this, use the 1G command (introduced earlier), which stands for "go to the first line of the file," and the cursor will be taken to the beginning of the file. Then you can search to the end of the file, and you'll be sure to find the expression you seek, if it's in the file.

You could also enter f and follow it with the character that you want to go to, and you'll be taken to the beginning of that text. (You can remember this command as "f is for find.") For instance, if you type f, (*f* followed by a comma), you'll be taken to the next comma. Move the cursor to the line beginning *A journey of a....* Now typing f, places the cursor as shown here:

```
Setting Off On A Roadtrip

A journey of a thousand miles begins, hopefully, with an empty
bladder and all the appliances turned off.
~
~
~
~
~
~
~
~
~
~
~
~
~
~
~
~
~
~
~
```

The t command does almost the same thing, except that it takes the cursor to the character immediately before the expression you type; so if you're at the beginning of the roadtrip file, in command mode, and you type tj, you'll be taken to the space immediately before the word *journey*. (This only works if the text you seek is on the line currently occupied by the cursor, and the text is between the cursor and the end of the line.)

```
Setting Off On A Roadtrip

A journey of a thousand miles begins, hopefully, with an empty
bladder and all the appliances turned off.
~
~
~
~
~
~
```

~
~
~
~
~
~
~
~
~
~
~
~

Making Changes to Text

Changing text in vi is considerably more difficult than it is in most modern word processors. You can't simply go to the word you want to erase and start pressing the Delete key to wipe out text and then "type over" where the old word was. In vi, you have to issue commands telling vi what text to change and how to change it.

Correcting One Letter

To correct one letter, the easiest thing to do is to go to the letter you want to change and press the r key—which puts you in "replace" command. Now type the new letter. As soon as you type the new letter, you're automatically taken out of the "replace" command, and you can enter other commands. (You can tell that you're out of the "replace" command because the $ goes away.)

Now try this on the roadtrip file. Press Esc to make sure you're in command mode. Move your cursor to the letter j in the word journey and press r. Enter J to capitalize journey to Journey.

Replacing a Few Letters

To replace a few letters, you can use the s command, which replaces letters starting with the one under the cursor. If you want to replace one character, type s, followed by the new text. When you press the s command, a dollar sign ($) appears in place of the letter you're replacing. The dollar sign is a visible marker for you.

You can also use the s command to replace several letters. You can do this by preceding s with the number of characters you want to replace. If you wanted to replace four characters, type 4s, and you could start replacing four characters, beginning with the letter where the cursor is positioned. Notice that, with 4s, the dollar sign is positioned on the letter three positions to the right of the cursor. This indicates that you changed four characters.

If you want to replace the next three letters, you could also do it by entering
and the next three characters are typed over. The same is true with the other
movement commands. If you want to replace three words, you could type 3cw.
The cw command is the "change word" command. Three words to the right of
the cursor you'll see the dollar sign. When you type three new words over them,
the old words are replaced.

Use this command on the roadtrip file to change the first occurrence of the word
a with *ten*. Start by moving the cursor to the word *a*. Type cw. You'll see the dollar
sign appear. Type the word ten, followed by pressing Esc to tell vi that you're
done with the r command.

Replacing a Lot of Text

Another replacement command, uppercase R, is useful for replacing a lot of text.
It replaces the character on which the cursor sits, and then continues to overwrite
the characters to the right of the cursor until you terminate the command by pressing Esc.

Deleting Text in *vi*

You can delete characters, words, or lines in vi. These vi commands are fairly easy
to remember. To delete characters, for instance, the commands are x and X. The
x command deletes the character marked by the cursor, and the X command deletes the character before the cursor.

To delete words, use dw for "delete word." This command deletes the first word
or part of a word to the right of the cursor. Note that vi considers a punctuation
mark, such as a period or question mark, to be a word.

Unfortunately, this ease of remembrance breaks down; if you need to delete a line,
the command is dd. (As they say in beer commercials, "Why ask why?")

Use these commands to delete lines and words in the file roadtrip. Note that punctuation counts as a separate "word" to vi, so you need to use dw twice when you
encounter a word followed immediately by punctuation. Use these commands to
delete everything in the roadtrip file. Then, after you're done practicing, you can
enter the :quit! command, which takes you out of vi and puts you back at the
UNIX command line without saving any changes to the file, so your file will be
the way it was before you started editing in vi. Then enter vi roadtrip, and you'll
be taken back to the unchanged file.

...anges Throughout a File in *vi*

...t to make a change throughout a file. For instance, if you were
...tor, you might use vi to create a file such as the following. As
...dy figured out, the first two and the last two lines of the ex-
...nds, not text to be entered.

```
        not be displayed on the screen>
        it our company is routinely shut down at 3:00a.m.
        working around 3:00a.m., you need to save your
        : or you lose it. If you are submitting programs
        t, you need to make sure that they terminate
well __        /0. If you're not done by 3:00, the system
administrator will not be responsible for lost work.
Esc<This key will not be displayed on the screen>
:w maintain
```

Create and save such a file using the commands shown. Use the filename
maintain, as shown. The screen should look like this:

```
The UNIX system at our company is routinely shut down at 3:00a.m.
If you are still working around 3:00a.m., you need to save your
work before that or you lose it. If you are submitting programs
to run overnight, you need to make sure that they terminate
well before 3:00. If you're not done by 3:00, the system
administrator will not be responsible for lost work.
~
~
~
~
~
~
~
~
~
~
~
~
~
~
~
~
~
"maintain" 6 lines, 364 characters
```

Now go to the top of the file using the 1G command. Pretend you're a system
administrator, and you've decided to change the standard maintenance time to
4:00 a.m. instead of its current 3:00 a.m. You look at the file and realize that all
you need to do is to change every occurrence of 3 to 4. Because you're changing
every 3 to a 4, you can do a *global* change. This means that every occurrence,
throughout the file, will be changed. When you're absolutely sure that you need
to change every occurrence of a particular pattern to the same new pattern, you
want to do a global change.

To change the 3 to a 4, enter : followed by %s/3/4/g. The : is the command-line mode of vi; %s tells vi to make the replacement for every occurrence of the pattern in the file; /3 is the pattern to search for, and /4 is the value to replace for the pattern. The last letter, g, tells vi to replace 3 with 4 for all occurrences on a line in the file. If you left the g off, the substitution would be restricted to the first occurrence on a line. For example, the following line has the word zachary twice. You want to replace lowercase z with uppercase Z. The first example replaces only the first occurrence of z because the g option is missing on the command line. The second example replaces all occurrences of z because the g option is added. Here is the original line:

```
zachary has a dog named Molly. zachary likes to pull Molly's hair.
```

Use :s/z/Z/ and here is the result:

```
Zachary has a dog named Molly. zachary likes to pull Molly's hair.
```

Use :s/z/Z/g with the original line and here is the result:

```
Zachary has a dog named Molly. Zachary likes to pull Molly's hair.
```

The full syntax for global substitution is this:

```
:%s/pattern to be changed/new pattern/g
```

Clue: Just in case you make a mistake and change your file in a way that you don't intend, it's always a good idea to save your work using the :w command before you use a global substitution. If you do make a mistake, you can always use the u command to undo the unwanted changes.

If, by chance, you start to use a command and then change your mind, the Esc key can help you. Pressing this key essentially erases the command you started to type and puts you back into the command mode of vi.

Doing Things Over and Over in *vi*

What if you have a huge file, and you want to delete 40 lines? Would you have to enter dd 40 times? No way! To delete 40 lines, you would simply precede the dd command with the number 40 (no space between them):

```
40dd
```

You can use this principle to delete four lines, starting at the top of the file. Begin with the basic command, and multiply it by the number of times you want the command repeated, in this case, four times. Try this on your maintain file. First, move the cursor to the top of the file using 1G:

```
The UNIX system at our company is routinely shut down at 3:00a.m.
If you are still working around 3:00a.m., you need to save your
work before that or you lose it. If you are submitting programs
to run overnight, you need to make sure that they terminate
well before 3:00. If you're not done by 3:00, the system
administrator will not be responsible for lost work.
~
~
~
~
~
~
~
~
~
~
~
~
~
~
~
```

Now enter the command, 4dd. You'll see four lines disappear:

```
well before 3:00. If you're not done by 3:00, the system
administrator will not be responsible for lost work.
~
~
~
~
~
~
~
~
~
~
~
~
~
~
~
~
~
```

Now enter the u command, which undoes the last command you issued by putting back the lines that were deleted. (More on this later in this chapter.)

You could also use this principle to delete two words or two lines. Many of the vi commands work this way; when I introduce a new command, I will point out whether it works this way. The following are the commands that you've already learned that behave this way:

a	append
cw	change word
i	insert
cw	change word
dw	delete word
dd	delete line
r	replace letter

Another type of repetition you can use for repeating change commands only is the & command, which means "make the same change you just made, again." After you've made a change using any of the change commands, you can go to the next place where you want to change something, enter &, and vi will make the same change again.

The dot command (made by entering a period) can also be used to repeat any change command. You simply make sure you're in command mode, go to the next place where you want to change something, and enter a period. If you have to make a change several times, this command can save you some time.

Moving Text in *vi*

To understand how to move text in vi, you need to understand the concept of a buffer in vi. A *buffer* is a place in computer memory where something is temporarily stashed or stored. In vi, you can have many different buffers, each storing a different previous version of your file.

To move text, you need to yank it into this temporary memory space—a buffer—using the yy command. Use this command to copy the first line of the maintain file by going to the first line of the file, then entering yy. You should see the file:

```
The UNIX system at our company is routinely shut down at 3:00a.m.
If you are still working around 3:00a.m., you need to save your
work before that or you lose it. If you are submitting programs
to run overnight, you need to make sure that they terminate
well before 3:00. If you're not done by 3:00, the system
administrator will not be responsible for lost work.
~
~
~
~
~
~
~
~
~
~
~
~
```

~
~
~
~
~

> **NOTE**
> Doing a "yank" this way uses the default buffer. There are quite a few
> commands that will overwrite this buffer (for example, dd). Remember to
> use the yanked line before you delete a line.

Unfortunately, on most systems, you won't see any effect of yanking the text, but
vi is remembering it just the same. This operation is the same as Copy in most
word processors.

If you don't believe me now, you will after you learn how to place the text you
just copied. You do this by using the p command, short for "put." Move the cursor to the end of the file and enter the p command. You should see the first line
added onto the end:

```
The UNIX system at our company is routinely shut down at 3:00a.m.
If you are still working around 3:00a.m., you need to save your
work before that or you lose it. If you are submitting programs
to run overnight, you need to make sure that they terminate
well before 3:00. If you're not done by 3:00, the system
administrator will not be responsible for lost work.
The UNIX system at our company is routinely shut down at 3:00a.m.
~
~
~
~
~
~
~
~
~
~
~
~
~
~
~
1 more line
```

Now enter 3p. Your file should have become longer. Now enter u to undo the last
change.

As you can see, you can precede the p and yy commands with numbers to specify
how many lines are to be yanked or put, or copied and pasted, as the rest of the
computer world would say.

Inserting One File into Another Using *vi*

Another extremely useful feature of `vi` is that you can insert an entire file into a file that you're editing. The command to do this is `:r filename`, where *filename* is the name of the file you want to insert. Of course, you need to be in command mode for this to work. Check out this feature by inserting the `maintain` file into your `roadtrip` file. A key thing to remember is that new text will read in at the last position of the character. You should position the cursor where you want to read in the new file. Start by firing up `vi`, if you haven't already:

```
$ vi roadtrip
Setting Off On A Roadtrip

A journey of a thousand miles begins, hopefully, with an empty
bladder and all the appliances turned off.
~
~
~
~
~
~
~
~
~
~
~
~
~
~
~
~
~
~
```

Now enter `:r maintain`. The file named `maintain` that you're reading in will be pasted into the file on which you were already working:

```
Setting Off On A Roadtrip
The UNIX system at our company is routinely shut down at 3:00a.m.
If you are still working around 3:00a.m., you need to save your
work before that or you lose it. If you are submitting programs
to run overnight, you need to make sure that they terminate
well before 3:00. If you're not done by 3:00, the system
administrator will not be responsible for lost work.

A journey of a thousand miles begins, hopefully, with an empty
bladder and all the appliances turned off.
~
~
~
~
~
~
~
~
```

```
~
~
~
"maintain" 6 lines, 364 characters
```

This is the easiest way to incorporate one entire text file into another. Later, this ability to insert a file directly will be very important in sending electronic mail and responding to other kinds of Internet messages.

Undoing Commands with the Undo (*u*) Command

The vi editor was one of the first to provide the capability to undo a change, which was extremely wise, human nature being what it is. After all, a smart person invented the pencil, but an even smarter one stuck an eraser on it. Don't worry about making a mistake, because if you do, you can undo it by entering u for undo immediately after you make the mistake.

> **WARNING**
>
> Make sure that you don't make any more changes before entering the u command. If you do make some other changes, you can't use a simple u command to get back to where you started.

If you accidentally undo a change that you subsequently decide you shouldn't have undone, you can even undo the undo command if you immediately press u again. Doing so undoes the last command—which, in this case, was the undo command itself—that changed the buffer or file. Thus, undoing the u command gets you back to where you started.

Undoing Several Changes at the Same Time

In the preceding section, you learned that if you want to use the u command, you can't make changes in the file, because the u command will only undo the last change you did before the u command. What if you don't immediately realize that you've made a mistake, and you make other changes?

Many of the people who worked on vi in the early days must have had the same problem. That's why they added the capability to undo deletions. If you enter p, vi retrieves the most recently deleted block of text and inserts it following the cursor.

That means that if you deleted something, then deleted something else with a second delete command, you couldn't use the u command to undo the first change. However, you could undo the first one by entering "2p.

Try this using the roadtrip file. Call up your roadtrip file (if you worked through the earlier examples, it may have the modifications shown here):

```
Setting Off On A Roadtrip
The UNIX system at our company is routinely shut down at 3:00a.m.
If you are still working around 3:00a.m., you need to save your
work before that or you lose it. If you are submitting programs
to run overnight, you need to make sure that they terminate
well before 3:00. If you're not done by 3:00, the system
administrator will not be responsible for lost work.

A journey of a thousand miles begins, hopefully, with an empty
bladder and all the appliances turned off.
~
~
~
~
~
~
~
~
~
~
~
"maintain" 6 lines, 364 characters
```

Now delete the first line using dd:

```
The UNIX system at our company is routinely shut down at 3:00a.m.
If you are still working around 3:00a.m., you need to save your
work before that or you lose it. If you are submitting programs
to run overnight, you need to make sure that they terminate
well before 3:00. If you're not done by 3:00, the system
administrator will not be responsible for lost work.

A journey of a thousand miles begins, hopefully, with an empty
bladder and all the appliances turned off.
~
~
~
~
~
~
~
~
~
~
~
~
~
```

Next, delete the second line using dd:

```
If you are still working around 3:00a.m., you need to save your
work before that or you lose it. If you are submitting programs
to run overnight, you need to make sure that they terminate
well before 3:00. If you're not done by 3:00, the system
administrator will not be responsible for lost work.

A journey of a thousand miles begins, hopefully, with an empty
bladder and all the appliances turned off.
~
~
~
~
~
~
~
~
~
~
~
~
~
```

Finally, delete the third line using dd:

```
work before that or you lose it. If you are submitting programs
to run overnight, you need to make sure that they terminate
well before 3:00. If you're not done by 3:00, the system
administrator will not be responsible for lost work.

A journey of a thousand miles begins, hopefully, with an empty
bladder and all the appliances turned off.
~
~
~
~
~
~
~
~
~
~
~
~
~
```

Now move your cursor to the letter w in work and restore the text you deleted first by entering "3p:

```
Setting Off On A Roadtrip
work before that or you lose it. If you are submitting programs
to run overnight, you need to make sure that they terminate
well before 3:00. If you're not done by 3:00, the system
administrator will not be responsible for lost work.
```

```
A journey of a thousand miles begins, hopefully, with an empty
bladder and all the appliances turned off.

~
~
~
~
~
~
~
~
~
~
~
~
~
~
```

Move your cursor to the letter S in Setting and then restore the second deletion by entering "2p:

```
Setting Off On A Roadtrip
The UNIX system at our company is routinely shut down at 3:00a.m.
work before that or you lose it. If you are submitting programs
to run overnight, you need to make sure that they terminate
well before 3:00. If you're not done by 3:00, the system
administrator will not be responsible for lost work.

A journey of a thousand miles begins, hopefully, with an empty
bladder and all the appliances turned off.

~
~
~
~
~
~
~
~
~
~
~
```

Finally, move your cursor to the letter T in The and you can restore the last change by entering p:

```
Setting Off On A Roadtrip
The UNIX system at our company is routinely shut down at 3:00a.m.
If you are still working around 3:00a.m., you need to save your
work before that or you lose it. If you are submitting programs
to run overnight, you need to make sure that they terminate
well before 3:00. If you're not done by 3:00, the system
administrator will not be responsible for lost work.

A journey of a thousand miles begins, hopefully, with an empty
bladder and all the appliances turned off.
```

~
~
~
~
~
~
~
~
~
~
~
~

You can see how this command is great for recovering from accidental deletions.

Of course, sometimes you've messed up so badly that you want to forget the whole editing session, and you want to get back to where you were before you last started editing. The command to do this is U. Note that this U command is uppercase. Think of it as being a bigger kind of undo command, because it undoes many changes, whereas u undoes only the last change.

Quitting *vi*

To quit vi, you can enter either :q to quit without saving your changes or :wq (the w stands for "write") to write, then quit. If you try to quit without saving using :q, you may get a message like the following:

```
:quit! overrides.
```

This means that you have to enter :q! or :quit!, with the exclamation point, to quit without saving your changes.

Clue: If you're smart, you'll save occasionally by using the :w command. You won't exit vi this way, but your work will be saved each time you use this command. Otherwise, if there is a power outage or your computer goes down for some reason, you'll lose all of the work you've done since you last saved your work, and if you haven't yet saved it, you'll lose the whole thing.

Using *:set*

For some commands, you enter a colon (:) to execute and access the command line. This is different from the command line for UNIX. The reason you need the colon is to tell vi not to interpret your typing either as letters to put into the file or as regular one- or two-letter commands.

The :set commands fall into this category. The :set commands are used to set up the vi environment by setting some variables on and off. Your system looks at these variables to set up your vi environment, so by setting these variables with :set, you have better control over your interactions with vi.

Having said that, I will point out that many of the :set commands are irrelevant for beginners and only become important when one is writing, say, C or Lisp code. A few of these commands—such as :set all, :set number, :set nonumber, and :set ignorecase—can make your life easier, so I'll cover them in this chapter.

To see what the choices are, enter :set all from within vi. You should see something like the following:

```
:set all
noautoindent        nonumber          noslowopen
autoprint           nonovice          nosourceany
noautowrite         nooptimize        tabstop=8
nobeautify          paragraphs=I      taglength=0
prompt                                tags=tags
noedcompatible      noreadonly        agstack
noerrorbells        redraw            term=vt100
flash               remap             noterse
hardtabs=99         report=5          timeout
noignorecase        scroll=11         nolisp
warn                nolist            shell=/bin/ksh  window=23
magic               shiftwidth=8      wrapscan
mesg                noshowmatch       wrapmargin=0
nomodeline          noshowmode        nowriteany
```

Don't panic. It looks intimidating, but we'll ignore most of these variables, which are more important for experienced programmers than for beginners, and focus instead on a few basic :set variables. The preceding response to :set all shows you all of the variables that can be set in your system's version of vi and their current settings. Some variables, such as warn, which controls whether you get a warning when you try to exit a file without saving your changes, are set on. Others, such as ignorecase, are set off, and that's why they're preceded with the word no. Others are set to a number, for instance, the scroll variable, which controls how far up and down the scroll commands take you whenever you press Control+D or Control+U.

Most of these variables are probably fine set as they are, but you may wish to reset some of the following variables, which are given here with their abbreviations and their meanings:

Abbreviation	Variable	Meaning
eb	errorbells	If this variable is on, you'll hear a beeping tone when you make a mistake in vi. This one is great for detecting mistakes early, but some people find this annoying, and if you're one of them, you should turn this off.
ic	ignorecase	When this variable is set, vi will ignore the case of what you type when you search for a particular piece of text.
(none)	novice	This variable changes the behavior of commands that start with colons so that they are a little bit more user-friendly. For instance, when this variable is enabled, there are more error messages and warnings, and more detail is often provided in these messages and in warnings.
nu	line numbers	If this variable is on, each line in the file will be numbered. This makes it easier to go to a particular line in the file.
wa	warn	You'll receive a warning when you try to quit without writing, if this variable is on.
wm=n	wrapmargin	Turning this variable on means that when you type a space or a tab within *n* characters of your right margin, vi will automatically wrap the text by generating a linefeed (the computer version of a carriage return on a typewriter).
ws	wrapscan	If this variable is on and you're searching for text, when vi reaches the end of the file, it will continue the search starting at the top of the file. This means that the entire file will be searched.

The abbreviations you see are acceptable wherever the variable name is, most importantly when you're setting and resetting the variables.

To set these variables, use the `:set` command, followed by the option you want to set. Thus, to set, say, `wrapscan` on, you would enter `:set wrapscan`.

Once it's set on, you can turn it off by entering the opposite command, `:set nowrapscan`. There is no space between `no` and the option you're trying to set.

Try using these techniques to turn on line numbering. *Line numbering* is the practice of numbering the lines in order; in other words, the first line is a 1, the second line a 2, the third line a 3, and so on. As usual, the command starts with `:set`. Follow this with a space, then the word `number`, then Enter:

```
:set number
```

Note two things. First, you could have also entered `:set nu`, because `nu` is the legal abbreviation for `number`, which turns on line numbering, within the `:set` command. Second, when the `:set` command terminates, which it does immediately and automatically, it takes you back to the same place and the same mode you were in when you invoked the `:set` command. You should now see line numbers on the far left side of the screen.

Now try this: press Esc to reset the mode, then press 2 followed by G. You'll be taken to the second line in the file. This is a useful feature when you need to maneuver quickly through a long file.

Finally, remove the line numbers by using the command `:set nonumber`. You could also enter `:set nonu`, although sometimes it's worth it to use the full word, because `:set nonu` looks weird enough that you could accidentally confuse yourself. Look at the file now. The numbers have disappeared.

Once you've set these variables, they will stay as they are until the next time you change them in the same editing session. That's why `:set` is not a command that you're going to use extremely often. Most of the time, you'll either accept the default settings or make an occasional change. Many `vi` users, in fact, never use the `:set` command at all, but some users like to have their environment set up just so, which is why I've explained it here.

Clue: If you would like the variable to remain set from one editing session to another, you can enter it into an `.exrc` file. Edit the `.exrc` file with `vi` and add your `set` variables. Here is an example:

```
set wrapmargin=7
```

```
set tabstop=5

set wrapscan
```

I'd like to be able to tell you that there's an easy way to get help if you're interested in learning more, but unfortunately, there are only two ways to get any information at all, and neither is very complete.

You already know the first way. Using :set all will give you some information and, depending on the quality of the documentation on your system, may give you more than the basic variables and their current values. The second way is to enter man vi at the UNIX command prompt, which on some systems will give you extra information on the :set command and the variables associated with it.

Using *vi* Command Summaries: Everybody Does It

Now that you know the basics of vi, you know exactly how user-friendly and easy-to-remember all of the commands are...NOT! That's why command summaries and cheat-cards are so popular. These summaries and cards give you the formats of all the commands, often on very compact cardboard cards that can be taped to the side of a workstation or to a table next to one. Even professionals use these cards, so there's no shame in it. If you think you're going to use vi, you should either get one of these if you like the card format or make a copy of the vi command summary included in the appendixes of this book. Keep it taped or tacked somewhere near your terminal.

Using Emacs

Another popular UNIX editor is Emacs (often lowercased as emacs). Many commercial companies sell versions of Emacs, but what has made the editor so common is the Gnu (also often lowercased) version of Emacs, distributed by the Free Software Foundation. This organization makes the editor available free to anyone who wishes to download it, but there is little customer support, so you're on your own if you find bugs. Nevertheless, the fact that it's free has made this editor very popular. If you choose to use this editor or if the choice is made for you by your employer, the following sections will teach you enough to do the things you need to do.

As previously mentioned, remember that if you use most popular word processors and save your work as text, you'll get the same effect, with a much friendlier user interface. Some people, however, don't have access to such tools, and if you're one of them, you can't beat the price of (free) Emacs. Also, many people want to know how to use Emacs for convenience or personal satisfaction.

To Start an Emacs Session

You start an Emacs session with your roadtrip file by entering emacs roadtrip (lowercase) at the command line, just as you would any other command name. You could have also entered emacs, without giving it a filename. Once you get into Emacs, you'll enter commands to help you enter text, change it, and manage windows.

The Emacs editor automatically opens up a window. This is an Emacs window; you can think of it as a temporary holding place, either for a file and its changes or for a temporary workspace. Your work isn't saved to a file until you specifically tell Emacs to do so.

Meta and Control Keys in Emacs

Emacs has commands that use the Control and Meta keys. You already know what a Control key is. A Meta-key command is similar, except that instead of pressing the Control key and holding it down, you press the Meta key, the Edit key, or the Esc key, whichever your computer keyboard has. In the rest of this chapter, I'll denote a Meta key as Esc, but if your computer has one of these other keys, remember to press it whenever you see Esc.

If you've already read the section on the vi editor, you'll see that one of the ways in which these two editors differ is that Emacs doesn't have several modes, as vi does. Anytime you press Control and Meta-key commands, Emacs assumes that you want to enter a command. Anytime you're entering text without such characters, Emacs assumes that it's text to be entered.

Getting Out of Emacs

To end an Emacs session, press Control+x Control+c.

Learning Emacs

One of the best ways to learn Emacs is to go through the online tutorial that is provided with Emacs. This tutorial is very easy to use and will probably take you only a few hours to complete. When you're done, you'll probably be able to get through any editing session with a little help from a command reference, such as the one included in the editor appendix of this book.

To start the tutorial, press Control+h t. That is, hold the Control key, press the h key, release the Control and h keys, and press the t key. This will fire up the tutorial, which will provide you with instructions from there. You don't have to press the Enter key in Emacs to give it a command, as you must when you're working at the UNIX command line.

Much of what follows is contained in the tutorial, which is highly recommended. The following explanations, examples, and summaries can be used to reinforce the tutorial. The best way to use this book, then, is as a supplement to the tutorial; when there is something about the tutorial that you don't understand, check here for more details.

Viewing and Moving Through Files

Luckily, the commands to move through files are easy to remember because the designers of Emacs purposely designed them that way.

To try out the move commands, fire up Emacs by entering emacs maintain at the prompt. If you haven't already created the maintain file, enter the command anyway, and type the following file in the resulting window:

```
The UNIX system at our company is routinely shut down at 3:00a.m.
If you are still working around 3:00a.m., you need to save your
work before that or you lose it. If you are submitting programs
to run overnight, you need to make sure that they terminate
well before 3:00. If you're not done by 3:00, the system
administrator will not be responsible for lost work.
```

You will be taken to an Emacs window with a copy of the maintain file in it. However, the window you see contains only a working copy of the file, called a buffer, and unless you save your work at the end of this session, the maintain file will remain unchanged. The following are the two most common commands that help you view files:

✖ Control+v scrolls the window forward, so to keep reading a file from the beginning to the end, keep using Control+v.

✖ Esc+v scrolls the window backward, so it's the opposite of Control+v.

NOTE

Esc+v means to press the Esc key, let go of the Esc key, and press the letter v.

Control+v means to hold down the Control key and press the letter v.

> Control+x 2 means to hold down the Control key and press the letter x, let go, and enter 2.
>
> This may sound complicated, but with a little practice you'll become an expert.

Of course, these are the commands that essentially move the window, which is roughly the same as moving a magnifying glass over a scroll; that is, you're moving the window to the place you want to look. These commands don't affect the position of the cursor at all.

You can also create another window and then switch between them. Two commands do this. Control+x 2 splits the selected window (the window where the cursor is) into two windows, one immediately above the other. Using Control+x 5, on the other hand, splits the selected window into two side-by-side windows.

Use Control+x 2 to split the window containing the roadtrip file into two windows. Each window contains a copy of the file. To switch between the two windows, press Control+X o. The cursor will move back and forth between the two windows.

You can also have your cursor in one window and scroll the other window forward. To do this, use the Esc+Control v command. This is useful when you're working with two files, cutting text from one file to paste into another.

Now that you know how to create windows and switch between them, get rid of one of the windows. Put your cursor in a window, and press Control+X 1. The window containing the cursor will disappear.

Help!

The following advice can help you if you're stuck or confused while in Emacs.

Clue: If you're stuck in Emacs, you can often get out of whatever weird state you're in by pressing Control+g once or twice. If you're really stuck, press Control+x Control+c, and you can exit immediately. You'll be asked if you want to save your work before you're taken out of Emacs.

If you're not exactly stuck, but are confused, you can get online help by pressing Control+h a, which will put you into the apropos help system. (*Apropos,* in which the *s* is silent, is French for "concerning" or "about.") You'll be asked to supply a word or phrase that might appear in documentation concerning the topic that you need to look up.

If you want to look up a command about manipulating windows, enter the word *windows*, and you'll be shown a list of the commands that work on windows, along with brief explanations of what the commands do. If you're looking for commands that let you insert or delete text, you can enter the words *insert* or *delete*, and you'll see a set of related commands.

If you enter a word that relates to a lot of commands, the apropos text may be too long to fit in the window. You can use the window commands to scroll through the documentation and to kill (get rid of) the window containing the help information. Thus, to scroll the selected window containing the help documentation forward, use Control+v. To scroll backward, use Esc+v. Perhaps most importantly, the command to remove the apropos text is Control+X k, followed by Enter. The help information will disappear from the window.

Reading the Help Information

To be able to get through some of the help information, you need to understand some key terms that are important to maneuver through Emacs and get real work done. Understanding these terms will also make it easier to decipher online help. The following terms are sometimes confusing for beginners.

Buffers

Buffers, as I mentioned before, are temporary chunks of memory that hold text on which either you or the computer are working. When you edit a file in Emacs, a copy of it is placed in a buffer, where you can work on it. Later, when you save the file, the buffer is copied into the permanent place on disk where your file is stored. Many people loosely use the word *file* when they mean *buffer*, because what you usually see in the buffers that are displayed in Emacs windows are copies of the files.

There are also other types of buffers besides the ones that hold files, but for most beginners, the other aren't important; only fairly advanced programmers really need them. In this chapter, the only other buffer I'll talk about is the minibuffer. You can assume that when a buffer is discussed, I mean a buffer that contains a copy of a file.

Major Modes

A *major mode* is a way of mapping the characters you type to the effect that the keystroke has. A major mode, in other words, defines how Emacs interprets your keystrokes. You can be in only one major mode at a time. There are many possible mappings, and they mostly fall into these categories:

✖ The one you will probably use exclusively is called Fundamental mode. This is the default major mode, and it's the one you'll use almost all of the time, unless you're using Emacs as part of a documentation or you're using a programming environment such as, for example, Lucid Inc.'s Energize.

✖ Others are designed especially for editing documents, such as those for ordinary text, outlines, and specialized UNIX document languages such as nroff.

✖ Some are designed for use with programming languages such as FORTRAN, C, C++, or LISP.

Minor Modes

Minor modes are similar to major modes, except that instead of defining a whole universe of key mappings, they control one small type of action. For instance, in the auto-fill minor mode, Emacs automatically inserts new-line characters when a line gets too long. Another big difference between major and minor modes is that several nonconflicting minor modes can be turned on at the same time, but you can only be in one major mode at a time.

The following are the most common, important minor modes:

✖ Auto-fill mode—If you're in this mode, Emacs automatically inserts new-line characters (returns) into your document when a line gets too long. To turn on this mode, press Esc followed by x, then, without a space, type `auto-fill-mode`. To turn it off, type the same thing again. Commands that work this way—switching between on and off, using the same command or action—are said to *toggle* between on and off.

✖ Auto-save mode—This one is a biggie. If you're in auto-save mode, Emacs periodically saves a copy of the file in the buffer. For most people, most of the time, there is almost never any reason to work with this one off; for beginners, not using this mode is a lot like bungee jumping without a chord. To get into this mode, type Esc+x `auto-save`. To get out of it, do the same.

✖ Overwrite mode—In this mode, when you're typing text into a document, the old text is overwritten. If you're not in this mode, text is merely inserted, and the old text is moved forward and down in the window, as needed. As a matter of fact, not being in this mode is a lot like being in insert mode in vi. To toggle between having this mode on and having it off, press Esc+x.

✖ Read-only mode—If you're in this mode, Emacs won't let you change a document. You can only read documents in this mode, and you can't make any modifications. To get in and out of this mode, press Control+x Control+q.

The Mark

The *mark* is a position in a buffer. You can loosely think of it as being a special placemarker in your file. Later, you'll learn how to use this special place to describe a section of text you wish to alter (to cut and paste, for instance).

The Minibuffer

The *minibuffer* is the small window at the bottom of the screen that shows you status information and displays commands that require you to type more than one key. One-key commands work right away, so you see their effect, not the command itself.

The Mode Line

The *mode line* is a line across the bottom of a window. It displays two characters at the far left of the line: double percent signs (%%) for read-only, double asterisks (**) for changed, and double hyphens (- -) for unchanged. You'll also see the name of the file shown in the window, the major and minor modes you're in, and the position of the text relative to the entire contents you're editing.

The Point

The *point* is the place where editing commands take place. Every window has its own point, and if you're looking at the same file in two different windows, each window can have a different point. For any window, this place is always immediately to the left of the cursor.

The Region

The *region* of a window is the area between the point and the mark. This definition will become important later, when you learn how to cut and paste text.

Moving the Cursor

So far, the commands you've learned have manipulated windows, but haven't dealt much with cursor movement. The following commands help you move the cursor:

✖ Control+b moves the cursor backward (to the left) a character at a time.

✖ Control+f moves the cursor forward (to the right) one character at a time.

✖ Control+n moves the cursor to the next line (down) a line at a time.

✖ Control+p moves the cursor (back or up) to the previous line.

✖ Esc+r moves the cursor to the line in the middle of the window. If you press Esc+r, followed by a plus sign (+) and a number, for example 5, the cursor will move to the fifth line from the top of the window. If you press Esc+r, followed by a minus sign and a 5, the cursor will be taken to the fifth line from the bottom.

✖ Esc+f moves the cursor forward a word at a time. Note the parallel to Control+f, which moves forward a single character at a time.

✖ Esc+b moves backward a line at a time. Notice that this is similar to Control+b, which moves the cursor backward a single character at a time.

You should experiment with these commands on the roadtrip file until you're comfortable with them and can remember them easily.

Cutting and Pasting Text

To understand cutting and pasting text, you need to understand a strange distinction that Emacs makes between two different ways of getting rid of text. In Emacs, you can either *kill* text or *delete* text.

Deleting Versus Killing Text

The main difference is that deleting text is a final act. Once you've deleted text, you can be assured that it has really, truly gone to that great electronic bit-bucket in the sky.

However, if you've merely killed the text, you can often bring it back to life. In other words, like some "Dungeons and Dragons" characters, some text can live to fight another day. Killed text in Emacs inhabits a netherworld called the *kill ring*, where recently killed text hangs out until it truly can move on to a higher plane of existence. Prepare yourself for "Zen and the Art of Kill-Ring Maintenance," or "The Ring of the Delete-ungen" (apologies to Wagner).

Deleting Text

The commands discussed in this section delete text; that is, they irrevocably remove it. You can't enter a command and easily get yourself back to the state in which you started.

Clue: Of course, if you did a disastrous delete, you could quit Emacs without saving your changes, but that approach would mean that you couldn't retain any of the changes that you made since you saved your work or since the computer automatically saved it in auto-save mode. That's entirely different from trying to get back a specific section of text, which will be discussed shortly.

These Commands Actually Erase, or Delete, Text

✖ Control+d deletes the character to the right of the point—in other words, the character that the cursor is on.

✖ The Delete key erases the character to the left of the point, which is the character immediately left of the cursor.

Killing Text

The following commands kill text. Each time text is killed, it is deposited on a kill ring, as if it were hanging on one of those rotating rings that were once used in restaurants to hold the orders that the waitress took from the customers. Just as the cook would take the order slips of paper off the ring, and the waitress would put more on, you will be putting new sections of text on this ring, where you can pull it off if you need to do so. The kill ring keeps track of the text you kill.

These commands are useful when you only have to kill a little bit of text:

✖ Esc+d kills the word to the right of the point.

✖ Esc+delete kills the word to the left of the point.

✖ Esc+k kills the whole sentence to the right of the point.

Use the Esc+d command to delete the first word of the roadtrip file. Then move two words to the right using the Esc+f command to move forward a word at a time, and kill the second word using Esc+delete. Now move two lines down and delete the line you're on using Esc+k.

Undoing Commands and Resurrecting Killed Text from the Kill Ring

Now you can undo the preceding commands to get back to the original file. The command to undo is either Control+_ (that is, press Control and underscore) or Control+x u, depending on your keyboard. You can use Control+_ first, because it requires fewer keystrokes, but the Control+x u command is the more common of the two, so that's what I will be using in the following examples.

Use Control+x u to undo the most recent change, which was your deletion of the third line. The line should come back.

Now press Control+x u to undo the next most recent change, which was your deletion of the second word on the first line.

Finally, press Control+x u to undo the first change you made, which was the deletion of the first word of the file. You should be back to the state of the file before you made changes.

You can undo a lot of different kill commands, up to the limit of the memory of Emacs, which is about 8,000 characters. If you save a file, Emacs will still let you undo the changes, as long as you haven't exceeded this limit, which is big for most people's purposes.

You can even undo the undo commands; but first, you have to do something to clue Emacs in to the fact that you want to undo the undo command, not just undo one earlier set of changes. The way most people do this is to take some trivial action that doesn't involve a change to the file, such as moving the mark, and thus the cursor, over by one position. This breaks the chain, so to speak, of deletes.

Now play with the undo command a bit more. Go to the end of the file and insert the following line:

```
The plans for the journey are in the temple, under the largest statue.
```

Now press Delete until you've deleted the entire word statue.

Now insert the word urn. Save your changes. Now use the undo command again. Emacs has undone the changes, even though you saved the file already.

Next, press Control+x u repeatedly, until you've gotten the entire word and the period back again.

To kill large amounts of text, you have to first specify the text to be killed. The way to do this is to put the mark in one place, the point in another, and kill everything in between. To do this, call Emacs together with the maintain file from the UNIX command line, and go to the second line in the maintain file.

Set the mark on the beginning of the second line in the maintain file. To do this, use Control+space (or, if that doesn't work, Control+@) to set the mark to the place where the point now is, immediately to the right of the cursor. Now move the cursor (and therefore the point) down two lines. Next, you're going to use the Control+w command to kill the region, which you'll recall is the text between the mark and the point. Do this.

Now you've killed the text, and that text has been yanked into the kill ring. Go (move the point) to the end of the file, and use the Control+y command (think of this as "yanking" text) to paste it in, starting where the point is.

On the other hand, you can also copy text rather than killing it. The only difference is that after you kill the text, before moving the cursor anywhere, you use Control+y to restore the text into the same place from which you deleted it. You can then paste it anywhere you want by repositioning the cursor to where you want to insert the text, then yanking or copying it into the new position.

Searching and Replacing Using Emacs

Searching and replacing text using Emacs is easy. Emacs queries you at key points in the search-and-replace operations, which makes it simple to know what to do next.

Searching

To simply search for a particular piece of text, use the following commands to look for the phrase in the forward and backward directions:

✖ Control+s Esc Control+w   Searches for text in the forward direction. When you type this command, Emacs will ask you what text you seek. You then type in the word, phrase, or letters for which you want Emacs to search. Use this command to start at the top of the file and look for the word *the* in the roadtrip file.

> **NOTE**
>
> The keystrokes Control+s Esc Control+w can be a little confusing, so here's a little refresher. To enter this command, you should hold down the Control key and press s. Let go and then press Esc. Then hold down the Control key and press w.

✖ Control+r Esc Control+w   Searches for text in the backward direction. When you type this command, Emacs will ask you what text you seek. You then type in the word, phrase, or letters for which you want Emacs to search. Now go to the bottom of the roadtrip file and use this command to do a backward search for the word *the*.

To replace a word or phrase everywhere that it occurs, use the following command:

✖ Esc+x replace-string   When you type this command, Emacs will ask you for the text you want to replace. Next, it will ask you to enter the text you want to replace. This command searches from the point to the end of the buffer (the file, loosely speaking) and makes the replacement everywhere it finds a match with the specified text.

To replace text some places and not others, you can use commands that find the selected text, ask you if you want to make a change, and then make the change if you want the text changed. The following command does this:

✖ Esc+%   This command searches for each occurrence of a specified piece of text and asks you whether you want to do each replacement.

When Emacs asks you what you want to do, you must respond. You can provide any of the following responses:

✖ Control+h or ?   Displays a list of all of the possible responses.

✖ space bar or y   Performs the replacement.

✖ Delete or n   Skips this occurrence.

✖ Esc   Exits without replacing any more text.

✖ !   Replaces the remaining matches without asking you any further questions.

Congratulations! You've now learned enough about Emacs to be dangerous. You should now be able to do all of the editing operations you'll need to perform regularly. Happy editing!

Stream Editing: Using *sed*

The sed editor is different from vi and Emacs. The latter two let you edit a file by scrolling up and down, back and forth, searching for text, and making changes as you go. The sed editor isn't like that. You use sed from the UNIX command line, instead of entering a workspace where you then enter vi or Emacs commands. Instead, when you enter a sed command at the UNIX prompt (a sed command is one that literally starts with the word *sed*), sed gets input from the file you specify by processing the file one line at a time. When sed is finished processing that line according to your instructions, it moves on to the next line and processes it, continuing until there aren't any more lines in the file to process. There is only one direction in which you can go—forward.

Thus, unfortunately, you have less control over which lines are changed than you do in vi or Emacs. The lines quickly stream through your screen, or perhaps you don't see them at all if you want to save the lines to a file. The only way you can control which lines are changed is by specifying them in some sort of regular way and letting sed work its magic.

> **NOTE**
>
> There are many types of streams, but for now you need to know only two of them: standard input and standard output. They are called *streams* because of the way the information flows—in a continuous fashion. You can redirect the streams with the redirection symbols you learned in Chapter 4, "Working in UNIX Environments."

You may ask, "If sed is less controllable than vi or Emacs, why would I want to use something like sed? If this input is going to come flying out of my file into some kind of editor magic that I can't even see, why would you use sed instead of Emacs or vi?"

People use sed for two reasons. The first is because it is fast, and changes that are regular in nature can be changed quickly. The second reason is that you can easily store sed commands in a file, and then quickly use them to process a text file. You'll learn more about this in a later chapter, when you learn about shell script programming; this feature of sed can be useful in shell script programming. Thus, if you have to make the same kinds of changes to many files, it can be easier to use sed to quickly and repetitively change your files.

You can specify the instructions you give sed in one of two ways. The first, as mentioned, is to store the sed commands in a file. The second is to issue sed commands from the command line.

Using *sed* Commands

The sed editor is unusual in that it takes as its input other commands. In other words, the form of the command is sed, followed by any options for sed that you wish to add (the options aren't required), followed by the command—usually a change and replace command—followed by the file that you want to change. Thus, the form of the sed command is this:

`sed options commands files`

There are only two options that you're likely to need often; they are the -e and -f options. The -e option tells sed that you're going to give sed a command from the command line. If you use this option, you need to follow the -e with a sed command, usually a change or delete command.

The -f option tells the system that it should look for a file that you specify for the inputs to sed. When this is the case, you don't have to give sed a command to execute, because the commands are in the file. Thus, all of the following commands are legal:

`sed -e 's/journey/trip/' roadtrip`	Changes the word journey, wherever it is found in the roadtrip file, to the word trip.
`sed 's/journey/trip/' roadtrip`	This is actually the same as the preceding command, and you'll soon see why.
`sed -f instructions roadtrip`	Uses the file instructions to make changes to the file roadtrip. (The instructions file could have any legal editing commands. You'll learn more about how to use this type of command when you learn about shell scripts in a later chapter.)

The -e option means that sed should expect a script. A *script* is a command or set of commands that you give to sed to tell it how to process a file.

The most common sed command is the s, or substitute, command. The general form of the command is `'s/old text/new text'`, or, if you want to substitute for every instance of old text, `'s/old text/new text/g'`, for global changes. It's also important that you place single quotes around this command when using sed, even though the quotes aren't technically part of the command itself.

You must also specify the file or files on which you want sed to operate. You can give sed one file, which is usually what you want to do anyway, or you can give it several files. If you give it several files, sed processes them one at a time, one right after the other, almost as if you'd given sed one long file with all of the files you specified stuck together.

Finally, you need to understand one last thing before you use sed for the first time: sed doesn't technically change a file just because you use the command. If you want to use sed to change your file, you need to redirect its output to a temporary file—say, a file called exper1 for experiment one—so you can look at the results to see if they're what you wanted. You can then copy this file to whatever filename you wish, including the original file on which you used sed.

Use sed to change all instances of the number 4 in your maintain file to 5, and save the results to a file called holdit. Enter the following command at the UNIX prompt:

```
$ sed -e 's/4/5/g' maintain > exper1
```

This command tells sed to use the s command to change all the 4s in the file to 5s (the g tells sed to do this everywhere in the file, that is, globally). The redirection operator puts the results into exper1.

You can look at your results using the UNIX more command. At the command line, enter more (and press the space bar to see more of your file, if not all of it, displayed). You'll see that, indeed, you have changed all of the 4s to 5s.

Picking and Choosing Lines from Files with *sed*

A common use of sed is to select or delete certain lines from a file. The selected lines can then either be put into a file or further processed in some way, or if the delete command is used, the original file can be purged of the deleted lines. The sed editor can do this easily.

To delete certain lines from a file using sed, use the delete command. It lets you specify a range of lines that are to be deleted from the processing of the sed editor. Note that they aren't removed from the original file, which will stay the same until you overwrite it.

For instance, you can tell sed that you want to delete all of the lines in the maintain file from the word The to the first 5. In this case, you're basically deleting the first line. To do this, call sed as follows:

```
sed -e '/The/,/5/d' maintain > exper2
```

The final d tells you that this is a delete operation. The first word between slash marks tells sed to start deleting lines beginning with the line that contains the first The. The comma should be read as "until." In other words, delete lines until the next line that contains a 5.

Thus, the form of the basic command is this:

```
sed -e '/word or phrase in first line to be processed/,/word or phrase in last
line to be processed/d' filename
```

Now use the more command to look at exper2, the file to which you redirected the output. Remember, had you not redirected the output, you would have seen the results just on standard out, which is your computer screen.

You should see the original file, minus the first line.

```
The UNIX system at our company is routinely shut down at 5:00 a.m.
If you are still working around 5:00 a.m., you need to save your
work before that or you may lose it. If you are submitting programs
to run overnight, you need to make sure that they terminate
well before 3:00. If you're not done by 5:00, the system
administrator will not be responsible for lost work.
```

Note that `sed` works on lines only, so if the first occurrence of a `5` was on the second line, both the first line and the whole second line would be deleted. You couldn't, in other words, use `sed` to delete individual phrases. The smallest unit that `sed` can process is the line.

Now, if you want to overwrite the revised file into the original file, you can enter `cp exper2 maintain`, and you'll get the desired effect. Remember to check the `maintain` file first to make sure that you've made the changes correctly.

What You've Learned

In this chapter, you have learned how to edit text files with the UNIX text editors. First was `vi`, which is the most common of all the editors because it is provided free on every installation of UNIX. Second was Emacs, which is very popular and is free, but may not be on every UNIX box. Last was `sed`, the stream editor; `sed` is excellent at making fast search-and-replace edits to files.

Rewards

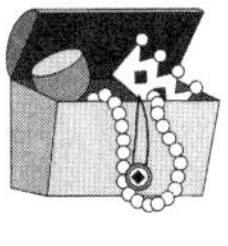

- ✖ The `vi`, Emacs, and `sed` editors are almost always included with UNIX.
- ✖ The Gnu version of Emacs is available without charge from the Free Software Foundation. You can order it by writing the Free Software Foundation.
- ✖ You learned how to use `vi` to do basic editing, such as:
  1. Use the `j`, `k`, `l`, `h`, `G`, and `b` commands to move through a file a letter at a time, a word at a time, or a line at a time.
  2. Insert text using `a` to add text after the cursor, or insert `i` to begin adding text before the cursor.
  3. Delete text using `dl` to delete lines, `dw` to delete words, or `dd` to delete lines.
  4. Make changes using `s` and `r`.
  5. Cut and paste text by using the `yy` (yank) and `p` (put) commands.
- ✖ You learned how to repeat many commands by prefacing them with numbers, such as `12dd`, which deletes 12 lines starting at the cursor.

- You learned how to set up your `vi` environment using common set commands.
- You understand that the Emacs editor is a popular alternative to the `vi` editor.
- In Emacs, you learned how to do some basic steps of editing, such as:
  1. Move through a file a letter at a time, a word at a time, or a line at a time.
  2. Insert text.
  3. Delete text.
  4. Make changes.
  5. Move text.
  6. Manage several different windows at the same time.
- A stream editor passes a stream of information—which could be a file fed into the editor sequentially—through an editor. The `sed` editor starts at the beginning (or top) of a file and continues processing information until it reaches the end of a file or files, and then automatically terminates and takes you back to the command line.
- The `sed` editor is often the most convenient to use when you have to make one or two kinds of global changes throughout a file. In such cases, it's more of a pain than it's worth to go into `vi`, make the changes, save the work, and exit. The `vi` and Emacs editors, on the other hand, are useful when you need to look at your text line-by-line or screen-by-screen and make individual decisions about where you want to make changes.
- The most common `sed` commands are the `s` and `d` commands, which change and delete lines. The `sed` editor can also be made to select some lines, and not others, from a file for processing or saving.

Pitfalls

- The `vi` editor doesn't have an indicator as to whether it is in command or insert mode. You can press Esc to make certain that you are in command mode. Afterward, you can enter insert mode.
- You can make a mess if you are in command mode and you thought that you were in insert mode. Press Esc to be sure.
- You might find it hard to undo a global change made in error. Save your file with the `w` command before you perform a big update.
- Emacs may not be on your UNIX system. You may need to download it from an FTP site on the Internet.

✖ Don't forget to redirect your output from sed to a file; sed does not automatically put your result in a file.

Using UNIX E-Mail Facilities

Driving Around the Parking Lot of the Information Superhighway

In This Chapter

* ✖ *What is a mailer?*

* ✖ *How do mailers work?*

* ✖ *What kinds of mailers are there, and how can you tell which one you have?*

* ✖ *What are the most common UNIX mailers?*

* ✖ *What do e-mail messages look like, and what's all that funny stuff at the beginning of all your messages?*

* ✖ *How do you send and receive e-mail using the most popular UNIX mailers?*

* ✖ *When you're in a hurry, how do you check to see if you have urgent e-mail, and how do you tell your mailer the right order in which to display your messages?*

✖ *How do you make carbon copies of e-mail messages?*

✖ *How do you save messages you've received?*

✖ *How do you reply to people who send you e-mail?*

✖ *Why do e-mail addresses look so funny? How do you send e-mail to people who use different e-mail services, such as CompuServe and MCI Mail?*

If You Can Learn to Drive Around the Block, You Can Drive to Zim

Learning how to send and receive electronic mail is much like learning to drive. After you master some basic skills, driving almost anywhere is pretty much the same. After you've mastered the basics of driving around the parking lot, learning the extra skills to drive in, say, the Cook Islands, is no big deal. After you've been driving a while, driving in a foreign country means that you have to remember that almost everything stays the same—signaling, using the clutch, parking—but you drive on the correct side of the road and you may have to use a traffic circle once in a while.

That's the way it is with e-mail and the Information Superhighway. When you've learned how to send e-mail to your buddy down the hall, you need only learn a few extra details and you'll be sending e-mail to Australia and South America.

In the chapter on getting started, you sent a simple e-mail message. You also learned how to read one. In this chapter, these processes will make more sense, and you'll learn how to control your mail more intelligently. In essence, you have driven around the parking lot a little bit, and now you will learn to travel the globe.

UNIX Mailers

There are many different UNIX mailers or e-mail programs, such as `mail` and `mailx`, and they fall into several different categories. Many of the free ones are used by typing commands at the UNIX command line. Others are based on using some kind of windowing software to achieve more user-friendliness. Some mailers are menu-driven. If you are lucky enough to have a menu-driven program, you can probably skip to the section, "How to Send Mail to People Who Use Popular

E-Mail Services," because your mailer doubtlessly has its own helpful, online documentation and menus to help guide you. You're driving the Cadillac of the Information Superhighway. If, however, you don't have access to such luxuries, you're probably stuck with the "plain vanilla" UNIX mailers, which are much like driving an AMC Pacer down the Information Superhighway. They work, and they'll get you there, but you won't exactly be riding in comfort.

Two of the most common mailers are the `mail` Seventh Edition Mailer and the `mailx` (Berkeley) mailer. The former is most closely associated with System V, Release 4 UNIX systems, while the latter is a common BSD mailer. They are fairly similar, but I'll point out some of the major differences.

To find out which mailer you have, enter `mail`. Do you see a prompt that says `Subject:`? If you do, you probably have the `mailx` mailer or some variant of it. You are not prompted for a subject in the `mail` program. (Enter Control+d, enter a period, or enter q to get out of the mail program.) If this doesn't work, enter `mailx` to see if it is actually the `mailx` mailer. (Enter q, Control+d, or a period to get out of the e-mail program.)

The *mail* Seventh Edition Mailer

The Seventh Edition Mailer is sometimes called *binmail* because it is placed in a standard UNIX directory called `/bin`.

Let's refresh your memory a little bit. The following is an e-mail message:

```
From lleaky Mon. Apr. 18 22:15 PDT 1994
Date: Mon, 18 Apr 1994 22:15:45 +0800
From lleaky (L. Leaky)
Message-ID <9404190515.AA0066900@origin.world.com>
To: Jgoodall

We set out for Ghombi next week. Can you have someone meet us on
the road to camp?

—LL
```

The top part is called the *header*, and it contains information that shows you who sent the e-mail, when the e-mail was sent, the computers that routed it and those associated times, the recipient (you), and the time you received it. The message itself is often referred to as the *body* of the message.

How to Start the *mail* Program

The good news is that learning to use the most user-unfriendly UNIX mailer isn't hard, and once you've learned one, the rest are easy. That's because various mailer have many similarities, and you need to know only how to do a few basic operations. Those basic operations include the following: start up the mail program, send e-mail, read new e-mail, read old e-mail, save e-mail to files, delete e-mail, get help, and quit out of e-mail. It's really not hard.

The bad news, however, is that the Seventh Edition Mailer included with some of the most popular UNIX systems today may be the most user-unfriendly mailer in the world. The mail program lacks some of the menu-driven screens of today's mailers. It is strictly command-line driven and can be very cryptic, but this book will help you learn how to use it. To start the program, you can enter mail, if you want to read mail, or, if you want to send mail, you can enter mail and an e-mail address (or a list of e-mail addresses, separated by commas, if you want to send mail to several people).

You can also enter mail, followed by some options. There are many options, depending on your system, but the most useful one for beginners is the -t option, which causes the mailer to insert into the message itself a line showing the names of the recipients of the message.

Clue: Sometimes programmers—who are themselves users of this mailer—modify the mailer to make this happen automatically, so you might get a recipient line without using the -t option. If this is the way it's done at your site, you don't need to use the -t option, but doing so won't hurt anything.

To use this option, enter mail -t, followed by your own e-mail address from the UNIX command line.

Now enter the following message:

```
$ mail -t lisas
Note to self: Remember to stop newspaper delivery before leaving for
Raratonga. And don't forget to buy mosquito repellant before you go.
.
$ _
```

Remember, though, that this mailer doesn't have line-wrap, so you'll need to press Enter every time you want to start a new line. When you're done, enter a period to send the message. After you've sent it, you'll see a question mark or maybe an ampersand. Now quit the mail program by pressing Enter, or, if that doesn't work, try Control+d.

Reading New Mail

To read mail, enter the word `mail` at the UNIX command line. Because you didn't enter any names after the word `mail`, the program assumes that you want to read your mail, not immediately send e-mail to someone.

Your mail is kept in two mailboxes: the incoming, primary mailbox, which is for all of your unread e-mail; and the secondary mailbox, which is a file called `mbox` in your `HOME` directory.

Clue: If you're curious about where your incoming mailbox is, you can enter `echo $MAIL` at the UNIX command line, and the full path will be displayed. The path will often tell you which mailer you have.

Here's a major difference between the Seventh Edition Mailer and the Berkeley mailer. In the Berkeley `mailx` mailer, when you read messages and don't delete them, they are automatically put in your `mbox` at most installations. You can look at them later, but they won't be shown to you automatically when you next start up `mailx`. After you've read a message, it won't be shown to you again unless you go looking for it.

In the Seventh Edition Mailer, however, messages hang around until you delete them. If you read a message and don't delete it, you'll see it again in your list of messages (along with any new messages you may have received in the meantime) the next time you read your mail, until you delete it or otherwise dispose of it.

If you have new e-mail (and you will, if you sent yourself the message in the example in the preceding section), you should see your first message. When I recently checked my e-mail, I saw a single message waiting for me:

```
$ mail
From loren Mon Apr. 18
Date: Mon, 18 Apr. 5:00 p.m. 0800
From: Loren L. art
Message ID: <9483787484.AA02109@KLUDGE.ENG.SUN .COM

CONTENT LENGTH: 29

Our reservations to Raratonga have been confirmed.

loren@sun.com

? _
```

After you've read your message, there are only a few logical responses. Most of the time, you'll want to read the next message, or to ask for help using the ? command, or to reply to the message you just received.

> **NOTE**
>
> The prompt for mail is the question mark (?). This can be confusing if you look at it from a help point of view. To get help, press ? at the ? prompt.

You do have some options when it comes to reading mail, but you must specify them when you start up mail. For instance, mail normally shows you your newest messages first. That is good, because if somebody sends you an urgent request for help, followed by a message saying, "Uh, never mind, I figured out the problem," you'll get the "nevermind" message first; you won't read the panicky message first and waste your time working on a solution. On the other hand, on some busy days you may want to read and respond to the messages that have been waiting the longest for your attention; you think that the more recent messages can be put off until later. In that case, you'd want to reverse the normal order, as the following command does:

```
$ mail -r
```

Everything else works the same when you use this option. The only thing that changes is the order in which you receive your e-mail.

Clue: To get help with mail or to see if there are special commands or utilities that work with your particular version of the mailer, remember that you can enter a question mark (?) at the mailer's prompt. You will be shown a summary of all the options and commands possible from your mailer. This works not only with the Seventh Edition Mailer, but with almost every command-line editor in the history of civilization. Thus, this is a universal lifesaver if you ever have to work on somebody else's computers.

Also, you can enter man mail—or mailx, if mail doesn't work on your system—at the UNIX command line (before you get into your mailer), and you can find out which options your mailer supports. This can be important, particularly if you have many extra features in your mailer that aren't generally available.

Replying to Mail

To reply to e-mail after you've read a message, enter r at the mailer's prompt. The mailer's prompt will disappear, and in some mailers (but not the Seventh Edition mailer), a subject line of the form Re:, followed by the subject line of the message to which you're responding, will automatically be generated. You compose the message normally, as you would if you had initiated the message. Now send the following reply to your own message:

```
Note to self: Remember to stop newspaper delivery before leaving for
Raratonga. And don't forget to buy mosquito repellant before you go.

? r
mail lisas
And also remember to go to the bank and get travelers' checks.

—Lisa
(lisas@uworl.com)
.
New mail loaded into letter 3.
? _
```

When you're done, terminate the message with a period. The reply is sent, and the mailer again gives you the mail prompt. Of course, to get out of the program, you can press Control+d, if that's what you want to do.

Clue: When you reply or send e-mail to other users, it's a good idea to include your e-mail address. Often, people can figure it out from the header information or can reply automatically to your address, but not always. It's best to help them respond to you.

To Continue Reading Messages

To continue reading messages, keep pressing Enter every time you see the mail prompt at the end of each message you read. Remember, every time you reply to a message, you'll see a prompt when you're done, and you can resume reading the message after the one to which you just replied. When you've read all of your messages, you press Enter at the mail prompt. You'll be automatically returned to the UNIX command line.

If you don't decide to read all of your messages at once, you can read the rest later. The ones that you haven't read are saved in the new messages file until you've read them. The messages that you've already read are stored in mbox.

Reading Old Messages

There are two ways to look at your old messages, the ones that you've a[l
The most advisable method—if it works on your system—is to e[n
the UNIX command line.

The other method you can use to read old messages is to use the more command to read the mbox file in your home directory. You can then keep pressing Return until you find the message you want. Thus, you go to your home directory and enter more mbox or give the full pathname of mbox to the more command, which in my case would be the following:

```
$ more /usr/lisas/mbox
```

In some mailers, if you look at the messages stored in mbox, you'll see only the messages you've saved. In others, you'll see every message you've ever received. If you want to, you can edit the mbox file to clean out old messages that you no longer want. Fire up your favorite word processor or line editor, and edit the file as you wish.

How to Save and Delete Messages

To save messages, read the message first. Then enter s at the mail prompt. If you want to save the message you sent yourself earlier, read it and enter the following command at the mail prompt:

```
? s Raratonga
```

The message will be stored in the file named Raratonga. If there isn't a file called Raratonga, the mailer will create one. On most systems, if you want to save the message to your mbox file, enter s, with no filename after it, and the message will be saved in your mbox file.

For Letters from Your Ex: How to Delete Mail

When you get a message you don't need or want to keep, you can delete it. After you've read ⁱ⁓   ˡ at the mail prompt, and the message will be deleted. For
          message from a seedy character who tried to pick you up in
          takes care of that message:

```
u at the Maui Wauwi Resort Hotel. You never showed!
```

175

eady read.
ter mail -f at

estiny with someone else. If, at this point, you want to
          dq would delete the message and quit the mailer.

s as you read them, but you can also delete messages
          you enter d, followed by the message number. The
          delete message number 3:

```
? d 3
```

If you're in the Seventh Edition Mailer, enter h, and you'll see the letter d on the header line of the message that you just deleted. When you exit normally, the message will be truly deleted, not merely marked for deletion, but until then, it's in limbo until you exit the mailer session. In the Berkeley mailer, though, the message isn't marked for deletion; it is removed entirely from the list of header lines, so it isn't displayed at all:

```
? h
2 letters found in /var/mail/lisas, 0 scheduled for deletion, 0 newly arrived
>   2    3280    lisas      Thu May  5 22:37 EST 1994
    1     352    lisas      Thu May  5 22:37 EST 1994
? _
```

Suppose you decide, after deleting poor Sammy's message, that Sammy isn't so bad, and you want to retrieve his message. If you haven't already quit the mail program, you can *undelete* it. If your change of heart comes immediately, you can enter u at the mail prompt that appeared after you deleted the message; entering u at this point will undelete the message. Then you can reply to it, if you want to.

If, before your change of heart, you had to think about Sammy's note a while and you had continued to read mail in the meantime, you must undelete the message by using its number. To do that, get the correct message number. Then, at the mail prompt, enter d followed by the number you want to delete. If you want to undelete message number 3, the following line does so:

```
? u 3
```

> **Clue:** If you can't remember the number of the deleted message, enter h a at the mailer prompt to see your deleted messages.

If you decide, for some reason, that you're sorry you deleted all of the messages in a particular session, you can quit and pretend that the entire session never happened; the result is that all of the messages that were unread at the start of the session are still considered unread when you exit.

The command to do this—to "forget" an entire session—is x. Enter x (for exit) at the mail prompt, and you'll exit as if your entire mail session had never happened.

```
? x
$
```

When you use this option, any messages that you've read are still considered unread. Any messages you'd saved to files or deleted are no longer saved or deleted.

Just Checking

There are ways to check your e-mail without actually reading it. If you have a graphical-user interface, a mailbox icon indicates that you have e-mail waiting. If you don't have such an interface, however, you may still want to know if messages are waiting, how many, who they are from, and how urgent they are—but all without actually opening and reading the messages. In that case, you can use the following instructions, and often you'll be able to tell who sent the e-mail and whether the e-mail you have is extremely important or can wait.

> **WARNING**
>
> One of the important differences between the Berkeley and Seventh Edition mailers is the order in which messages are displayed. In the Seventh Edition Mailer, the oldest messages appear first in the list unless you use the `mail -r` command at the UNIX command line to call the mail program. In the Berkeley mailer, the newest messages appear first.

Enter `mail -h` (remember, `h` is for header) at the UNIX command line to see something like the following, which my husband recently saw while reading his e-mail:

```
$ mail -h
3    362  jimb      Mon. Apr. 18   22.28 PDT 1994
2    348  ellen     Mon. Apr. 18   22.17 PDT 1994
1    404  rob       Mon. Apr. 18   22:00 PDT 1994
? _
```

The numbers on the far left indicate the message number; these are handy if you want to delete or save mail. The dates and times indicate when the message was received. In the Berkeley mailer, you'll also see a subject line, a nice feature.

The preceding command works if you know—when you're still at the UNIX command line—that you want to see headers; but it won't help you if you start by entering `mail` and later decide you want to see the headers. Later, when you're actually in the mailer, you see the headers by entering `h` at the mail command line. This shows you the headers of the messages before and after the current message.

Some similar commands, all of which are entered at the mail command line (not the UNIX command line), include the following:

h   Shows the header of the message.

h a Shows the headers of all messages in your primary mailbox.

h d Shows you the headers of deleted messages. Deleted messages are marked with a d in the Seventh Edition Mailer.

For example, in the following example, I have listed the headers of messages 1 and 2, deleted a message, listed the headers of messages in my primary mailbox, and looked at the header of the deleted message:

```
? h 1
3 letters found in /var/mail/root, 0 scheduled for deletion, 0 newly arrived
     3     879    root        Fri May  6 06:18 EST 1994
     2     840    root        Fri May  6 06:18 EST 1994
 >   1     358    root        Fri May  6 06:18 EST 1994
? h 2
3 letters found in /var/mail/root, 0 scheduled for deletion, 0 newly arrived
     3     879    root        Fri May  6 06:18 EST 1994
 >   2     840    root        Fri May  6 06:18 EST 1994
     1     358    root        Fri May  6 06:18 EST 1994
? d
From root Fri May  6 06:18 EST 1994
Date: Fri, 6 May 1994 06:18:42 +0500
From: Mailer-Daemon (Mail Delivery Subsystem)
Subject: Returned mail: Host unknown
Message-Id: <9405061118.AA27015@excelsior-bb.>
To: Postmaster
Content-Length: 466

    — — Transcript of session follows — —
421 Host mailhost not found for mailer ether.
550 lisas@vasanet... Host unknown

    — — Message header follows — —
Return-Path: <root>
Received: by excelsior-bb. (5.0/SMI-SVR4)
        id AA27013; Fri, 6 May 1994 06:18:42 +0500
Date: Fri, 6 May 1994 06:18:42 +0500
From: root (0000-Admin(0000))
Message-Id: <9405061118.AA27013@excelsior-bb.>
Errors-To: root
Content-Type: text
Content-Length: 42
Apparently-To: lisas@vasanet

? h a
3 letters found in /var/mail/root, 1 scheduled for deletion, 0 newly arrived
     3  d  879    root        Fri May  6 06:18 EST 1994
 >   2     840    root        Fri May  6 06:18 EST 1994
     1     358    root        Fri May  6 06:18 EST 1994
? h d
3 letters found in /var/mail/root, 1 scheduled for deletion, 0 newly arrived
     3  d  879    root        Fri May  6 06:18 EST 1994
? _
```

Common Types of E-Mail Addresses

There are several common kinds of e-mail addresses. Understanding their formats and how to send e-mail between different types of addresses is often convenient.

The Form of E-Mail Addresses

The following are some typical e-mail addresses. They all have the most common format that you'll encounter.

```
rodriguez@netcom.com
vice-president@whitehouse.gov
president@whitehouse.gov
cservice@computercorp.com
smith@stanford.EDU
chen@nasa.gov
```

This most common form of e-mail address consists of an *identifier*—such as a name or department of a company, or a personal name or set of initials—followed by an organization name.

These designations at the end are a by-product of the history of the worldwide computer network called the Internet, and if your message goes outside of your area, it probably uses part of this network to travel on its electronic path. Because the Internet is the descendent of ARPAnet, the government-subsidized communications network for people who worked on defense and weapons research—primarily university researchers, government workers, and the commercial companies that designed and produced the projects—Internet addresses end in .edu for education, .com for commercial, and .gov for government.

These days, almost anyone can get an e-mail address that ends in .com. These services are provided by third-party companies—such as Portal, Netcom, and America Online—who provide accounts for a small fee ($15–$40, approximately). These accounts are similar to electronic post-office boxes; many people who work at companies that give them accounts, but who change jobs often, have accounts on these third-party services in order to have a permanent address.

How to Send Mail to People Who Use Popular E-Mail Services

Some computer services use numbers, instead of names, for the addresses of their members. For instance, CompuServe members typically have addresses composed of a five-digit number, followed by a comma, followed by a four-digit number, for example, `78910,1234`. You can use such an address if both you and the message recipient are on CompuServe; if you aren't, however, you must convert such an address to a format that computers on the Internet can recognize.

To convert an address, take the CompuServe address, change the comma into a period, and add `@compuserve.com`. The preceding e-mail address would become `78910.1234@compuserve.com`. The following are some sample conversions:

`74623,1387` becomes `74623.1387@compuserve.com`

`78921,2133` becomes `78921.2133@compuserve.com`

A similar method works to convert MCI Mail addresses to Internet-friendly addresses. If someone is named `nancyk` on MCI Mail, you can reach her at `nancyk@mcimail.com`. If someone's account number is `23455452`, you can reach him at `23455452@mcimail.com`. Here are some examples:

`kathyr` becomes `kathyr@mcimail.com`

`maria_cordova` on `mcimail` becomes `maria_cordova@mcimail.com`

`91849878` on `mcimail` becomes `9184978@mcimail.com`

CompuServe and MCI Mail are two popular e-mail services, and you've learned how to convert their members' addresses into something that can be reached from Internet-style addresses, which are very common on UNIX systems.

Rewards

- ✖ You know that a mailer is a program that helps you send, receive, and manage your electronic mail.

- ✖ Mailers manage primary mailboxes, which keep current messages, and secondary mailboxes, which usually hold older messages.

- ✖ The two most common mailers included free with UNIX machines are the Seventh Edition Mailer—shipped with most System V, Release 4 UNIX systems—and the Berkeley mail reader. There are a few differences, but in the most basic and common commands, they work similarly.

- ✖ The times, dates, and e-mail addresses included at the beginning of e-mail messages are called headers. The rest of the message, the part that you compose, is called the body of the message.

- ✖ You can get help on almost any mailer in the world by entering a question mark (?) at the mailer command line. You can also enter `man mail` at the UNIX command line if you want more information about the available options.

✖ To send e-mail, enter mail, followed by the recipients of the message that you want to send. Then enter the body of your message, followed by a period (.). To exit, press Enter again or Control+d.

✖ To read messages, you can enter the message number, or you can enter mail and keep pressing Enter until you're done reading messages.

✖ To save e-mail messages, enter s.

✖ To reply to the person who sent you e-mail, enter r. To reply to everybody to whom the message was sent (including those who were sent copies), enter R.

✖ To read old messages, you can scroll through your mbox file using the more mbox command from the UNIX command line. In some mailers, entering mail -f shows you all of the undeleted messages that you've already received and read.

✖ There are easy ways to send e-mail to people who use different e-mail services, such as CompuServe, America Online, and MCI Mail.

Pitfalls

✖ Answering e-mail can take a considerable amount of time. I recommend that you search for urgent messages and leave the rest for a special time of the week that's set apart to answer mail.

✖ Disorganization can lead you into the e-mail Pit of Despair. Delete messages frequently or save them in another mailbox for later. You will be amazed at how much e-mail is junk e-mail.

✖ Don't let your words lead you to a pink slip and to the unemployment line. Be ethical and considerate online. You never know where you e-mail will end up.

A Beginner's Guide to Reading UNIX Internet Newsgroups

Or, How to Mine the Net for Fun, Romance, and Profit

In This Chapter

- ✖ *What are newsgroups?*

- ✖ *How are newsgroups used?*

- ✖ *What is a newsreader?*

- ✖ *What are the common newsreaders, and how are they used?*

- ✖ *From computer groups to religion to romance and sex: How do you find the newsgroups that interest you?*

- ✖ *How do you subscribe to a newsgroup?*

▶

✖ *How do you browse through and read newsgroups?*

✖ *How do you read messages on newsgroups?*

✖ *How do you reply to postings?*

✖ *What are threads in newsreaders?*

✖ *How do you post messages to newsgroups for others to read?*

Seeking Love, Friendship, and Sacred Wisdom in Newsgroups

Looking for friends? information? love? Want to learn about the latest in computers, sports, hobbies, and the sciences? Do you just want to talk? Newsgroups are where people can meet, talk, argue, share, discuss, look for jobs, and fall in love.

You already know one use of the Internet. It carries your e-mail, as you learned in a previous chapter. Whenever you send e-mail to someone outside your company, you are using part of the Internet.

Another use of the Internet—one most people don't realize—is to get information and make friends using *newsgroups*. Newsgroups are like electronic versions of supermarket-style bulletin boards, except that there are thousands of newsgroups and they can all be accessed in the same way. For beginners, this is particularly important, because one way to get help from UNIX gurus and to keep up on the latest developments in UNIX is to ask the experts electronically.

Surviving Natural Disasters

Newsgroups can do so much more, both for you and for the rest of humanity. For instance, newsgroups help people cope with traumatic events in their lives. In places such as the San Francisco Bay Area and Los Angeles, for example, people used newsgroups as electronic public bulletin boards to exchange information and moral support in the aftermath of the Loma Prieta and Northridge earthquakes.

During the breakup of the Soviet Union and during the events leading up to the massacre at Tiananmen Square, people in these places were able to get word out to the world about what was happening by posting messages to newsgroups, and their governments were powerless to censor their messages.

Today, most high-tech businesses—as well as many businesses that have nothing to do with defense—let their employees read newsgroups to communicate with other employees, keep up on the latest computer research, and to do marketing and customer service.

> **NOTE**
>
> As you read other reference material about newsgroups on the Internet, you will see that newsgroups are sometimes referred to as *the news.*

People use newsgroups in all kinds of fascinating ways. Some are looking for love in all sorts of strange places, some want gardening advice, some are seeking information from the most knowledgeable people in their field, some are into becoming politically aware, and others are seeking religion. Such people can "hang out on the Net." In particular, celebrities—actors, actresses, athletes, and politicians—often hold extended conversations with total strangers on The Well, which is a popular provider of access to newsgroups.

The Incendiary Internet Connection

Perhaps the most worthwhile use of newsgroups is political organizing and the fight for freedom. If Madison, Jefferson, and Franklin were alive today, the Declaration of Independence might have been posted to a newsgroup.

Because governments everywhere are having trouble controlling personal computers—even in totalitarian regimes such as China and the former U.S.S.R.—newsgroups are a great place to foment rebellion. During the breakaway of the Baltic Republics from the former Soviet Union, I read postings from people who watched demonstrations in Lithuania, Estonia, and Latvia. People who watched sessions of the illegal, breakaway parliaments posted full transcripts of these sessions, as well as frequent updates describing what was happening in the political fronts. It was impossible for the Soviet Union to totally stifle these movements, because observers could send messages to computers across the Gulf of Finland, as well as to Sweden and Norway, where these messages could be broadcast worldwide.

Because newsgroups are numerous and finely divided into particular specialties and interests, it's fairly easy to find some of the foremost experts in any given field. Think of that: the world's experts are at your fingertips, and you have a way to find out what they're thinking. This is particularly important in fields where technical research is heating up; although the most current information is not available in books or in technical journals, it is being discussed among peers on the Internet.

For instance, researchers working on the Human Genome Project, which aims to discover what each part of each gene controls in humans, have created separate newsgroups for the discussion of each aspect of the project.

Another newsgroup is focused on researchers who are working on nanotechnology—the creation of microscopic machines that may someday do everything from absorbing toxic wastes to performing surgery.

Are you interested in ecology or mass transit? You can try the environmental groups, where many of the people who are on the front lines in the ecology movement congregate. Do you want to learn how to use a particular kind of computer? No matter how old or how uncommon your computer is, you'll probably be able to find a newsgroup of people who use the same computer and have probably faced the same problems as you do. Does your job depend on learning to use a particular software well? There is probably a newsgroup for users of that software, so if you become a regular reader, you can often get help from experienced users.

Overcoming That Nerdy Image

Unfortunately, many beginners shun newsgroups as being too "nerdy" or too "techno-weenie," as some of them put it. Those who take this attitude are making the rather common mistake of confusing the method of communication with the messages delivered. In other words, the way that newsgroups are read does involve high-tech equipment, but the messages that people share are as important and as "human" as any that are exchanged through fountain pens, parchment, and stamps.

As a matter of fact, I have several New Age friends who would never be caught dead showing any enthusiasm for computers. But they work at high-tech companies that automatically give everyone access to the news, so they are Internet enthusiasts and regularly read the gardening and horticultural newsgroups. My friends believe in saving and planting heirloom seeds, old varieties of plants that people have passed down for years. By posting messages telling people what kinds of seeds they have and what kind they're seeking, they're able to grow their own rare varieties of plants and to pass on some of their best "finds" to others. The newsgroup they regularly hang out on is called `alt.sustainable.agriculture`. By no means are any of these people obsessed by technology; in fact, if anything, they wish they could get closer to nature. They realize, however, the power of the tool to help them achieve their goals and are willing to learn how to use it so they can reap the benefits.

How Do Newsgroups Work?

The Internet handles messages of all types. E-mail is one type of message you can receive. Newsgroup postings are another. Both types of messages reach your computer after traveling, in some cases, around the world.

Newsgroups differ from regular e-mail because of the way these messages are posted. Posted messages in newsgroups can be read by anyone, whereas regular e-mail messages are posted in private from you to your friend somewhere on the Internet.

If you are interested in a newsgroup such as alt.startrek, a newsgroup focused on the *Star Trek* TV series and movies, you can join this group. When you join this newsgroup, you can read messages from other Trekkies. These messages are called *postings*. As you read these messages, or postings, your computer keeps track of where you left off reading messages. The next time you read this newsgroup, you will see only messages posted since your last visit.

What Is a Newsgroup?

The backbone of newsgroups consists of messages, but unlike e-mail, these messages aren't directed at particular people, but at a public "electronic space." A newsgroup is the electronic equivalent of a public bulletin board at a laundromat, school, or grocery store. People electronically "post" messages, and using software at your end, you can read these messages. When you read the messages, you may choose to read them and go onto the next one; or you may choose to post a message of your own to this public space, where anybody who is interested can read it. Finally, you could respond to the poster with an e-mail message, which behaves as does any other e-mail message, going straight to the e-mail addressee; in this case, your response is a private communication you and the person who posted the message that you read.

You may wonder how newsgroups are created and by whom. The answer is that anybody can set up a newsgroup on the Internet. There is a voting process, and people can vote *yes* or *no* as to whether the new group should be created. A certain number of *yes* votes must be achieved, and the ratio of *yes* to *no* votes must be high enough, or the newsgroup can't be legitimately started.

Actually, though, nothing technological prevents anybody from starting whatever newsgroups he or she may want. That's why you may see a number of "renegade" newsgroups created solely for fun or, in some cases, as practical jokes or malicious swipes at real people or fictional characters. Usually, these are easy to spot by looking at the names of such newsgroups. You will occasionally see newsgroups such as alt.barney.die.die.die or alt.sexy.bald.captain (a reference to one of the main characters of the TV series *Star Trek: The Next Generation*). Read them at your own peril. They are usually empty, the result of the exuberance of youth or of the gray-haired young-at-heart.

Newsreaders

Earlier, you learned that UNIX had built-in technical features for communication. This is true, but the facilities to read newsgroups weren't built into the UNIX operating system per se. Most UNIX installations add this capability with an installation of one of a number of utility programs that enable people to read newsgroups. These utility programs are called *newsreaders*. Before you go any further in this chapter, you should make sure that you have such facilities on your network. Because these programs vary significantly in the exact way you perform the basic newsreading operations, you also need to discern which mailer you're using.

The best way to do this is to check with your system administrator to verify that you do have these facilities and to find out which newsreaders you have on your network, where they are located, and how to start them up. The second-best way to figure out which newsreaders you have is to use the man command on the common mailreaders—rn, readnews, tn, tin, news—and see which ones have man pages on your system. However, this doesn't mean you have access to the newsreaders.

The third and the least preferable way to figure out what newsreaders you have on your UNIX system, if any, is to enter the following commands: tin, rn, readnews, tn, rtn, and news. If, after entering any one of these commands, you get a response from the system, then you have that newsreader on your system. Many installations have several mail readers so that users can use whichever mailer they prefer. To get out of these newsreaders, press Control+d until you're taken back to the UNIX command line.

Most installations having newsreaders at least have the rn program. That is why this newsreader is covered in detail in this chapter; it's not the best newsreader, but it's probably the most common.

If you have rn, it's a good idea to go through this chapter using it. Then you'll understand the basics and can easily use more user-friendly newsreaders either with a little help from others or by reading the man pages for your alternative newsreaders. If you have other newsreaders, you'll be able to quickly adapt what you've learned to those newsreaders, because all newsreaders perform the same kinds of actions. They differ in the exact commands used, and once you've learned the concepts behind newsreading, it's not hard to learn a slightly different way of doing it.

If you don't have rn at all, but you do have access to some other newsreader, it's best to read this chapter, then use either the man command or the help feature within your newsreader to figure out what the equivalent commands are in your newsreader. More detailed discussion of some of the common newsreaders—for example, nn and trn—is provided in Appendix B, "Commonly Used Newsreader Commands," and in these books:

The Internet Unleashed by Sams Publishing, ISBN 0-672-30466-X

Navigating the Internet, Deluxe Edition by Richard J. Smith and Mark Gibbs, ISBN 0-672-30485-6

Teach Yourself the Internet: Around the World in 21 Days by Neil Randall, ISBN 0-672-30519-4

NOTE

If you're not working in a corporate network environment or your environment doesn't support newsgroups, you can do one of two things. You could set up your own machine to be an Internet site, but that would be hard for a beginner and is far beyond the scope of this book. You could also do what most people do: Obtain a connection from an Internet provider that will provide you with a personal account connected to the Internet. These providers give you access to newsgroups and much more. This will usually require a personal computer and a modem, or you can Telnet to their site to read mail. Popular Internet providers include the following:

Netcom, (800) 501-8649 or (408) 554-8649

PSINet, (703) 620-6651

UUNet's AlterNet, (703) 204-8000

Portal, (408) 973-9111

Some of these services, such as Netcom and UUNet, provide not only access but "menu-driven front-ends," which do the same things as newsreaders, but are much more user-friendly to most beginners. These services cost about $15–30 a month, with start-up fees of about $20–40, that is, about the same as basic telephone service. If you decide to read newsgroups this way, you'll do all of the same basic operations discussed in this chapter, but you'll have to follow the instructions given to you by the service and to use the menus where provided.

The *.newsrc* File and Getting Started

I've sold you on the idea of reading news, and you know that you can find all kinds of treasures in newsgroups. Unfortunately, the most difficult part of learning to read news comes at the beginning, when you have to tell your newsreader which newsgroups you want to read regularly. This process is called "setting up your subscriptions," or "subscribing" for short. After you've done this, reading news becomes a simple matter of browsing through all of the messages posted to each newsgroup to which you've subscribed since you last read your newsgroups.

> **NOTE**
>
> You need to think of these start-up tasks as building a tunnel into a dark, damp cave searching riches to mine. Once you have the tunnel braced and tracks laid, extracting gold or silver is a much easier ongoing task.

The reason it's so hard to read news in the beginning is that all newsreaders must create a special file called the .newsrc file. This will take a little time. This file contains all of the newsgroups available at your site, and for each newsgroup, the file contains notation that indicates whether you subscribe to that newsgroup. Your newsreader relies on this file to tell it which groups you want to read. The problem is that you have to set up the newsreader in the beginning, and this involves either making a decision on each and every newsgroup—and there are now at least 5,000 newsgroups on the Internet—or being clever about how you tell the .newsrc file what you want.

Clue: You can cheat a little on the setup of the newsreader by coping a .newsrc from a friend. Of course, you will be subscribed to your friend's newsgroups, but it will be easy to unsubscribe these newsgroups.

The rn newsreader is one of the oldest newsreaders; it has grown up with UNIX and has been around long enough that it has been incorporated into many UNIX installations. Because it was created so long ago—at a time when few people could imagine there being more than a few hundred newsgroups and when practically the only people on the Internet were computer scientists—it was not designed to handle all of the thousands of newsgroups now available upon startup.

You start up your newsreader, and the newsreader queries you as to whether you want to read each newsgroup. In the beginning, you're subscribed to all of them, and you must usually enter u—meaning *unsubscribe*—for each newsgroup that you don't want to read. I'll show you how to do so using rn, but if you do unsubscribe in this way, you'll have to reserve several hours to get through all of the newsgroups the first time. After that, you'll only have to worry about unsubscribing to newsgroups added to the Internet since the last time you read news, which is usually 10 or fewer each day. Using this method to select newsgroups is easier than the other, but it takes a long time.

The slightly more difficult way involves editing the .newsrc file directly, using an editor to unsubscribe to everything in the beginning (the opposite of the default), and then to subscribe individually to the few that you do want to follow. This way is a little bit more difficult to understand conceptually, but it takes far less time at startup.

My advice to you is to read the following two sections and choose the route you're more comfortable taking. Then go through your selected method step-by-step, following the examples and performing the instructions.

Before you move on, here are some things you'll need to understand before you pick your newsgroups.

First, some companies have polices about newsreading. You should familiarize yourself with such policies. Some policies ask that you restrict yourself to job-related newsgroups, such as perhaps the computer-related newsgroups. Others ask that you put yourself on the honor system and read non-work-related newsgroups only outside of work hours. Some use the computer system (a cron entry, actually) to lock people out of reading news during specific hours; companies do this because, even with the best of intentions, employees can easily become addicted to newsreading, to the exclusion of doing real work. Most companies that support newsreading, however, put people on the honor system and are willing to tolerate employees who usually use newsreading for business purposes—people who read computer-related newsgroups, for example—but who occasionally read one or two newsgroups purely for pleasure.

> **WARNING**
>
> As you make your selection, please understand that it's very easy for your system administrator or other co-workers to find out which newsgroups you're reading. (It's written down in one of your files, as will be discussed later.) In particular, most sites give the system administrator a report that tell him or her at least which newsgroups were read in, for example, the last week and how many people at the site read each group. Sometimes,

this report is distributed to the other people at the site who read news; these others know how many people on-site read each group. Why am I telling you this? In essence, I'm trying to explain why it's not a good idea to read `alt.sex.bondage` (or similar newsgroups) at work. It's a good idea to read this one from a more private computer.

Even if nobody is interested in which groups you personally are reading, the existence of a published list of the groups read at your site can cause tension in the workplace. For instance, a small startup company I once worked for used to publish the newsreading reports. The reports showed that there were two people who read `alt.sex.fetishes`, `alt.skinheads`, and `alt.sex.bondage`. No names were given, just the groups and the number of readers for each group. Because everybody in the company knew everyone else, some of the people I worked with used to wonder to themselves who was reading these newsgroups. Had I ever found out who was reading these newsgroups, I think I might have wondered how the readers viewed me, people of color, and the other women who worked there. Such tension in the workplace can be very counterproductive.

The general rule you should follow is a high-tech modification of an old one you've doubtlessly heard: If you wouldn't want a particular newsgroup that you read to appear on the front page of the Sunday paper, it's probably not a good idea to subscribe that newsgroup at work.

A few other guidelines can help you find the newsgroups you want to read. The groups referring to computers all start with `comp`. Recreational groups start with `rec`. Groups that deal with lifestyles usually contain `alt` or `soc`. Groups that deal with meeting and "talking" to people about a particular topic start with `talk`, whereas groups dealing with science start with `sci`.

There are also geographical groups. If you don't belong to a particular geographical region and never expect to go to that region, it's probably not worth reading. For example, if you never plan to live in California, `ca.environment` and `ca.jobs` are probably irrelevant; so are the `ba` newsgroups, which stands for the San Francisco Bay Area. Some sites automatically exclude groups that are concerned with faraway geographical areas; users at such sites don't have to unsubscribe to such groups because the newsfeed has been "screened out" at the machine that receives it.

Clue: You should remain subscribed to `news.announce.newgroups`, `news.announce.newusers`, and `news.answers`, if they are available from your site. These newsgroups are good places to read about new newsgroups and to find answers to questions that beginners usually ask. In particular, the group `news.announce.newusers` has much good information, including advice on the etiquette and "rules" involved in reading news. Reading the information here can save you from accidentally committing an Internet faux pas. Remember, the Internet has millions of readers, a population greater than some small countries. As a result of this mass of humanity, it also has its own culture and social norms, as well as its own way of making those who violate these norms feel uncomfortable, so "read up on the natives" as you first start to travel.

Using *rn*—Readnews

The next sections teach how to use rn in two completely different ways. Most of this has to do with the way you use rn from the start.

Using *rn* the Easier (But Longer) Way

Here's the easy-to-understand way to begin using rn, which will probably take you hours to complete the startup procedures. You will be asked what you want to do about every single newsgroup, so you always know what you're doing and are, therefore, less likely to get lost or confused.

Begin by typing rn at the command line:

```
$ rn
Trying to set up a .newsrc file — running newsetup...

Creating /u3/lisa/.newsrc to be used by news programs.
Done.

If you have never used the news system before, you may find
the articles in news.announce.newusers to be helpful. There
is also a manual entry for rn.

To get rid of newsgroups you aren't interested in, use the 'u' command.
Type h for help at any time while running rn.


Checking for new newsgroups...
```

You are now asked whether you wish to read the messages in each and every newsgroup. You'll also see a prompt, [ynp], which stands for *yes, no,* and *previous.* If you enter y, you'll be shown the messages for that particular group. If you enter n, you'll be asked about the next group. The p means to read the previous newsgroups. Because you're starting at the beginning, you don't have any previous newsgroups yet, so don't worry about this one. You aren't restricted to these three options. You can enter any of the rn commands at the prompt, and this time, you want to enter u for *unsubscribe* when you're not interested in the group. It's important to realize, by the way, that entering n for *no* doesn't unsubscribe you; entering n means simply that you are not shown the messages in that group now.

You should see something like the following, although the newsgroups may be different or displayed in a different order:

```
****** 150 unread articles in news.announce.newgroups — read now? [ynq] n
****** 25 unread articles in news.announce.newusers — read now? [ynq] n
****** 3195 unread articles in news.answers — read now? [ynq] n
```

By entering n at each query, I've postponed reading the mentioned newsgroups, but I've remained subscribed.

If you want to unsubscribe to some newsgroups, type u at the prompt:

```
****** 3354 unread articles in news.groups — read now? [ynq] u
Unsubscribed to newsgroup news.groups

****** 231 unread articles in news.misc — read now? [ynq] u

Unsubscribed to newsgroup news.misc

******  13 unread articles in news.newsites — read now? [ynq] u

Unsubscribed to newsgroup news.newsites
```

Now, every time you see a question about subscribing to a particular newsgroup, decide whether you want to read it. Enter u to unsubscribe to the groups to which you don't want to subscribe. (You're automatically subscribed to each group unless you unsubscribe with u.) When you're done, enter q to exit the newsreader, or stay in the news program and move forward to the section in this chapter titled "Browsing and Reading Newsgroups" for how to read newsgroups using rn.

Using *rn* the Shorter (But Harder) Way

Here's the hard-to-understand way to begin using rn. You will use it long enough to build a .newsrc file, then you'll exit rn and doctor the file yourself. To do this, begin by entering the rn command:

```
$ rn
Trying to set up a .newsrc file — running newsetup...

Creating /u3/lisa/.newsrc to be used by news programs.
Done.

If you have never used the news system before, you may find the articles
in news.announce.newusers to be helpful. There is also a manual entry for rn.
```

```
To get rid of newsgroups you aren't interested in, use the 'u' command.
Type h for help at any time while running rn.
```

As soon as you see the line Trying to set up a .newsrc — running newsetup, you know rn is building for you a .newsrc file in which you are subscribed to every newsgroup your site can receive. In this example, my .newsrc file is being created in the directory /u3/lisa. As soon as you see the line saying Done, you can quit by entering Control+d, although the succeeding lines will probably fill the screen before you can exit the program. You're now subscribed to several thousand newsgroups. That's a little much, even for the most dedicated Internet news fan.

Now that you're back at the UNIX prompt, the next thing you do is make several copies of your .newsrc file. That way, if you mess up your .newsrc file, you don't have to remove it entirely and go back into rn to rebuild it.

```
$ cp .newsrc .newsrcsave
$
$ cp .newsrc .newsrc_old
```

You've saved the file to two places. Next, so that the next changes makes sense, you need to look at the file using more or cat to see the original contents of the .newsrc file. At the UNIX prompt, enter either more .newsrc or cat .newsrc. You should see something similar to the following (the individual entries aren't important, just the format):

```
$ cat .newsrc
ca.usenet:
ca.wanted:
na.forsale:
news.admin:
news.admin.misc:
news.admin.policy:
news.admin.technical:
news.announce:
news.announce.conferences:
news.announce.important:
news.announce.newgroups:
news.announce.newusers:
news.answers:
news.config:
news.future:
news.groups:
news.lists:
news.lists.ps-maps:
news.members:
news.misc:
news.newsites:
       .
       .
       .
```

The lines you see are the names of different newsgroups followed by colons.

Notice that all of the newsgroups to which you subscribe—all of them, now—have colons next to them. If you were to go back into rn now, the program would try to show you the messages in all of these groups, sequentially.

You don't, however, want that. You have a life and better things to do than read newsgroups all day long. You want to unsubscribe to all but a few newsgroups. You should limit yourself to no more than 40 or 50 newsgroups. More than this is recommended only for high-tech monks, not for regular people. To unsubscribe, you need to change the colons into exclamation points, which indicates to the rn program that you don't want to read any of the exclamation-point marked groups. Now you are going to use your old friend sed to unsubscribe. Enter the following sed command, which replaces the colons in your .newsrc file with exclamation points:

```
$ sed -e 's/\:/\!/g' .newsrc_old > .newsrc
$ cat .newsrc
ca.usenet!
ca.wanted!
na.forsale!
news.admin!
news.admin.misc!
news.admin.policy!
news.admin.technical!
news.announce!
news.announce.conferences!
news.announce.important!
news.announce.newgroups!
news.announce.newusers!
news.answers!
news.config!
news.future!
news.groups!
news.lists!
news.lists.ps-maps!
news.members!
news.misc!
news.newsites!
        .
        .
        .
```

As you can see, the sed command replaces the colons with exclamation points, thus unsubscribing you from these newsgroups.

Clue: If you mess up your .newsrc file, copy the one you saved in .newsrcsave into .newsrc by entering the following command:

```
$ cp .newsrcsave .newsrc
$
```

If you mess up both the .newsrc and the copy you made of it in .newsrcsave, remove the file entirely and use your newsreader to re-create one for you and then start at the top of this section. Also, realize that because all newsreaders make .newsrc files, if you make or alter a .newsrc file with one newsreader, it still works with any other, and you'll still be subscribed to the same groups to which you subscribed using the first newsreader.

Deciding Which Groups to Read

Now you're going to decide which newsgroups you want to read. First, you need to decide what types of things interest you. Think of some words that you'd like to read about and some synonyms. Maybe your interests are subjects, maybe they're people (last names are easiest to search for), or maybe they're rock bands.

Next, you're going to grep through your .newsrc file to find the groups relating to your subject. If, for example, you picked unix as a keyword (remember to lowercase the words, because the newsgroups are all in lowercase letters), the following command finds all of the newsgroups that contain the word unix:

```
$ grep unix .newsrc
ca.unix!
comp.security.unix!
comp.sources.unix!
comp.std.unix!
comp.sys.amiga.unix!
comp.unix!
comp.unix.admin!
comp.unix.advocacy!
comp.unix.aix!
comp.unix.amiga!
comp.unix.appleiigs!
comp.unix.aux!
comp.unix.bsd!
comp.unix.cray!
comp.unix.dos-under-unix!
comp.unix.i386!
comp.unix.internals!
comp.unix.large!
comp.unix.misc!
comp.unix.msdos!
comp.unix.osf.misc!
comp.unix.osf.osf1!
comp.unix.pc-clone.16bit!
comp.unix.pc-clone.32bit!
comp.unix.programmer!
comp.unix.questions!
comp.unix.shell!
comp.unix.solaris!
comp.unix.sys3!
comp.unix.sys5.misc!
comp.unix.sys5.r3!
comp.unix.sys5.r4!
comp.unix.sysv286!
```

```
comp.unix.sysv386!
comp.unix.ultrix!
comp.unix.unixware!
comp.unix.user-friendly!
comp.unix.wizards!
comp.unix.xenix.misc!
comp.unix.xenix.sco!
comp.windows.x.i386unix!
alt.bbs.unixbbs!
alt.bbs.unixbbs.uniboard!
alt.unix.wizards!
arc.ccf.unix!
brasil.unix!
cix.unix.2home!
clari.nb.unix!
de.alt.sources.huge.unix!
de.comp.os.unix!
de.comp.sources.unix!
de.comp.sys.amiga.unix!
fj.questions.unix!
fj.unix!
fj.unix.wizards!
milw.unix!
no.unix!
orst.cs.unix.reading!
orst.oce.unix!
pb.unix.sun!
resif.info.unix!
sfnet.atk.unix!
su.computers.unix!
sub.os.unix!
sub.sources.unix!
swnet.unix!
tamu.unix.general!
tn.unix!
umn.cs.systems.unix!
umn.itlab.systems.unix!
umn.local-lists.tc-unix!
umn.local-lists.techc-unix!
unix-pc.bugs!
unix-pc.general!
unix-pc.sources!
unix-pc.uucp!
ut.unix.sysadmin!
ut.unix.user!
uw.unix!
za.unix.misc!
za.unix.sco!
$
```

That's a lot of newsgroups! The Internet grew up around UNIX, so most of the people who have been using the Internet have at least some interest in UNIX. You may want to pick a few of the newsgroups and see how you like them.

The following code looks for groups having to do with gardening:

```
$ grep 'garden' .newsrc
rec.gardens!
$
```

Only one group on the Internet has the word garden in it. That's probably because most people who read news don't have time to grub around in the dirt; they're too busy reading their newsgroups. Now use grep to find agriculture:

```
$ grep 'agriculture' .newsrc
alt.sustainable.agriculture!
$
```

You get the idea. You can continue "grepping" through the file, as UNIX gurus say, until you've built a list of newsgroups to which you'd like to subscribe. Keep track of these, either by redirecting the output of grep to a file or files or by writing them down on paper.

Subscribing to Newsgroups

When you've found the names of the newsgroups to which you'd like to subscribe, you need to alter your .newsrc file to subscribe. Remember, you unsubscribed to all the newsgroups when you edited .newsrc with the sed command. Start by firing up rn:

```
$ rn

No unread news in subscribed-to newsgroups. To subscribe to a new
newsgroup use the g<newsgroup> command.

****** End of newsgroups — what next? [qnp]
```

Note the [qnp] prompt. This stands for *quit, next,* and *look at previous unread message.* If you don't want to do any of these, you can instead enter any rn command at the prompt, including h for help, which you should use if you get stuck or lost.

As expected, you are subscribed to no groups, but you've been prompted as to what to do. If you want to read the newsgroup for archaeology, enter g sci.archaeology, which means "go to the newsgroup sci.archaeology." You'll be asked whether you want to resubscribe, and you'll enter y for *yes*:

```
g sci.archaeology
Newsgroup sci.archaeology is unsubscribed — resubscribe? [yn] y

****** 150 unread articles in sci.archaeology — read now? [ynq] n
******* End of newsgroups — what next? [npq]
```

This technique can be used with any newsgroup. Keep going. Subscribe to whatever groups you wish. For demonstration purposes, you should also subscribe to rec.gardens:

```
g rec.gardens
Newsgroup rec.gardens is unsubscribed — resubscribe? [yn] y

**** 175 unread articles in rec.gardens — read now? [ynq] n
***** End of newsgroups — what next? [npq]
```

201

You get the idea. You're telling rn to go to the newsgroup you want, and then you are responding to the prompt that asks you whether you want to subscribe.

The g command is a good one to use when you know which newsgroups you want to read. If you don't know the exact name of the newsgroup you seek, you can look for all of the groups that contain a related word or string and then make a decision as to whether you'd like to read each of the groups you've found. To do this, enter a, followed by the word or part of a word that you want to find. Use this technique to search for the string road-trip:

```
***End of newsgroups — what next? [npq] a road-trip

Newsgroup alt.travel.road-trip is unsubscribed — resubscribe? [yn] y

***   48 unread articles in alt.travel.road-trip — read now? [ynq] n
```

You're now subscribed to alt.travel.road-trip, a newsgroup dedicated to adventurous road travel. To unsubscribe, when you're asked whether you want to read your postings in this group, type u for *unsubscribe*. Use the same technique to subscribe to sci.archaeology:

```
What next? [npq] a archaeology

Newsgroup sci.archaeology is unsubscribed — resubscribe? [yn] y

****** 132 unread articles in sci.archaeology — read now? [ynq] n
Restriction archaeology still in effect.

****** End of newsgroups — what next? [npq]
```

Now try it with a general phrase, such as *bio*, and you'll find all of the groups dealing with biology:

```
a bio

Newsgroup bionet.general is unsubscribed — resubscribe? [yn] n

Newsgroup bionet.jobs is unsubscribed — resubscribe? [yn] n

Newsgroup bionet.journals.contents is unsubscribed — resubscribe? [yn] n

Newsgroup bionet.population-bio is unsubscribed — resubscribe? [yn] n

Newsgroup bionet.sci-resources is unsubscribed — resubscribe? [yn] n

Newsgroup bionet.software is unsubscribed — resubscribe? [yn] n

Newsgroup bionet.users.addresses is unsubscribed — resubscribe? [yn] n

Newsgroup sci.bio is unsubscribed — resubscribe? [yn] n

Newsgroup bionet.software is unsubscribed — resubscribe? [yn] n

Newsgroup bionet.biology.tropical is unsubscribed — resubscribe? [yn] y
```

```
***    4 unread articles in bionet.biology.tropical — read now? [ynq] n
Newsgroup bionet.journals.contents is unsubscribed — resubscribe? [yn] y

***    1 unread article in bionet.journals.contents — read now? [ynq] n
****** End of newsgroups — what next? [npq]
```

Now try using this technique to look for groups containing the word *adventure*, to subscribe, and then to start reading the newsgroup:

```
****** End of newsgroups — what next? [npq] <a adventure>

Newsgroup comp.sys.ibm.pc.games.adventure is unsubscribed —
resubscribe? [yn] y

****** 1047 unread articles in
comp.sys.ibm.pc.games.adventure — read now? [ynq] y
```

You should see a message, although not necessarily this one:

```
Reading comp.sys.ibm.pc.games.adventure #15684 (738 more) Organization:
Penn State University Date: Thu Feb 24 11:41:25 PST 1994 From:
<CWB109@psuvm.psu.edu>

Subject: Help again in castle. Where is the king? Lines: 15


OK, Where is King Richard, and what must combine with the ruby so
that I may keep Scotia from polymorphing? I tried to kill her without
this item, but that third form is utterly indestructable! Also, whats
up with dawn? I freed her from the crystal ball and haven't seen her
since. Where do I need to go? Finally, what are the statuettes used for?
I have three and haven't found a use for them.
```

Don't you hate it when that happens? Some days, a video-game hero can't win for losing. You thought you had problems! This newsgroup is dedicated to discussions of IBM PC computer games.

You can quit this newsgroup by entering q once, and you can quit rn by entering q again, if you wish.

```
End of article 15684 (of 16428) — what next? q

Restriction adventure still in effect.

****** End of newsgroups — what next? [npq] q

$
```

Browsing and Reading Newsgroups

Now that you've done your subscriptions, you can read your newsgroups. Each time you read them, you'll mark different postings as read, so that the next time you check your newsgroups, you'll only see the ones that have reached your site since you last read news.

Next, you're going to read a few messages. Keep in mind as you read that your messages—and the number of messages you have—will be different from those used in the examples here. What's important is the method you use to read news.

Fire up rn again, if you aren't already in the program. When I next read news, I'll see a display similar to the following:

```
$ rn
Unread news in ca.environment                        13 articles
Unread news in sci.archaeology                      154 articles
Unread news in sci.environment                      317 articles
Unread news in rec.gardens                          415 articles
Unread news in alt.spam                             108 articles
etc.
```

Yes, there is a newsgroup dedicated to that meat product called Spam. I don't wish to read most of these articles, so when the system asks whether I want to read these groups, I select n from the three options—*yes, no,* and *quit*—abbreviated [ynq]:

```
****  13 unread articles in ca.environment — read now? [ynq] n
**** 154 unread articles in sci.archaeology — read now? [ynq] n
**** 317 unread articles in sci.environment — read now? [ynq] n
**** 415 unread articles in rec.gardens — read now? [ynq] y
**** 106 unread articles in alt.spam — read now? [ynq] n
```

I do want to read the postings from rec.gardens. Note that because I haven't read any of the backlog of messages, I have more than 415 of them. I want to read all of them now. If, on the other hand, I didn't want to read any of these "old" messages, I could enter c for *the catch up* command and I would be caught up. Then, the next time I read news, I'll get only messages that have come in since I used the "catch up" mode. I recommend that you do this whenever possible when you're just starting, or you'll never feel as though you can keep up.

I've entered y when asked whether I want to read rec.gardens.

The first message—or *posting,* as the messages posted to newsgroups are called—is displayed. Again, if you are reading this newsgroup, there is no guarantee that this is exactly the message that you will see, but you should see something on the topic:

```
From: edward@mace..
Subject: resource document for rotational gardening
Date: Tue Feb 22 09:47:41 PST 1994
Organization: public mailing list
Lines: 15
Distribution: world

I'm in the process of developing a resource document for the archives
of the discussion list HERBS-L on the topic of rotational gardening
and have already amassed a wealth of information. The document will
```

```
consist of a list of books, other publications, videos, software,
etc. that would be of use to producers, extension agents, etc.
requiring information about rotational gardening.

I'd like to request your assistance in the completion of this
document. If you are aware of any such resource materials that would
be suitable for inclusion in this document, please contact me via
email with particulars.

Thank you.

Edward Peabody
edward@mace


(Mail) End of article 268 (of 272) — what next? [npq]
```

Here are a few notes about the preceding posting. First, note its similarity in form to electronic mail. It has a header showing who it is from, the time, and date.

What's different? If you look closely, you'll see that the posting has a distribution line that says *world*. This means that this posting is to be distributed worldwide. Some messages, on the other hand—those that announce local events or items for sale locally, for example—should only be distributed locally or within a state at most. Newsreaders that let you decide the distribution (not all do) query posters at the time of posting as to what distribution they wish to give a particular posting. For example, distribution options may include *local*, *state*, *USA*, and *world*. Otherwise, the header information looks like an e-mail message.

Typing n for *next*, I get the following message:

```
From: wayne@fbn.edu (Jen Wayne)
Subject: Dogtoothed Violet
Date: Tue Feb 22 05:14:15 PST 1994
Distribution: usa

Does anyone know of a source for the seeds of dogtooth violets
(Erythronium dens-canis)? They're listed in Parks' catalogue,
but when I tried to order them they weren't available. Thanks for
any tips.
        —
Jen Wayne
Dept. of Research., Knight Univ.    wayne@fbn.edu
End of article 368 (of 802) — what next? [npq]
```

Now, I can continue reading through the postings in this newsgroup using n and p, or I can move on to the next newsgroup and repeat the procedure. To move on, I enter q to quit this newsgroup. I'll then be prompted as to whether I want to read messages in the next newsgroup.

These are the basic operations for reading news. A detailed command summary for rn is provided at the end of this chapter. Many of these commands are shortcuts that do nifty variations of what you've already learned; they aren't usually absolutely necessary, but they're nice amenities to have.

To end your session and to get out of news, enter q until you see the UNIX prompt.

Now, for kicks, you might want to look at your .newsrc file. You'll notice that the newsgroups you read now have numbers next to them. The numbers next to each group indicate the numbers of the messages that you've read. The numbers are site-dependent; message number 345 at your site could be a different message at another site. Thus, if you were to move your .newsrc to another site—a place with a different computer in charge of reading news, not just to a different computer—the new site's newsreader would have a different idea of which messages you'd read and which ones you hadn't. For example, list out the .newsrc file:

```
$ cat .newsrc
ca.environment: 1-13
sci.archaeology: 1-154
sci.environment: 1-317
rec.gardens: 1-415
alt.spam: 1-106
```

You can see that these are the newsgroups that you subscribe to, and rec.gardens: 1-415 indicates that you have read postings 1 through 415 of the rec.gardens newsgroup.

You're now past the most difficult part of reading news, and you understand how to browse through the groups. From now on, you'll check your subscriptions by entering rn, and you will doubtlessly settle into a routine of newsreading.

At Your Next Login: Dealing with New Newsgroups

The rate growth of new newsgroups is astounding. Several new ones are created almost every day. Therefore, each day you read news, you are likely to see something like the following upon starting up:

```
$ rn

Checking for new newsgroups...

Newsgroup netnews.alt.airhead.jon-doe not in .newsrc — subscribe? [yn] n
```

I don't know who poor Jon Doe is, but this is definitely not a newsgroup I wish to pursue; and presumably, neither would you. Enter n, and you'll be unsubscribed. The prompts continue until you've made a decision on all of the new groups.

```
Newsgroup alt.binaries.pictures.erotica.furry not in .newsrc
  — subscribe? [yn] n
```

Furry erotica? Enter n to unsubscribe.

The following newsgroups have achieved new levels of irrelevance:

```
Newsgroup alt.impeach.clinton not in .newsrc — subscribe? [yn] n
```

```
Newsgroup alt.alt.alt.alt.alt not in .newsrc — subscribe? [yn] n
```

Of course, if you wanted to read any of these newsgroups, you'd enter y or Y, and you'd be subscribed.

Responding to News Postings

You now know enough to read newsgroups, which means that you know enough to *lurk*, as news fans say. Lurking means that you read news, but you don't respond in any way. Despite the sinister sound, lurking is a good idea for beginners; the best thing to do when you're trying to fit into a different culture is to observe a while before engaging people, to avoid possibly responding inappropriately.

You can make two kinds of responses to postings: e-mail and postings. If you respond by e-mail, you keep the interaction one-on-one between yourself and the poster. If you post to a newsgroup, the entire world may be able to see it, so you need, first, to make sure you know how to post news; second, to make sure you know the subject matter; and third, make sure you're prepared to get a lot—maybe hundreds—of transmissions of e-mail.

Responding to News Postings Using E-Mail

Most of the time, you'll respond to postings. For instance, if you happen to know how to keep Scotia from polymorphing or the true purpose of the statuettes, you could answer the following posting by entering r for reply:

```
(Header Information)

Subject: Help again in castle. Where is the king? Lines: 15


OK, Where is King Richard, and what must combine with the ruby
so that I may keep Scotia from polymorphing? I tried to kill
her without this item, but that third form is utterly indestructable!
Also, whats up with dawn? I freed her from the crystal ball and haven't
seen her since. Where do I need to go? Finally, what are the statuettes
used for? I have three and haven't found a use for them.

(signature information)

r
```

You'll then see something like the following:

```
r
Prepared file to include [none]: <enter>
```

You are asked if you want to post a file; that's what you would want to do if you'd already written a response and saved it to a file. If you enter y for *yes*, you can post that file. If you say n for *no*, you'll be automatically plunged into vi, where you'll edit your response:

```
To: CWB109@psuvm.psu.edu>
Subject: Subject: Help again in castle. Where is the king?
(Other header information deleted)
Cc:
Bcc:


~

"/u3/lisa/.letter" 10 lines, 287 characters

Check spelling, Send, Abort, Edit, or List? s
```

As shown in this example, you're in the text editor, and you can use all of the standard vi editing tools. You can edit the message, then enter :wq to get out of vi. You'll see the line asking you whether you want to check spelling, send, abort, edit, or list. Abort gets rid of the message; list shows you the message; check spelling shows you the misspelled words; and send speeds the message on its way to the recipient. As you see, after you've entered r in response to a message, you're prompted every step of the way until you've sent the message.

Posting Your Own Messages to Newsgroups

Sometimes, you may want to communicate with many people at the same time. For example, say you've read a posting that asks for help in finding rare carnivorous plants, your passionate hobby. You want to post the information, not mail it, so that anyone who might be curious about where such plants can be bought can receive the information. That's when you would want to post a message of your own. To start this process, read the original article using rn. When you see the following End of article message, respond by entering f:

```
End of article 29696 (of 29974) — what next? f
```

The f will begin the process to post the message. You'll be asked whether you're starting an unrelated topic. Because you're responding to a message, not starting your own topic, you enter n for "no:"

```
Are you starting an unrelated topic? [ynq] n
```

If you are posting a message unrelated to anything you've read in your newsgroup, you could enter f at any time, not just after you've read a posting. You'll see something like the following:

```
This program posts news to many machines throughout the country.
Are you absolutely sure that you want to do this? [ny] y
```

```
Prepared file to include [none]: enter
```

If you want to include a text file that you've already prepared, you would respond y to this one, and then you would be asked to enter the name of the file.

Now, you're placed into vi, where responses can be edited using any of the vi commands. When you're done, enter :wq. The rn program responds by taking you to the next message or newsgroup, and then you'll be asked what you want to do next:

```
Your article's newsgroup:
rec.gardens              Gardening, methods and results.

Check spelling, Send, Abort, Edit, or List? s
```

If you've changed your mind, enter a to abort the posting, and nobody will know that you wrote the message. Entering e puts you back into vi, where you can further edit your message. Entering l shows you your message, and entering s sends your message. In this case, I entered s, and my message was posted to the current newsgroup.

If I had wanted to abort the message, I would have entered a, and I would have seen a message indicating that my posting had not been sent.

The following is an example of a posting that I posted to rec.gardens regarding a question about yellow pear tomatoes:

```
End of article 29696 (of 29974) — what next? f

Are you starting an unrelated topic? [ynq] n


This program posts news to many machines throughout the country.
Are you absolutely sure that you want to do this? [ny] y

Prepared file to include [none]:

Newsgroups: rec.gardens
Subject: Re: Yellow pear tomatoes
References: <CLzzvJ.4C0D@hawnews.watson.ibm.com>
Distribution: usa
Organization: Portal Communications Company — 408/973-9111 408/973-8091
(data)

"/u3/lisa/.article" 13 lines, 274 characters

<Yellow pear tomatoes are a little bit difficult to get to germinate,
but once they get started, look out. They are very prolific, and a
joy to grow and to eat.

—Lisa Stapleton
lisa@shell.portal.com

<:wq>
"/u3/lisa/.article" 19 lines, 496 characters
```

209

```
Your article's newsgroup:
rec.gardens               Gardening, methods and results.

Check spelling, Send, Abort, Edit, or List? s
```

If that looks like a lot of work, remember that posting news is probably the most difficult of all of the things you've learned in this chapter. You've now seen two simple examples and are capable of posting your own news.

Threads

Some newsreaders incorporate a concept called *threads*. Threads are so named because they're the news equivalent of threads of conversation. They're helpful in managing news conversations.

How do they work? Suppose that someone posted the following message to `sci.archaeology`:

```
I'm going on an expedition to Nepal to look for an ancient culture.
I'm looking for contacts there who could supply interpreters, guides,
provisions and transportation, etc. Thanks in advance to all who
respond.

Mary Jones
mjones@anywhere.com
```

Someone else responds with information about tour guides. Someone else posts a list of professorial contacts. Yet another person posts a list of temples. All of this information would be interesting, except that you've got $25 in your travel budget for the next three years, and you're tired of reading about a trip to a place that you can't hope to visit for a few years. It would be nice if you could use a command to tell your newsreader to "unsubscribe to the thread" or "kill the thread." You'd still be able to read all postings that were unrelated to this original posting, but you wouldn't have to read about the trip of Mary Jones to Nepal. Any messages that came in after you killed the thread would be filtered out by the newsreader, so you would never see them.

In the most common versions of rn, there is no threading. However, trn, a revised version of rn, uses many of the commands of rn and has, in addition, threads and commands to manage them. Another popular newsreader is tin; check to see if your site has it. In threaded newsreaders, the capability to kill a thread is a useful tool in cutting down on messages you don't want to read.

What You've Learned

In this chapter, you have learned what newsgroups are and how they can help you with such things as planting flowers and cooking with Spam. You have learned basics of rn (readnews) and how to join newsgroups. You have learned how to read and post messages in your favorite newsgroups. For a listing of rn commands, see Appendix B.

Rewards

✖ An Internet newsgroup is like an electronic bulletin board. People read messages, post messages, and respond to messages. The messages that they post are called postings.

✖ When you sign up for a newsgroup, you subscribe to it, just as you would to a magazine or newsletter. Every few minutes or hours, the computer that connects your site to the Internet checks for and stores incoming postings and e-mail. It may also pass the incoming information on to other sites that receive a "feed" from your computer. This computer keeps track of which messages you've read and which you haven't.

✖ A newsreader is a program that helps you read Internet newsgroups. The most common operations are to subscribe, unsubscribe, read, post, reply to a posting, move forward and backward through groups, read the next message, and kill a thread.

✖ When you subscribe to a newsgroup, your subscription goes onto the file that your Internet connection computer checks for incoming postings. Postings for groups that are not read at your site are not pulled off the Net or stored.

✖ There are newsgroups for virtually every interest: commercial, recreational, and educational. Some of the most common categories are computer-related newsgroups, hobbies, and social and political groups.

✖ Among the most common newsreaders are rn and readnews. Common threaded newsreaders include tn, trn, and tin. To start up a newsreader, enter its name.

✖ For rn, the most commonly used operations are these:

c	Catch up (mark all articles as read).
A	Abandon read/unread changes to this newsgroup since you started rn.
n	Go to the next newsgroup with unread news.
N	Go to the next newsgroup.

p	Go to the previous newsgroup with unread news.
P	Go to the previous newsgroup.
-	Go to the previously displayed newsgroup.
1	Go to the first newsgroup.
^	Go to the first newsgroup with unread news.
$	Go to the end of newsgroups.
f	Post a message in a newsgroup.
g *name*	Go to the named newsgroup. Subscribe to new newsgroups this way too.
/*pat*	Search forward for newsgroup matching pattern.
?*pat*	Search backward for newsgroup matching pattern.
l *pat*	List unsubscribed newsgroups containing pattern.
m *name*	Move named newsgroup elsewhere (no name moves current newsgroup).
o *pat*	Display only newsgroups matching pattern. Omit pattern to unrestricted newsgroups.
O *pat*	Like o, but skip empty groups.
a *pat*	Like o, but scan for unsubscribed newsgroups matching pattern.
y	Do this newsgroup now.
.cmd	Do this newsgroup, executing cmd as first command.
+	Enter this newsgroup through the selector (like typing .+<CR>).
=	Start this newsgroup, but list subjects before reading articles.
U	Enter this newsgroup by way of the Set unread? prompt.
u	Unsubscribe from this newsgroup.
L	List current .newsrc.
x	Quit, restoring .newsrc to its state at startup of rn.

✖ For command summaries of newsreaders other than rn, see Appendix B.

✖ Anyone can set up a newsgroup on the Internet. There is a voting process, and people can vote about whether the new group should be created. A certain number of *yes* votes must be achieved, and the ratio of *yes* to *no* votes must be high, or the newsgroup can't be legitimately started. Many illegitimate groups are created as practical jokes. These are usually evident from their names.

✖ You learned how to respond to postings by using r to reply to the poster by e-mail and f to do your own postings to the current newsgroup.

✖ Some newsreaders employ a concept called *threads*. Threads of messages in newsreaders are much the same as threads of conversation. Each thread represents an electronic conversation, and threaded newsreaders let you decide which threads you want to follow and which ones you no longer want to read. Deciding that you don't want to read messages associated with a given thread is sometimes called killing the thread or unsubscribing to a thread.

✖ Many companies are setting up internal newsgroups that can be read only by company personnel. Common functions of these groups are public suggestion boxes, communication between people working on the same project, and corporate communications. These newsgroups work like all outside newsgroups, but people outside of the company do not have access to the company's internal newsgroups.

Pitfalls

✖ There are more than 7,000 newsgroups on the Internet, so don't forget to sleep.

✖ Newsgroups can consume a considerable amount of time. You must be very selective in your newsgroup membership. You should keep your membership to fewer than 40 newsgroups.

✖ Setup can be tedious and time-consuming in the beginning. You can use shortcuts, such as borrowing a .newsrc file from a friend, to save time.

✖ Novices stick out like sore thumbs on the Internet. When you join a newsgroup, watch and listen for a few days before you join in on the fun.

213

Finding the Holy Software Grail and the Sacred Wisdom of the Ages

9

Communicating with Other Computers and Navigating the Internet

In This Chapter

✖ *How do you use the* rlogin *command to connect to other computers to use them to do work on the UNIX operating system?*

✖ *What is the Internet?*

✖ *How did the Internet get started?*

✖ *How do you use* telnet *to log into other computers on the Internet?*

✖ *How do you use* ftp *to find and download files?*

▶

✖ *What kinds of programs are* archie *and* veronica, *and how can you use them to hack your way through the jungles of information available on the Internet?*

✖ *How can you use e-mail to get on interesting mailing lists?*

What Is the Internet?

The Internet is a very large, worldwide computer network. Originally started as a government-subsidized computer web that tied the country's computer scientists and defense researchers together, it has become much more than that. Today, it helps people find information, free software, and like-minded people who share the same religion, sexual orientation, hobbies, taste in TV programs, brand of computer, or interest in politics.

NOTE

I've said that the Internet can help people find others who are interested in the same subjects, such as entertainment and politics. Here is a very brief sample of information sources to which users can subscribe. You'll learn more about various information sources and how to access them later in the chapter.

✖ Movies. FTP to penguin.gatech.edu to get movie ratings. Also, subscribe to newsgroups, for example, rec.arts.movies and rec.arts.movies.reviews. (You learned about newsgroups in Chapter 8, "A Beginner's Guide to Reading Internet Newsgroups.")

✖ Sexual Orientation. See the different sex-content discussions in newsgroups under .alt.sex, or for more scholarly approaches, see newsgroup clari.news.sex or mailing list SSSSTALK. (To subscribe by e-mail, enter listserv@tamvm1.tamu.edu. In the body of the message, enter SUBSCRIBE SSSSTALK *first-name last-name*.)

✖ TV Programs. See different television-show discussions in newsgroups under .alt.tv, for example, .alt.tv.melrose-place or alt.tv.seinfeld.

✖ Computers. For discussions of computer-related information, see newsgroups under the .comp. Here are a few:

.comp.binaries.ibm.pc Programs for the IBM PC.

.comp.unix.questions A place to find UNIX help.

> `.comp.answers`   A place to find answers on general computer-related topics.
>
> There is a mailing list for computer-related help called TIPSHEET. To subscribe by e-mail, enter `listserv@wsuvm1.csc.wsu.edu`. In the body of message, enter SUBSCRIBE TIPSHEET *first-name last-name*.
>
> ✖ Politics. A large topic, for many interests. Mailing lists and newsgroups to make you laugh or see red, including
>
>> POLITICS—Serious discussion of political issues. To subscribe by e-mail, enter `listserv@ucf1vm.cc.ucf.edu`. In the body of the message, enter SUBSCRIBE POLITICS *first-name last-name*.
>>
>> `.alt.politics.clinton`—Newsgroup devoted to discussing President Clinton.
>>
>> `.alt.rush-limbaugh`—Newsgroup devoted to discussing Rush Limbaugh.
>
> Again, this sample of topics is very limited. The information resources of the Internet are indeed vast.

There are thousands of computers on the Internet that have archived files, lists, and even databases that you can use for research or to get free, public-domain software. You can often send e-mail to get on mailing lists or to get access to some of these resources; the rest are accessible through other methods discussed later in this chapter.

Many libraries put their card catalogs and other resources online, and some will let you electronically file your requests for interlibrary loan materials. UNIX has commands that enable you to access this wealth of information. There are also programs—such as veronica and gopher—that help you navigate through this sea of neat stuff.

There's also the new world of electronic publishing on the Internet. Many people and organizations publish online periodicals—proceedings, conferences, or online magazines, also called *'zines* (rhymes with *teens*). You can get an electronic subscription to any of these either by sending e-mail or using UNIX commands and utilities to download them. Some are free, others are not.

Some private companies make money by providing individuals with their own e-mail addresses and connections to Internet newsgroups. These companies are invaluable for many people who don't have connections to the Internet through their workplaces. It's also great for many others who do have access to newsgroups at work but who change jobs frequently. People who use these services pay for an Internet connection through these private companies, and for such people, these private companies provide the equivalent of an electronic post-office box.

You've no doubt heard about the Information Superhighway, also called the Data Superhighway. What you may not know is that one of the best things about UNIX is its easy access to the Internet. Communications capabilities were built into UNIX at its inception, so, using UNIX, you can get onto the Internet easily.

> **NOTE**
>
> Even though you may find Microsoft Windows packages that can connect to the Internet—so you don't necessarily have to connect to the Internet from a UNIX machine—it is, nevertheless, a fact that more UNIX machines than any other kind are already connected to the Internet. Virtually every UNIX-based computer comes with a mail program and a connection.

The Internet is a loosely constructed network of literally thousands of computers. Usually, to connect their machines to the Internet, companies offer either to pay a fee or to volunteer to be an Internet site for other people and companies. Then they become a site. There is no central point or administration of the network, nobody who can say *yes* or *no* to a site. Today, most companies and government entities are willing to volunteer part of their computer's time, money, and memory to become an Internet site; it's a voluntary arrangement.

> **NOTE**
>
> Companies are joining the Internet at a staggering rate every day. In many cases, they are joining to do business on the Internet. Some are doing online ordering and customer support. Many companies join to allow their employees to benefit from the various information resources of the Internet.

How Do Messages Get Transmitted on the Internet?

You send an e-mail message. It goes from your computer or a terminal and probably goes to a different computer in your company that connects to the Information

Superhighway. Your message then hops to another computer on the Internet, and if that computer isn't the destination of the message, it passes the message on to another computer that's in the path from your computer to the destination. That computer then forwards the message to another computer, until it gets to the final destination. If you're curious, you can look at the path your e-mail took. For instance, the following shows the path of one e-mail message:

```
From zachary@netcom Fri May 19 06:20:44 1994 -0400
Flags: 000000000005
Received: from noc (noc.halcyon.com) by halcyon.com with SMTP id AA18151
(5.65c/IDA-1.4.4 for <scott@halcyon.com>); Mon, 16 May 1994 14:37:26 -0700
Message-Id: <199405162137.AA18151@halcyon.com>
X-Sender: sda@halcyon.com
Mime-Version: 1.0
Content-Type: text/plain; charset="us-ascii"
Date: Mon, 16 May 1994 14:35:56 +0900
To: zachary@netcom.com
From: scott@halcyon.com
Subject: Chameleon and Windows for Workgroups
Cc:
X-Mailer: <PC Eudora Version 2.0.1>

[Zachary- No secret, but not obvious either. Hope this is helpful --Scott]

No secret really
```

Think of it this way: Your e-mail is a letter. You live in Montana, and you want to send the letter from your home to your friend Ghengis Smith, who lives in Outer Mongolia. You walk down the street to a public gathering, and say "I have mail for my friend Ghengis in Outer Mongolia." Someone at the gathering says "I'm flying to San Francisco, so I'll get it that far." You hand her the letter. She flies to San Francisco, goes to the airport lounge, and says she has a letter that needs to go to Outer Mongolia. A man in the lounge says, "I'm going to China; I'll take it that far." When he gets to the airport in Shanghai, he says, "I've got a letter that needs to go to Outer Mongolia." A teenager in the crowd says he'll take it to the village in Outer Mongolia. He gets it safely to the village and tells the local monk that he has a letter for Ghengis. The monk takes the letter, walks up the path, and hands it to Ghengis, who, I might add, would be very upset if his mail were misdelivered.

NOTE

Your e-mail letter could have taken a number of different routes. For example, it could have gone from Seattle, Washington to Juneau, Alaska to St. Petersburg, Russia to Outer Mongolia. No matter the route, the Internet provides several possibilities for delivering mail.

The point of this analogy is that you specified the recipient, but there was no pre-determined route. The actual carriers who sent the message along at each point could have been anyone. The same is true of the Information Superhighway; this feature is what gives the Superhighway its incredible flexibility. Any computer on the Internet can be used to forward your private message, so, if for some reason—maybe because it's busy or temporarily out of order—a particular computer can't forward your message, another computer can take the message and pass it on. Similarly, public messages—such as newsgroup messages—are broadcast throughout the Internet shotgun-style and can be intercepted by any computer set up to receive them.

SKIP THIS, IT'S TECHNICAL

It doesn't take much in the way of software or machine capability these days to become an Internet site, and it takes even less—a PC and a modem—to hook up to a private provider such as Netcom or Portal. Many providers are beginning to offer software to access their services from PCs.

The Form of Internet Addresses

The following are some typical Internet addresses:

```
rodriguez@netcom.com
vice-president@whitehouse.gov
president@whitehouse.gov
cservice@computercorp.com
smith@stanford.edu
zachary@harrys.bar.com
cameron@p160.f17.n3.1.fidonet.org
chen@nasa.gov
```

An Internet address is composed of a user id, the @ sign, a site, the period, and a domain: *userid@site.domain*. The *userid*—such as zachary—is this person's account name at his site. A site may be one such as Netcom, Delphi, and Northwest Nexus. These sites belong to domains, such as commercial (com), education (edu), and government (gov). In the preceding examples, you can see several Internet addresses that have commercial, education, and government sites. The address zachary@netcom.com would be zachary at the netcom site under the commercial domain.

SKIP THIS, IT'S TECHNICAL

The domain designations are a product of the history of the Internet. The Internet is the direct descendent of ARPANET, a government-subsidized communications network for people who worked on defense and weapons research. Because the people who worked on such projects were primarily university researchers, government workers, and the commercial companies that actually designed and produced the projects, Internet addresses usually end in `.edu` for education, `.com` for commercial, and `.gov` for government.

There Must Be 50 Ways to Use the Internet

There are many ways to use the Internet, but in the popular press, everything from e-mail to newsgroups to `ftp` sites is lumped into a rather amorphous thing called the Internet. It is true that the underlying *infrastructure*—the networks and computers that make up the Internet, as well as the computers that serve up requests and results to users—is common to all of these types of communication.

There are, though, important differences in the many types of access you can get to information stored on the Internet, and these are even a little different from the ways you can use the computers in your local corporate networks.

In what follows, you'll learn what the different types of access are, how they're used, and how you can use each of these to get work done and information to flow your way.

The Lay of the Land

What types of access to other computers might you want, and which tool should you use for each?

Perhaps the simplest kind of access you can get to other computers is to log into other computers on your own local network. If you're working on a UNIX computer that's connected to other companies in your organization, you can use a UNIX command called `rlogin` to log in remotely to other local computers.

The next level of access is `telnet`, which you can use if your site has a direct connection to the Internet and the remote computer that you want to use also has a direct connection.

Clue: Some third-party providers enable you to use `telnet` as well, even though your computer may not be directly connected to the Internet. *Their* computers have this direct connection to the Internet, which they then share with you.

Essentially, `telnet` is a way to log in remotely to other computers directly connected to the Internet. It's a sort of `rlogin` on steroids; the main difference is that it will take you places where `rlogin` never could. If `rlogin` is a push-scooter on which you cruise your local neighborhood, then `telnet` is an airplane. It is `telnet` that can take you to the card catalogs of many of the greatest libraries of the world. It can also tell you where to find many other sources of information that you can request by e-mail.

But these are relatively pedestrian uses of the Internet, and I've only explained how to do work. You want to know about the fun stuff.

Well, you already know how to manipulate files on your local computers. But did you know you can download files from computers in England to Australia, on topics that range from computers to biodiversity to jazz? The UNIX command to do this is `ftp`, which stands for *file transfer protocol*, and you can use it to reach out and download whatever you want. You can also use `ftp` to download free software stored on other computers.

But if you're like most new users, you'll rapidly find that you're either overwhelmed by the wealth of information out there or that you're having trouble finding pointers that tell you what's on the Internet and how to get it. That's why people invented little information "rodents" called *Gopher clients*. They root through the Internet looking at Gopher servers for information you requested. `Gopher` is a menu-driven program that will help you organize your searches and show you what's available. It's pretty easy to use, and many people say it's all that stands between them and the mass confusion of the Internet.

Over time, Gopher servers have become numerous, making searches for information more complex and tedious; so, in came a Gopher option called `Veronica`. `Veronica` stands for *very easy rodent-oriented net-wise index to computerized archives*. It enables you to enter keywords, such as `oranges` and `mangos`, to search the Gophers. On your trip out on the Internet, you might run into `Jughead`. Seriously! `Jughead` (*Jonzy's universal gopher hierarchy excavation and display*) is another kind of Gopher index. It indexes your Gopher menus and directories.

There is also a program called `Archie`, used to explore documents that are stored, or archived, on machines on the Internet. Many people, however, find `Archie` frustrating to use (many versions are awkward or buggy), so I'll skip it here. Most beginners find that when they use the other programs and methods described in this chapter, they are so awash in interesting information that the mere thought of adding one more drop induces a sensation of seasickness.

What's Mine Is Mine and What's Yours Is Mine, Too, with *rlogin*

If your machine is becoming a little slow from too many users, you might want to connect to another machine with a bigger CPU and more memory. Your machine might be a terminal connected to a larger machine or a standalone UNIX box. Whatever the machine, you will find that even the best of the best will sometimes have performance problems.

Luckily, there's an easy UNIX command that you can use to login to other people's computers (and they can use to log into yours). It's called `rlogin`, which is sort of an abbreviation for *remote login*.

To use it, you need to know the name of the machine (yes, machines have names) to which you want access, and an account and associated password on that machine. This may sound like a lot, but it's not really. Many system administrators automatically set up user accounts for people on several machines that they might need to use. Before you try to use `rlogin`, save yourself some frustration: find out the machine name you need, your account name (or whatever name you should use) on that machine, and the password for that account.

> **NOTE**
>
> Companies often have interesting naming conventions for their machines. One Silicon Valley company names its machines after disasters: `tmi` (Three Mile Island), `hiroshima`, `black sox`, `Medea`, `krakatoa`, and `sodom`. Hewlett-Packard names its machines after islands: `tahiti`, `bora-bora`, `japan`, and so on. One system administrator names his company's machines after *Star Trek* starships, such as `enterprise` and `excelsior`.

To use `rlogin`, enter `rlogin` at the UNIX prompt, followed by the machine name. To log into a computer named `tahiti`, you'd enter the following:

```
$ rlogin tahiti
```

You are asked for your account name and password. However, on some systems, you might find the rlogin takes you right to the shell prompt. Your system administrator and the other machine's or host's system administrator could have decided to discard normal login and password procedures. Your machine is then considered a trusted host. Here is a example of the login and password prompts:

```
login: lisa

password: <what you type here is not displayed>
        .
        .
        .
$ _
```

You're now logged in, just as you would be to your own machine. Now you can examine files stored in that remote machine, or you can take advantage of its greater memory capacity to use programs too large for you to use on your own machine.

To end an rlogin session, enter either logout or the command. You'll be back on your own machine, as usual. To return to your machine, enter this command:

```
$ logout
Logged out from enterprise at 10:35:30 Thu May 19 1994
$ _
```

Sometimes, you'll have permission from someone to log in using his or her name and password. In that case, use rlogin -l, and proceed as before, giving the other person's name and password if you're asked for it.

```
$ rlogin -l zachary
password: <what you type here is not displayed>
$ _
```

The Foreign Equivalent of *rlogin*

Now you know how to use computers on your local network. Are you ready to take a spin on the open road? If so, telnet, which is the Internet equivalent of rlogin, is a good place to start.

You can use the telnet command to access any computer or computer network that's connected directly to the Internet. Not every computer that can send and receive e-mail is connected directly to the Internet, but luckily, tens of thousands are, so there's plenty you can do.

To use telnet, you enter telnet and the name of the computer. Thus, if you want to connect to a computer called java, you'd enter the following at the UNIX prompt:

```
$ telnet java
Trying...
```

```
Connected to java.
Escape character is '^]'.
UNIX(r) System V Release 4.0 (java)

login: zachary
Password: <what you type here is not displayed>
Last login: Wed Feb  2 06:55:53 from java
Sun Microsystems Inc.   SunOS 5.3      Generic September 1993
you have mail
$ _
```

Once you've entered the preceding command, you're connected to the computer you want to use, and you will be prompted for an account name and password. All of your UNIX commands work as they would were you entering them at your own terminal or workstation.

There are also special `telnet` commands, which you can learn about if you enter `man telnet` at the UNIX prompt. Most UNIX users live their entire lives without having to use these commands, if they know simply how to start and end a `telnet` connection. In between, the UNIX commands you already know work well, so there's nothing extra to learn.

To end your `telnet` connection, enter one of the following:

```
$ logout
Logged out from java at 10:35:30 Thu May 19 1994
$
```

or

```
$ exit
Logged out from java at 10:35:30 Thu May 19 1994
$ _
```

That's all there is to it.

So Who Cares?

You may ask why anyone would want to use `telnet`. There are three reasons: poverty (or frugality, for some), computing resources that some other computer has that yours doesn't, and the capability to list files and directories that might be interesting to you.

We've already covered the idea that you might want to use someone else's computer to get access to special computing resources or gizmos that they can use. What about the other two reasons?

To see what I mean by frugality, consider that you pay no telephone tolls when you use `telnet` as you would if you used a modem to dial into a computer; `telnet` works on any computer hooked onto the Internet, which means that it doesn't make any difference whether the computer you're calling is a block away or an ocean away. Down the street or in Sidney, Australia, you pay nothing, which would clearly not be the case if you had to pay trans-Pacific telephone tolls to call a computer in Sidney.

Clue: Many students use `telnet` to cut down on telephone costs. In the San Francisco Bay Area, for instance, Stanford University is in a telephone area code different from that of many of the bedroom communities where many students live. A student I knew would often make a local call with his modem and personal computer, connect to a local UNIX computer, and then use that UNIX connection to `telnet` to a Stanford machine where he had a student account. Thus, he paid no long-distance telephone charges or message-unit costs.

WARNING

Some beginners think that they can download files using `telnet`. You can't. You can list them using `ls` because `telnet` lets you use any UNIX command, but to download the files, you need to use a separate utility such as `ftp`. Also, don't confuse `telnet` with *Telenet*. Telenet is a commercial communications service that provides connections to a variety of commercial services, such as Dialog, whereas `telnet` is a UNIX utility.

Let's do something exciting: let's use `telnet` to look at the computer at the library of the University of California at Berkeley, and search its online card catalog. How would you find the name of the computer that gives you access to the library? Well, you could look it up in many of the books that provide information resources, look in the online resources section of this book for a brief list of some of the more interesting sources, or get it from online lists of resources, which I'll show you how to do later in this chapter. In this case, I looked up the name online, and I found that the name of the computer at the library is `gopac.berkeley.edu`. To reach the computer, I entered the following:

```
$ telnet gopac.berkeley.edu
```

If you try it, you'll see something like the following, which tells you that you're connected to the service (called GLADIS) and gives you some instructions:

```
Trying...
Connected to gopac.berkeley.edu.
Escape character is '^]'.
NETWORK ACCESS TO GLADIS — UCB's Online Library Catalog
```

```
************************************
GLADIS is available 24 hours a day!
************************************

**IMPORTANT POINTS FOR NETWORK USERS:**
1) If you should encounter garbage characters, use the Reset Screen (RS)
command. Typing "RS" and pressing the return key will repaint the current
screen.

2) You will be connected to GLADIS via a "generic" terminal type (i.e., without
cursor control). Once you are in GLADIS, you can use the SET TERMINAL command
to change the terminal type. HOWEVER, it is probably best to use the Generic
terminal type for printing or saving to disk. Once in GLADIS, type HELP SET
TERMINAL for more information.

3) When you finish searching, type LOGOFF to end your GLADIS session.

_ _ _ _ _ _ _ _ _ _ _ _ _ _ _ _ _ _
Press RETURN to start using GLADIS.
_ _ _ _ _ _ _ _ _ _ _ _ _ _ _ _ _ _
```

Press Enter, then you'll see the following menu:

```
                        WELCOME TO GLADIS
        The University of California at Berkeley's Online Library Catalog

*****************************************************************************
                Type NEWS for a list of Library news items.

*****************************************************************************

Enter one of these two letter codes, then press the RETURN key:

FI FIND (to do a search)
HE HELP (for online help)
NE NEWS (for online news)
CO COMMENTS (to send the library your comments)
ST START or STOP (returns you to this screen)
```

To get help with a command, enter help, followed by the command at the GLADIS
prompt, which is ===>. You'll see something like the following:

```
===> help fi

Search GLADIS by typing a "search statement," which consists of: FIND [a search
code] [your search term] <return>. The FIND command (may be abbreviated F)
instructs GLADIS to conduct a search, and should be followed by one of the
search codes listed under HELP GLOSSARY, followed by the desired search term.
Examples of search codes and search statements follow:

SEARCH CODES:
        TI  Title (book title, journal title, etc.)
        PN  Personal Name (person as author, subject, editor, etc.)
        CN  Corporate name (organization or conference name as author or subject)
        SU  Subject (for names as subjects, use PN or CN)
        SE  Series name (for works in series. For journal title, use TI)
        CA  Call number
```

```
SEARCH STATEMENTS:
    F TI JOURNAL OF MULTIVARIATE ANALYSIS
    F PN SHAKESPEARE WILLIAM
    F CN GENERAL MOTORS CORPORATION
    F SU BIOFEEDBACK
------------------------------------------------
COMMANDS:  F  [search code]  [your search term]
              HELP [search code] = more information about that code
              HELP GLOSSARY = list of help screens
------------------------------------------------
```

Use GLADIS to search for information about the Internet:

```
===> find su internet
```

You'll see something like the following:

```
Your search for the Subject: INTERNET
retrieved 8 subject entries.

    Subject List
    - - - - - -
    1.   Internet (Computer network)
    2.   Internet (Computer network)—Congresses.
    3.   Internet (Computer network)—Directories.
    4.   Internet (Computer network)—Handbooks, manuals, etc.
    5.   Internet (Computer network)—Periodicals.
    6.   Internet (Computer network)—Social aspects.
    7.   Internet (Computer network)—Terminology.
    8.   Internet—Periodicals.


------------------------------------------------
Type a line # from the above, a prior, or a subsequent screen.
COMMANDS:  Press RETURN for next screen     HELP = assistance
           PS = previous screen             FIND = begin a new search
------------------------------------------------

===> 5
```

Just for fun, look for periodicals on the subject:

```
Your search for the Subject: INTERNET COMPUTER NETWORK PERIODICALS retrieved 1
record.

1.      Internet world.
        Westport, CT : Meckler Corp.
        Continues: Research & education networking

Libr School   TK5105.5.R448
                Library has:  3:7(Sept 1992)-
```

Bingo! You found something. Now you'll see something like the following:

```
------------------------------------------------

COMMANDS: RETURN = next screen   NR = next record    DET  = detail display
          PS = previous screen   PR = previous record LIST = previous list
          LO = full display      HELP = assistance    FIND = begin new search
------------------------------------------------
===>
```

Now go to the previous screen by entering LIST:

```
===>LIST

Your search for the Subject: INTERNET
retrieved 8 subject entries.

      Subject List
      - - - - - -
        1.   Internet (Computer network)
        2.   Internet (Computer network)—Congresses.
        3.   Internet (Computer network)—Directories.
        4.   Internet (Computer network)—Handbooks, manuals, etc.
>       5.   Internet (Computer network)—Periodicals.
        6.   Internet (Computer network)—Social aspects.
        7.   Internet (Computer network)—Terminology.
        8.   Internet—Periodicals.




- - - - - - - - - - - - - - - - - - - - - - - - - - - - - - - - - - -
Type a line # from the above, a prior, or a subsequent screen.
COMMANDS:  Press RETURN for next screen       HELP = assistance
           PS = previous screen               FIND = begin a new search
- - - - - - - - - - - - - - - - - - - - - - - - - - - - - - - - - - -
===>
```

Enter 3 at the prompt to search for Internet directories, and you'll see something like the following:

```
===> 3

Your search for the Subject: INTERNET COMPUTER NETWORK DIRECTORIES
retrieved 2 records.

      Author/Title List
      - - - - - - - -
        1.   Newby, Gregory.
               — Directory of directories on the Internet : a guide to
                  information sources / Gregory B. Newby. <1994>
        2.   The Internet directory. <serial>



- - - - - - - - - - - - - - - - - - - - - - - - - - - - - - - - - - -
Type a line # from the above, a prior, or a subsequent screen.
COMMANDS:  Press RETURN for next screen       HELP = assistance
           PS = previous screen               FIND = begin a new search
- - - - - - - - - - - - - - - - - - - - - - - - - - - - - - - - - - -
```

Now break the telnet connection:

```
===> quit
Connection closed by foreign host.
$
```

You're now back at your own prompt and on your own computer, and you've found several interesting sources for information. You could now request any of the sources through cooperative interlibrary loan or look for them at your local library.

Dragging Files Down to Your Level with *ftp*

As you explore the Internet, you'll find files that contain interesting information. Many of these are available to anyone through a process called *anonymous* ftp. Anonymous ftp enables you to download files—that is, make copies of files and put them on your machine—by logging into other computers as an anonymous user.

To use the ftp command, you need to know the name or address of the machine that has your desired file. To find out this information, you can check outside directories or you may read somewhere that a certain file is available at a named site via anonymous ftp. For instance, I found out about a site that had information for new users.

This is how to download the information. To use the ftp command, enter ftp, followed by the machine name, which in this case is nysernet.org:

```
$ ftp nysernet.org
```

You'll see something like the following, which confirms the ftp connection (when you are prompted to enter an account name, enter anonymous):

```
Connected to nysernet.org.
nysernet.org FTP server (Version wu-2.4(1) Thu Apr 14 15:16:34 EDT 1994) ready.
Name (nysernet.org:loren): anonymous
```

When you see the following message, follow its directions:

```
Guest login ok, send your complete e-mail address as password.
Password:
-
-Welcome to nysernet.org!
-
-Questions or problems with this system can be mailed
-to consult@nysernet.org.
-
-See the README file for more information.
-
-(To have README appear on the screen without FTPing it, type
-get README ¦ more. This will enable you to view README on the _screen.)
-

Guest login ok, access restrictions apply.
```

You'll see the ftp prompt, which is ftp>. As with any other prompt, you can enter commands when you see it. The new user information is in the directory /pub/resources/guides, so I enter the following commands:

```
ftp> cd /pub/resources/guides
```

You'll see something like the following:

```
CWD command successful.
```

Now enter ls -F to get a neat, columnar listing that shows you strange characters in the file and directory names:

```
ftp> ls -F
PORT command successful.
Opening ASCII mode data connection for /bin/ls.

.message                          internet.tour.txt
Guide.V.2.2.text                  new.user.guide.v2.2.txt
agguide.dos                       nren.for.all.txt
agguide.wp                        polly.lita.txt
guide_to_internet                 speakers_on_internet.txt
ftp.list                          surfing.2.0.3.txt
internet.faq                      whatis.internet
internet.faq2                     zen-1.0.ps

Transfer complete.
remote: -F
279 bytes received in 0.14 seconds (1.9 Kbytes/s)
```

The Transfer complete message is confirmation that the ls command has been processed. Two commands are useful to beginners in downloading files: get, followed by the filename, downloads a file; and mget, followed by the filename and some wildcard, gets several files. You can quickly add several files to be downloaded by answering y to the filename prompts:

```
ftp> mget surf*
mget surfing.2.0.3.txt? y
```

Enter y to mark the file for transferring to your machine, and you'll see something like the following:

```
PORT command successful.
Opening ASCII mode data connection for surfing.2.0.3.txt (60661 bytes).
Transfer complete.
local: surfing.2.0.3.txt remote: surfing.2.0.3.txt
62015 bytes received in 13 seconds (4.8 Kbytes/s)
```

You're still in ftp mode, so download the file guide_to_internet:

```
ftp> mget guide_to_internet
mget guide_to_internet? y
PORT command successful.
Opening ASCII mode data connection for guide_to_internet (363797
bytes).
```

```
Transfer complete.
local: guide_to_internet remote: guide_to_internet
371251 bytes received in 47 seconds (7.7 Kbytes/s)
```

Now quit the `ftp` command, and the system will say goodbye and take you back to your own machine:

```
ftp> quit
221 Goodbye.
$ _
```

That wasn't so bad, was it? Now you should have copies of the files on your machine. Enter the `ls` command, and make sure that you have the files.

```
$ ls -l
total 9
drwxrwxrwx   1 lisas     vip        37 Feb 16 15:22 mydir
-rw-r--r--   1 lisas     vip       106 Feb 16 13:36 roadtrip
-rw-r--r--   1 lisas     vip       106 Feb 16 14:22 roadtrip2
-rw-r--r--   1 lisas     vip       106 Feb 16 14:19 roadtrip3
-r--------   1 lisas     vip       106 Feb 16 15:57 roadtrip4
-rw-r-----   1 lisas     vip       106 Feb 16 15:57 roadtrip45
-rw-rw----   1 lisas     vip       106 Feb 16 15:57 roadtrip5
-rw----r--   1 lisas     vip       106 Feb 16 15:57 roadtripA
-rw----rw-   1 lisas     vip       106 Feb 16 15:58 roadtripB
-rw-------   1 lisas     vip       106 Feb 16 15:58 roadtripC
-rw-------   1 lisas     vip       106 Feb 16 15:58 guide_to_internet
-rw-------   1 lisas     vip       106 Feb 16 15:58 surfing.2.0.3.txt
-rwxr-xr--   2 lisas     vip       664 Feb 16 15:58 change.it
$
```

Here's another example. This is how you would `ftp` into `ds.internic.net` to get a copy of some documents describing Internet resources.

```
$ ftp ds.internic.net
```

You'll see the following:

```
Connected to ds.internic.net.

InterNIC Directory and Database Services
-
-Welcome to InterNIC Directory and Database Services provided by AT&T.
-These services are partially supported through a cooperative agreement
-with the National Science Foundation.
-
-Your comments and suggestions for improvement are welcome, and can be
-mailed to admin@ds.internic.net.
-
-AT&T MAKES NO WARRANTY OR GUARANTEE, OR PROMISE, EXPRESS OR IMPLIED,
-CONCERNING THE CONTENT OR ACCURANCY OF THE INTERNIC DIRECTORY ENTRIES
-AND DATABASE FILES STORED AND MAINTAINED BY AT&T. AT&T EXPRESSLY
-DISCLAIMS AND EXCLUDES ALL EXPRESS WARRANTIES AND IMPLIED WARRANTIES
-OF MERCHANTABILITY AND FITNESS FOR A PARTICULAR PURPOSE.
-
-
-                    ****************************
-
```

```
-DS0 will be rebooted every Monday morning between 8:00AM and 8:30AM est.
-
-                     ****************************
-
 ds.internic.net FTP server ready.
```

Now log in as anonymous and enter your account name and site, for example zachary@netcom.com. Change to the correct directory, in this case the one named resource-guide:

```
Name (ds.internic.net:lisa): anonymous
Guest login ok, send ident as password.
Password:
Guest login ok, access restrictions apply.
ftp> cd resource-guide
CWD command successful.
```

Now use the directory command dir to list files (the ls command doesn't always work on all computers in ftp-land, so you must use dir). The wildcard characters still work, though, so to list all of the files containing the letters txt, you can use *txt* to get everything that has something before the letters txt and something after them:

```
ftp> dir *txt*
PORT command successful.
Opening ASCII mode data connection for /bin/ls.
-rw-r--r--  1 101       30         35852 Mar 17  1993 chapter1-txt.tar.Z
-rw-r--r--  1 101       30         36485 Mar 17  1993 chapter2-txt.tar.Z
-rw-r--r--  1 101       30         53960 Mar 17  1993 chapter3-txt.tar.Z
-rw-r--r--  1 101       30          7974 Mar 17  1993 chapter4-txt.tar.Z
-rw-r--r--  1 101       30         73679 Mar 17  1993 chapter5-txt.tar.Z
-rw-r--r--  1 101       30         14262 Mar 17  1993 chapter6-txt.tar.Z
-rw-r--r--  1 101       30         20448 Mar 17  1993 chapterM-txt.tar.Z
-rw-r--r--  1 101       30        215935 Mar 17  1993 resource-guide.txt.tar.Z
-rw-r--r--  1 101       30           547 Nov 11  1992 toc.txt
-rw-r--r--  1 101       30        578238 Mar 17  1993 wholeguide.txt
Transfer complete.
remote: *txt*
bytes received in 0.23 seconds (3.1 Kbytes/s)
```

Just for kicks, enter the help command at the ftp prompt to see which commands you could use. (For further directions on a specific command, you'd enter help followed by the command.)

```
ftp> help
Commands may be abbreviated.  Commands are:

!           cr          macdef      proxy        send
$           delete      mdelete     sendport     status
account     debug       mdir        put          struct
append      dir         mget        pwd          sunique
ascii       disconnect  mkdir       quit         tenex
bell        form        mls         quote        trace
binary      get         mode        recv         type
bye         glob        mput        remotehelp   user
case        nash        nmap        rename       verbose
```

```
cd            help          ntrans        reset          ?
cdup          lcd           open          rmdir
close         ls            prompt        runique
```

Now, looking at the file listing, you will probably realize that toc.txt is probably a table of contents to the rest of the files. So you'll download it first, then list its contents:

```
ftp> get toc.txt
PORT command successful.
Opening ASCII mode data connection for toc.txt (547 bytes).
Transfer complete.
local: toc.txt remote: toc.txt
607 bytes received in 0.31 seconds (1.9 Kbytes/s)
ftp> !cat toc.txt

                              Table of Contents

                 Chapter 1:    Computational Resources

                 Chapter 2:    Library Catalogs

                 Chapter 3:    Archives

                 Chapter 4:    White Pages

                 Chapter 5:    Networks

                 Chapter 6:    Network Information Centers

                 Chapter M:    Miscellaneous


           November 10, 1992         NNSC         Table of Contents
```

You decide, for example, it would be useful to have all of these chapters, so you'll use mget followed by a wildcard expression, and the machine will then ask whether you want to download each of the files (for example, mget chapter1-txt.tar.Z):

```
ftp> mget chapter1-txt.tar.Z
mget chapter1-txt.tar.Z? y
PORT command successful.
Opening ASCII mode data connection for chapter1-txt.tar.Z (35852 bytes).
Transfer complete.
local: chapter1-txt.tar.Z remote: chapter1-txt.tar.Z
36034 bytes received in 1.4 seconds (25 Kbytes/s)
mget chapter2-txt.tar.Z? y
PORT command successful.
Opening ASCII mode data connection for chapter2-txt.tar.Z (36485 bytes).
Transfer complete.
local: chapter2-txt.tar.Z remote: chapter2-txt.tar.Z
36666 bytes received in 1.2 seconds (29 Kbytes/s)
mget chapter3-txt.tar.Z? y
PORT command successful.
Opening ASCII mode data connection for chapter3-txt.tar.Z (53960 bytes).
Transfer complete.
local: chapter3-txt.tar.Z remote: chapter3-txt.tar.Z
54210 bytes received in 1.8 seconds (29 Kbytes/s)
```

```
mget chapter4-txt.tar.Z? y
PORT command successful.
Opening ASCII mode data connection for chapter4-txt.tar.Z (7974 bytes).
Transfer complete.
local: chapter4-txt.tar.Z remote: chapter4-txt.tar.Z
8002 bytes received in 0.58 seconds (13 Kbytes/s)
mget chapter5-txt.tar.Z? y
PORT command successful.
Opening ASCII mode data connection for chapter5-txt.tar.Z (73679 bytes).
Transfer complete.
local: chapter5-txt.tar.Z remote: chapter5-txt.tar.Z
74063 bytes received in 2.1 seconds (35 Kbytes/s)
mget chapter6-txt.tar.Z? y
PORT command successful.
Opening ASCII mode data connection for chapter6-txt.tar.Z (14262 bytes).
Transfer complete.
local: chapter6-txt.tar.Z remote: chapter6-txt.tar.Z
14311 bytes received in 0.67 seconds (21 Kbytes/s)
mget chapterM-txt.tar.Z? y
PORT command successful.
Opening ASCII mode data connection for chapterM-txt.tar.Z (20448 bytes).
Transfer complete.
local: chapterM-txt.tar.Z remote: chapterM-txt.tar.Z
20552 bytes received in 1.1 seconds (19 Kbytes/s)
```

Now you'll close the ftp connection by using the quit command:

```
ftp> quit
Goodbye.
$ _
```

SKIP THIS, IT'S TECHNICAL

As you become more experienced with ftp, you will eventually want to send files from your site to another Internet site; ftp has two commands, put and mput (multiple put), that are the opposites of get and mget. The put and mput commands transfer files to another Internet site; mput enables you to transfer multiple files with one command. Here is a short summary of ftp commands:

dir	Displays a listing of the current directory on the remote Internet site. You can use ls -l to get the same results.
cd *directory-name*	Changes directory on the remote site.
quit	Logs you out of the remote site and exits ftp.
get	Transfers a file from the remote site to your account.

mget	Stands for *multiple get*. Transfers several files from the remote site to your account. You answer y (yes) to transfer file or n (no) to skip file. You can use wildcard symbols, such as * and ?. The first, *, is for multiple characters to match, and the second, ?, is for a single character match.
put	Transfers a file from your account to the remote site.
mput	Stands for *multiple put*. Transfers several files from your account to the remote site.
ascii	Sets transfers to ascii format. You can transfer only text files. This is the default.
binary	Sets transfer to binary format. If you are transferring programs, compressed files, and so on (nontext files), then you need to set ftp to binary. If you don't, the file transfer will not execute properly.

Using *gopher* to Keep Control of It All

The gopher program shows the worldwide computer resources available to you. Created by the University of Minnesota, gopher is a great place to start looking for things when you only have a vague idea about what you seek. Because it's a menu-driven program that leads you through the different choices, it's easy to use.

There are many gopher sites, places where you can get a copy of this free program. Also, because gopher isn't a standard UNIX program or utility and is therefore not sold with every version of UNIX, there are many versions of gopher; each one has its own set of features, and there are different versions for PCs and UNIX computers. But the versions have much in common, and the menus are easy enough to use. If you've seen an example, you'll be able to maneuver like a pro almost from the beginning.

Many versions of gopher have menu items such as veronica and jughead (a play on words deriving from the archie archival utility). These utilities enable you to search the worldwide computer web for keywords in which you're interested. Some older versions of gopher, however, don't have these utilities.

The following example shows you how gopher is typically used. I've chosen the version that resides at "gopher central," the University of Minnesota. Your version may be slightly different, but it will be close. Begin by entering the word gopher on a computer that has gopher. You may have to telnet to a computer that has it, or you may have to download gopher from a free software server. In this case, I decide to specify the exact computer and version of gopher that I want, and I'm using the one at the University of Minnesota, so I enter the following:

```
$ gopher gopher.tc.umn.edu
```

You'll see something like the following. The first time you use gopher, you should choose the first option, Information About Gopher:

```
— — — — — — — — — — — — — — — — — — — — — — — — — — — —
                Internet Gopher Information Client 2.0 p15

                   Root gopher server: gopher.tc.umn.edu

     1.  Information About Gopher/
     2.  Computer Information/
     3.  Discussion Groups/
     4.  Fun & Games/
     5.  Internet file server (ftp) sites/
     6.  Libraries/
     7.  News/
     8.  Other Gopher and Information Servers/
     9.  Phone Books/
     10. Search Gopher Titles at the University of Minnesota <?>
     11. Search lots of places at the University of Minnesota  <?>
     12. University of Minnesota Campus Information/

Press ? for Help, q to Quit, u to go up a menu
```

Move the gopher arrow by using the up-arrow and down-arrow keys, then press Enter. (In some systems, you enter a 1, and in others you'd use a mouse to select Information About Gopher.)

You'll see the following menu, so choose About Gopher:

```
                    Page: 1/1
— — — — — — — — — — — — — — — — — — — — — — — — — — — —
                Internet Gopher Information Client 2.0 p15

                        Information About Gopher

     1.  About Gopher.
     2.  Search Gopher News <?>
     3.  Gopher News Archive/
     4.  GopherCON '94/
     5.  Gopher Software Distribution/
     6.  Commercial Gopher Software/
     7.  Gopher Protocol Information/
     8.  University of Minnesota Gopher software licensing policy.
     9.  Frequently Asked Questions about Gopher.
```

```
10. Gopher+ example server/
11. comp.infosystems.gopher (USENET newsgroup)/
12. Adding Information to Gopher Hotel.
13. Gopher T-shirt on MTV #1 <Picture>
14. Gopher T-shirt on MTV #2 <Picture>
15. How to get your information into Gopher.
16. Reporting Problems or Feedback.
```

```
Press ? for Help, q to Quit, u to go up a menu          Page: 1/1
```

You'll see something like the following, which gives you some useful information about how to use gopher:

— —

```
This is the University of Minnesota Computer & Information Services
Gopher Consultant service.

   gopher  n.  1. Any of various short-tailed, burrowing mammals of
   the family Geomyidae, of North America.  2. (Amer. colloq.)
   Native or inhabitant of Minnesota: the Gopher State.
   3. (Amer. colloq.) One who runs errands, does odd-jobs, fetches
   or delivers documents for office staff.  4. (computer tech.)
   Software following a simple protocol for tunneling through a
   TCP/IP internet.


If you have questions or comments, you can get in contact with the
Gopher development team by sending e-mail to:

        gopher@boombox.micro.umn.edu

If you are interested in news about new gopher servers and software
you can subscribe to the gopher-news mailing list by sending e-mail
to:
        gopher-news-request@boombox.micro.umn.edu


If you find gopher-news too technical or too high-volume, you might
try subscribing to another mailing list called gopher-announce; send
your request to:
        gopher-announce-request@boombox.micro.umn.edu.
Gopher-announce is moderated (hence low-volume), and only for
announcements of new gopher software or services.

There is also a USENET news discussion group called
    comp.infosystems.gopher
where Internet Gopher is discussed.

If you want to get the most recent releases of the gopher software,
you can get these via anonymous ftp from boombox.micro.umn.edu in the
    /pub/gopher directory.


Press <RETURN> to continue.
```

Follow the instructions, and press Enter to continue. You should see this menu:

```
--------------------------------------------
              Internet Gopher Information Client 2.0 pl5

                    Information About Gopher

        1.   About Gopher.
        2.   Search Gopher News <?>
        3.   Gopher News Archive/
        4.   GopherCON '94/
        5.   Gopher Software Distribution/
        6.   Commercial Gopher Software/
        7.   Gopher Protocol Information/
        8.   University of Minnesota Gopher software licensing policy.
        9.   Frequently Asked Questions about Gopher.
        10.  Gopher+ example server/
        11.  comp.infosystems.gopher (USENET newsgroup)/
        12.  Adding Information to Gopher Hotel.
        13.  Gopher T-shirt on MTV #1 <Picture>
        14.  Gopher T-shirt on MTV #2 <Picture>
        15.  How to get your information into Gopher.
        16.  Reporting Problems or Feedback.



Press ? for Help, q to Quit, u to go up a menu          Page: 1/1
--------------------------------------------
```

Select option 5, `Gopher Software Distribution`, from the preceding menu, then
select option 5 from the following menu, so you can look at `ftp` sites:

```
Root gopher server: gopher .tc.umn.edu

1.    Information about Gopher/
2.    Computer Information/
3.    Discussion Groups/
4.    Fun & Games
5.    Internet file server (ftp) sites/
6.    Libraries/
7.    News/
8.    Other Gopher and Information Servers/
9.    Phone Books/
10.   Search Gopher Titles at the University of Minnesota <?>
11.   Search lots of places at the University of Minnesota <?>
12.   University of Minnesota Campus Information/

Press ? for Help, q for Quit, u to go up a menu
```

You'll see the following menu:

```
              Internet Gopher Information Client 2.0 pl5

                    Internet file server (ftp) sites

        1.   About FTP Searches.
        2.   InterNIC: Internet Network Information Center/
        3.   Popular FTP Sites via Gopher/
```

239

```
4.  Query a specific ftp host <?>
5.  Search FTP sites (Archie)/
6.  UnStuffIt.hqx <HQX>
```

Pick menu item 3, Popular FTP Sites via Gopher/, and you'll see something like the following:

```
                    Internet Gopher Information Client 2.0 p15

                        Popular FTP Sites via Gopher

        1.  Read Me First.
        2.  Boombox - Home of Gopher and POPmail/
        3.  Case Western Reserve University FREENET/
        4.  Indiana University Mac Gopher Client App (beta)/
        5.  Indiana Windows Archive/
        6.  Interest Group Lists/
        7.  Internet Resource Guide (tar.Z files)/
        8.  Latest Disinfectant (ftp.acns.nwu.edu)/
        9.  Lyrics/
       10.  NCSA - Home of NCSA Telnet/
       11.  National Science Foundation Gopher (STIS)/
       12.  Newton Archives at Johns Hopkins University (bnnrc-srv.med.jhu.edu../
       13.  OCF Document Archives/
       14.  OSS-IS Info Archives (slow)/
       15.  SUMEX-AIM Archives - (Includes Info-Mac: a large collection of Mac../
       16.  Scholarly Communications Project of Virginia Tech/
       17.  Software Archives at MERIT (University of Michigan)/
       18.  Sonata NeXT software archive (sonata.cc.purdue.edu)/

Press ? for Help, q to Quit, u to go up a menu                    Page: 1/2
```

Use gopher to look at the list of gopher and other information servers by selecting menu option 7 for a list of Internet resources:

```
                    Other Gopher and Information Servers

        1.  All the Gopher Servers in the World/
        2.  Search titles in Gopherspace using veronica/
        3.  Africa/
        4.  Asia/
        5.  Europe/
        6.  International Organizations/
        7.  Middle East/
        8.  North America/
        9.  Pacific/
       10.  Russia/
       11.  South America/
       12.  Terminal Based Information/
       13.  WAIS Based Information/
       14.  Gopher Server Registration.
```

At this point, you could use menu selection number 2, a veronica search, to look for information by specifying keywords. You could use jughead to do a similar thing. Essentially, you enter the option and follow the menu directions, which involve searching for keywords. I recently did such a search by first specifying that

I wanted sources about women, and then I looked through the results to find a selection "Women and Computers," which gave me more information than I could use. It was wonderful! So gopher and the associated tools are great research aids.

E-Mail Information and Serials

Whew! You've been through a lot of multi-step programs. If you're looking for something simpler, consider this. You can take advantage of many different resources simply by sending e-mail to the right place. In response, you'll be mailed a single document, information about how to subscribe to a serial, or the serial itself. Many electronic magazines are distributed this way; some are free, whereas some require you to send money to be added to the distribution list (if you are added to the list, you will receive a copy of new issues by e-mail).

For instance, say you want to get on the mailing list for *Amazons International*, a news digest dedicated "to the image of the female hero in fiction and in fact, as it is expressed in art and literature, in the physiques and feats of female athletes and in sexual values and practices"—Thomas Gramstad. (I am not making this up; if you thought the Internet only caters to computer nerds, you're in for a shock.)

To do that, you'd send a short request to be put on the mailing list to amazons-request@math.uio.no, and thereafter, you'd receive regular digests about athletic, heroic women.

Some of these mailing lists are handled by people, others by computers. If it's handled by a person, you can send a short note explaining that you want to be added to the list. If it's managed automatically by a computer, you can often e-mail a message containing just the word *help*, and you'll get information mailed back to you that tells you how to subscribe.

Other mailing lists have distinct ways for querying information; to get directions, you can look for the list of Publicly Available Mailing lists, which is posted to the newsgroups news.newusers and news.groups. Check with some of the resources listed in the resources appendix to this book, or ftp to vm1.nodak.edu and look at the list of new mailing lists, called NEW-LIST.

What You've Learned

In this chapter, you have learned to travel the Internet highway with telnet, rlogin, ftp, and gopher. With telnet, you have seen that you can be a user on another site and have all the benefits of being there. The rlogin is a connection between friendly sites, and ftp enables you to shuttle files from far away lands to your own back door.

Rewards

✖ You've learned about the history of the Internet and the Information Superhighway. It started as a tool for defense workers, and now almost anyone with a computer can use it.

✖ You've explored some of the more interesting ways of using remote computers. The following table summarizes when to use each program or utility discussed in this chapter:

Program	Use
rlogin	This stands for *remote* login. It is used to log in to other UNIX computers on your local network—for example, other computers at your worksite, school, or home. For these other computers, you must have an account, the machine name, and a password. You can then use other UNIX commands on the remote machine.
mail servers	By sending e-mail with the single word *help* in the body of the message, you can often get other computers to put you on their mailing lists or to send you information about how to use files and receive electronic periodicals, including the electronic magazines called *'zines*. Some computers can figure out (by looking at the header on your message) how to mail these resources directly to your e-mail address. Some lists are administered by people, and you need to send a short note to the appropriate e-mail address.
telnet	This is used to log in to computers on the Internet, that is, computers outside your company or home. Once you've used the telnet command, you can use UNIX commands on the foreign machine. Some telnet sites require passwords and special accounts, but many do not.
ftp	This stands for file transfer protocol. This UNIX command is used to download files that reside on other computers on the Internet. Some ftp sites require a special password to transfer files; sometimes you can use a procedure called anonymous ftp to log in as a user, so that you can use the files.

Program	*Use*
gopher	This is a menu-driven program that can be downloaded for free; it helps you find ftp and telnet sites on the Internet. This program is not part of the standard UNIX utility packages, so you may have to use ftp to download a free but bare-bones version of the program, then run it on your UNIX system by entering gopher. A number of commercial software vendors sell more souped-up, user-friendly versions of gopher. You can use gopher to find interesting sites, then use the telnet feature of the program to actually use the computer or download a file, respectively.
veronica	A menu option under gopher, veronica helps you to do subject searches of computer resources.

Pitfalls

✖ Using the Internet can become time-consuming and addictive. Be frugal with your time on the Internet. Set time limits to read Internet mail and to travel to distant lands.

✖ NO MORE DISK SPACE! It is easy to download zillions of files and have fun to your heart's content, but keep tabs on your memory. Be frugal about what you download.

✖ VIRUS BEWARE! Beware of executables from the Internet. You could get a bad apple that contains a computer virus. Computer viruses can wipe out your files and programs. They are devastating, so get a virus checker.

10

UNIX
Shell
Scripts

*She Sells Bourne Shells,
and Much More*

In This Chapter

- ✖ *What is a shell procedure?*

- ✖ *How do you write short shell procedures to save yourself
  some typing and hassle?*

- ✖ *What is a shell script?*

- ✖ *How do shell scripts compare to, say, C programs?*

- ✖ *How are shell scripts used, and why are they important?*

- ✖ *How do you pass variables to shell programs and shell scripts
  to make them more flexible and useful?*

- ✖ *How do you handle conditions in shell scripts?*

- ✖ *How can you handle loops without going loopy?*

- ✖ *Can you make shell script "answer" to your beck and call?*

- ✖ *Where can you learn more about shell scripts?*

Why Do People Use Shell Scripts?

In Chapter 5, "Scoping Out the Territory," I discussed how to use the shell prompt for the Bourne shell and the C shell. You entered commands such as cd, ls, and echo from the shell prompt. In your everyday use of UNIX, you might use a series of commands (procedures) repeatedly and in a certain order. If we take these series commands and put them in a file to automate their execution, we have a *program*. These programs are called *shell scripts*.

People use UNIX shell scripts for everything from system administration to software development. System administrators who add many users to the system use shell scripts to automate the task of adding users. Programmers use shell script to automate compiling (making a program). You too can do this! Even if you've never written a program before, you'll be surprised at how quickly you'll learn.

It isn't hard to learn how to do some simple shell programs, but only you can decide whether you really want or need to read this chapter. If you're learning UNIX to become a system administrator or programmer, the answer is an unequivocal *yes*. Shell programming is going to be a major part of your life, and it's also a gentle introduction to programming languages.

Many UNIX end-users, however, live perfectly happy and useful lives without ever having to learn shell programming. For example, if you're a technical writer or businessperson, you can probably get away with skipping this chapter entirely. Other people will write shell programs to manage your company's computer system, and usually, you'll no more have to understand how these programs work than you have to understand how your car works.

Of course, even if you don't plan to become a technoid, one can make the argument that it's nice to know how to look under the hood when something's wrong. Likewise, it's sometimes useful to know enough of another language that you can occasionally read a menu in that language or read foreign road signs when you travel. So too, it's occasionally useful to be able to look at a particular shell script and know what it does; that way, you can modify it a little bit to fix a problem or make life more convenient for yourself.

Over the years, computer scientists have developed several shell languages. In this chapter, you'll use a very popular one, the C shell. I'll show you how to use it to do some interesting and basic things. Then I'll develop a fairly long shell script to show you how to develop such a program over time. At the end of this chapter, you'll understand what a shell is, how to use it, and how to write and execute useful shell programs.

What Is a C Shell Program?

A *C shell program* is a set of instructions that you store in a file so they can be used later. These instructions can be of any length. Some such programs are merely a single line that may be tedious to type or hard to remember and so merits being put in a shell script to reduce your typing. You can call the shell script something short, such as phone or even just p. Shell scripts can take long commands or hundreds of commands to be executed and put them in a file to be called by a shorter name, such as phoneinfo.

Don't Ya Just Hate It When...

Little annoyances can become big ones when you have to live with them every day. For example, maybe you are in a situation where you must use the list command many times every single day, and you find that typing the long form of the list command is tedious.

Wouldn't it be nice if you could type l only and do the same thing? You can. The following shell procedure, which you'll store in a file called l, does it for you. Put the following instructions into a text file using your favorite editor:

```
#!/bin/csh
ls -l
```

Clue: I realize that preceding shell script is a very short example. You can make an alias to do the same thing: alias ls ls -l. In some cases, an alias is a big help.

This looks like hieroglyphics, don't you agree? Don't worry; think of it as a secret message that you need to decipher.

Start with the first line. It's a standard line used whenever you use the C shell. It tells UNIX that all of the commands in the file are to be interpreted as C shell commands.

The second line is the list command with the -l option, which means that you'll do the long form of the listing.

How to Turn Files into Programs

Now that you understand what the commands in the file do, you need to turn the file into a program, or make it "executable."

There are two ways to make it executable. The first way is to precede the 1 with /bin/csh. Then, every time you want to run the program, enter the following:

```
% /bin/csh 1
```

You enter /bin/csh, followed by the filename, and your file will be executed right away. If you want to run it this way again, you'll have to run it using the /bin/csh before the command. Thus, it's not much of an improvement over ls -1, is it? But there's also a permanent way to make it executable.

Enter the following command to make this file executable by you:

```
% chmod o+x 1
% _
```

The chmod command, as you have learned, changes the permissions of a file. The preceding example changes the permissions for the file 1 to be owner executable; o stands for owner (you), and x stands for execute.

You've turned a shell command into a shell script, because you've written it down as a stand-alone program that can be stored, then used again and again.

How to Use Variables

The 1 program lists the directory you're in, because the ls -1 command, without any arguments, always lists the current working directory. But what if you wanted to list some other directory?

Try it. First, enter the following:

```
% ls -1
total 9
drwxrwxrwx   1 lisas      vip           37 Feb 16 15:22 mydir
-rw-r--r--   1 lisas      vip          106 Feb 16 13:36 roadtrip
-rw-r--r--   1 lisas      vip          106 Feb 16 14:22 roadtrip2
-rw-r--r--   1 lisas      vip          106 Feb 16 14:19 roadtrip3
-r--------   1 lisas      vip          106 Feb 16 15:57 roadtrip4
-rw-r-----   1 lisas      vip          106 Feb 16 15:57 roadtrip45
-rw-rw----   1 lisas      vip          106 Feb 16 15:57 roadtrip5
-rw----r--   1 lisas      vip          106 Feb 16 15:57 roadtripA
-rw----rw-   1 lisas      vip          106 Feb 16 15:58 roadtripB
-rw-------   1 lisas      vip          106 Feb 16 15:58 roadtripC
```

```
-rw-------   1 lisas    vip         106 Feb 16 15:58 guide_to_internet
-rw-------   1 lisas    vip         106 Feb 16 15:58 surfing.2.0.3.txt
-rwxr-xr--   2 lisas    vip         664 Feb 16 15:58 change.it
-rwxr--r--   2 lisas    vip         664 Feb 16 15:58 l
%_
```

What happens? You get a long listing of your current working directory, right?

Now, say you want to get the long listing for a file. Make sure that you've made the l file executable, then enter the following:

```
% l roadtrip
total 9
drwxrwxrwx   1 lisas    vip          37 Feb 16 15:22 mydir
-rw-r--r--   1 lisas    vip         106 Feb 16 13:36 roadtrip
-rw-r--r--   1 lisas    vip         106 Feb 16 14:22 roadtrip2
-rw-r--r--   1 lisas    vip         106 Feb 16 14:19 roadtrip3
-r--------   1 lisas    vip         106 Feb 16 15:57 roadtrip4
-rw-r-----   1 lisas    vip         106 Feb 16 15:57 roadtrip45
-rw-rw----   1 lisas    vip         106 Feb 16 15:57 roadtrip5
-rw----r--   1 lisas    vip         106 Feb 16 15:57 roadtripA
-rw----rw-   1 lisas    vip         106 Feb 16 15:58 roadtripB
-rw-------   1 lisas    vip         106 Feb 16 15:58 roadtripC
-rw-------   1 lisas    vip         106 Feb 16 15:58 guide_to_internet
-rw-------   1 lisas    vip         106 Feb 16 15:58 surfing.2.0.3.txt
-rwxr-xr--   2 lisas    vip         664 Feb 16 15:58 change.it
-rwxr--r--   2 lisas    vip         664 Feb 16 15:58 l
%_
```

You get the same thing that you did before, don't you? That's because the shell script that you created knows how to do only one thing, and that's ls -l.

> **NOTE**
>
> If you are using the C shell, you may find your command doesn't work even after you make it executable. This is because the C shell makes a list of all the commands it has available on your path when you log in. It uses this list until it is told to update the list with the rehash command. Try using this if you are having problems:
>
> ```
> $ chmod +x l
> $ l
> l: Command not found.
> $ rehash
> $ l
> total 26
> drwxrwxrwx   1 lisas    vip          37 Feb 16 15:22 mydir
> -rw-r--r--   1 lisas    vip         106 Feb 16 13:36 roadtrip
> -rw-r--r--   1 lisas    vip         106 Feb 16 14:22 roadtrip2
> -rw-r--r--   1 lisas    vip         106 Feb 16 14:19 roadtrip3
> -r--------   1 lisas    vip         106 Feb 16 15:57 roadtrip4
> -rw-r-----   1 lisas    vip         106 Feb 16 15:57 roadtrip45
> ```

```
-rw-rw----    1 lisas    vip          106 Feb 16 15:57 roadtrip5
-rw----r--    1 lisas    vip          106 Feb 16 15:57 roadtripA
-rw----rw-    1 lisas    vip          106 Feb 16 15:58 roadtripB
-rw-------    1 lisas    vip          106 Feb 16 15:58 roadtripC
-rw-------    1 lisas    vip          106 Feb 16 15:58 guide_to_internet
-rw-------    1 lisas    vip          106 Feb 16 15:58 surfing.2.0.3.txt
-rwxr-xr--    2 lisas    vip          664 Feb 16 15:58 change.it
-rwxr--r--    2 lisas    vip          664 Feb 16 15:58 l
```

Wouldn't it be great if you could give the l command that you created the name of any directory, and it would list that directory using the ls -l command?

You can. This is the way to write your request:

```
#!/bin/csh
ls -l $*
```

Now you've added the "$*" at the end of the ls -l command. What does it mean? The $* sign stands for the filename after the command. In UNIX terms, it's called a *variable* because it can change each time it's called.

Say that you enter l mydir, where mydir is a directory. Then mydir is what "goes into" or "expands to" the variable represented by $*. Think of the $* as grabbing the value that you give the shell script and holding that value until your program wants to use it.

NOTE

A good way to see how shell variables are expanded is to use the echo command. Try adding the following lines to your l script and save it:

```
#!/bin/csh
echo 'This is the output from $*...'
echo $*
echo '...'
echo 'This is the output from ls...'
ls -l $*
```

Now enter l road* and you'll see this:

```
% l road*
This is the output from $@...
roadtrip roadtrip1 roadtrip2 roadtrip3 roadtrip4 roadtrip45 roadtrip5
roadtripA roadtripB roadtripC
...
This is the output from ls...
-rw-rw-rw-    1 lisas    vip          497 May 11 06:25 roadtrip
-rw-rw-rw-    1 lisas    vip          106 May 11 06:25 roadtrip1
-rw-rw-rw-    1 lisas    vip          106 May 11 06:25 roadtrip2
-rw-rw-rw-    1 lisas    vip          106 May 11 06:25 roadtrip3
```

```
-rw-rw-rw-    1 lisas      vip          106 May 11 06:25 roadtrip4
-rw-rw-rw-    1 lisas      vip          106 May 11 06:25 roadtrip45
-rw-rw-rw-    1 lisas      vip          106 May 11 06:25 roadtrip5
-rw-rw-rw-    1 lisas      vip          106 May 11 06:25 roadtripA
-rw-rw-rw-    1 lisas      vip          106 May 11 06:25 roadtripB
-rw-rw-rw-    1 lisas      vip          106 May 11 06:25 roadtripC
% _
```

There's only one thing left to figure out. What do the quotes mean? They mean
that whatever is within them is to be taken literally, and any spaces or special characters are supposed to be taken exactly as they are. Why do you need the quotes
here? If you had entered 1 followed by several filenames, you'd have spaces between the filenames, and the spaces might have been misinterpreted. Now that
you've done one, you can try a few variations.

What do I mean by variations? Try changing some of the switches on the ls command, and make a different shell program for each. Remember to make each file
executable before you run the program. (In case you're wondering, nothing bad
would happen if you forgot this step; you just wouldn't be able to run the program.)

Here are some ways to experiment. The following variation is similar to the previous version, except that if you have any strange characters in any of your files,
this command will display them to the screen as ?, too:

```
#!/bin/csh
ls -lq $*
```

This one lists files and directories in the reverse order of their time stamps, the
oldest files first:

```
#!/bin/sh
ls -lrt $*
```

Using Arguments
and Variable Lists

Suppose you had a procedure called rescue that worked on dogs, maidens, and
children. You could call it using dogs, then call it using maidens, then call it using children, but that's pretty tedious. What you really want to do is call it once
with all of those things: rescue dogs maidens children. The dogs, maidens, and
children in C shell programming lingo are called *arguments*. Arguments are

values that can be passed to programs. You have been using arguments all along. When you entered ls -l, the -l is an argument for ls. The ls command can take many arguments, such as -l and filenames to list. So let's make your shell script handle more than one argument:

```
% rescue dogs maidens children
```

The shell has a way for you to refer to each of the things on which you ran the shell script. It puts each of these things into a *parameter*, which is something that stands for the things that you specify when you run the shell script. You can then refer to these things in your program, because they've already been set. In the previous example, the symbol referring to dogs would be $1. The second argument that you specified is maidens, and it would be $2. So what would children be? You guessed it, $3.

You can construct an instructive sample shell script to display your arguments called mirror, which takes the arguments that you give it, reverses their order and displays the results to the screen. Create the following script and put it in a file called mirror. Then make it executable:

```
#!/bin/csh
# mirror example
echo $8 $7 $6 $5 $4 $3 $2 $1
```

Anything following the # symbol is considered a comment. You can "comment" your shell scripts to help you remember what they do before you execute them. The echo command "echoes" back whatever variables that you give it. Let's set the permissions on the file to executable and enter mirror mirror on the wall who is the fairest.... You should see the following (I have made the arguments italicized so you can tell the argument from the shell script):

```
% chmod o+x mirror
% mirror mirror on the wall who is the fairest...
fairest... the is who wall the on mirror mirror
%
```

The shell script that you wrote collected the arguments with which you called it, kept track of what was where, and then did what you told it to do with them. (Wouldn't it be nice if people could be so easy to work with?)

You may wonder why I didn't finish the famous saying, with who is the fairest of them all. There is a reason. The shell can keep track of only nine arguments at a time. If that's not enough for you, you can cause the arguments to shift, so that you throw away the first one and cause all the others to shift their number by one, so that $2 becomes $1 ($1 is thrown away). At the same time, $3 becomes $2, and $4 becomes $3.

You can also access all of the arguments at the same time by using the $* notation, which expands to all of the arguments that you used to call the script initially. If

I modified the mirror script a little, as follows, and then called it mirror2 and made it executable, I could get the whole question in:

```
#!/bin/csh
# mirror2 example
echo $*
```

Make it executable, then enter the entire question:

```
% chmod o+x mirror2
% mirror2 Mirror mirror on the wall who is the fairest of them all
Mirror mirror on the wall who is the fairest of them all
% _
```

Special Argument Variables

There are several special shell-script symbols that you must learn. They are called parameters, which are very similar to variables in that they stand for something that can change each time a shell script is used.

The first of these is the variable count—usually called the argument count (the same thing)— which is the number of variables; count is written $#argv.

The variable $* stands for all of the arguments. If you have a command following by 50 arguments, it would take all 50 arguments. It saves you from entering $1 $2 $3 $4 ... $46 $47 $48 $49 for each of the 50 arguments.

The $* variable is often used when you want to specify that something is to be done in exactly the same way for every argument in the command line. There's more on that later in this chapter.

The variable $argv stands for the string containing all of the arguments. You've already used this for the l command, and it's this variable that enables you to list many files and directories with your l script.

Let's see a demonstration of how these variables work. The following changes to the l shell script will help you see each of the special argument variables.

Add the following lines to your l script, and run it:

```
#!/bin/csh
echo 'This is the output from $*...'
echo $*
echo '...'
echo 'This is the output from $argv...'
echo $argv
echo '...'
echo 'This is the output from $#argv...'
echo $#argv
echo '...'
echo 'This is the output from ls...'
```

```
ls -1 $*
$ 1 road*
This is the output from $*...
roadtrip roadtrip1 roadtrip2 roadtrip3 roadtrip4 roadtrip45 roadtrip5
roadtripA roadtripB roadtripC
...
This is the output from $argv...
roadtrip roadtrip1 roadtrip2 roadtrip3 roadtrip4 roadtrip45 roadtrip5
roadtripA roadtripB roadtripC
...
This is the output from $#argv...
10
...
This is the output from ls...
-rw-rw-rw-  1 lisas      vip            497 May 11 06:25 roadtrip
-rw-rw-rw-  1 lisas      vip            106 May 11 06:25 roadtrip1
-rw-rw-rw-  1 lisas      vip            106 May 11 06:25 roadtrip2
-rw-rw-rw-  1 lisas      vip            106 May 11 06:25 roadtrip3
-rw-rw-rw-  1 lisas      vip            106 May 11 06:25 roadtrip4
-rw-rw-rw-  1 lisas      vip            106 May 11 06:25 roadtrip45
-rw-rw-rw-  1 lisas      vip            106 May 11 06:25 roadtrip5
-rw-rw-rw-  1 lisas      vip            106 May 11 06:25 roadtripA
-rw-rw-rw-  1 lisas      vip            106 May 11 06:25 roadtripB
-rw-rw-rw-  1 lisas      vip            106 May 11 06:25 roadtripC
%
```

While you're messing around with variables, try creating the following program, phonelet, that changes letters to digits in phone numbers. Let's dissect it, line by line; this is a good way to read a new shell script that you've never seen.

First, though, you need to understand a basic utility called tr. When you use tr, you put two arguments after it and it converts the first argument to the second argument everywhere it occurs, one letter at a time. In our example, tr basically looks at each letter, asks if it's the one to be replaced, and if it is, tr replaces the letter with the a digit.

Now consider phonelet:

```
#!/bin/csh
echo $*
digits="2223334445555666777888999"
letters=ABCDEFGHIJKLMNOPRSTUVWXYabcdefghijklmnoprstuvwxy
echo $* | tr "$letters" "$digits$digits"
```

The first line is the standard shell line. The second line echoes the arguments that were fed into the program at the command line. The third line is a line of numbers, and you'll notice that there are three of each digit. (The 1 and the 0 are left out because they don't have letters associated with them on a phone dial.) The fourth line is a string containing both the upper- and lowercase characters of the alphabet. Now that you've set up the program, the echo command takes the letters of the phone number you enter—say, CALLIBM—and pipes them to the tr command. The tr command, in turn, replaces the letters with digits, and because it's being echoed to the screen, the user sees a phone number that is numbers only.

If you enter phonelet CALLIBM, you'll get back the following:

```
% chmod +x phonelet
% phonelet callibm
callibm
2255426
$ _
```

Testing Conditions with the *if* Statement

Sometimes, you want to specify that if a variable falls into a certain category or range, you want to perform some task based on that variable, but if not, then you want to do some other task. This situation is very common, so there's a way to do it in shell programming. Let's give you a real situation. If the day of the week is Saturday or Sunday, I will sleep in until noon; if not, I will wake up at 7 a.m. and trudge off to my job.

The general form of the if statement is the following:

```
If (this test or command is successful) then
    execute everything from here

      .
      .
      .

    down to the following "fi"
fi
```

The fi, in case you hadn't guessed, is *if* spelled backward; it helps you remember that it ends the if statement.

The following are some examples of if statements:

```
if ((mv door /house/door) == 0) then
    echo "I moved the door"
fi
```

If the mv command was successful, then the echo command will print I moved the door. Otherwise, nothing will happen.

You can also specify what will happen if the command is unsuccessful. The form of that command is this:

```
if (this command or test is successful) then
do all of the commands up to the next "else."
      .
    .else (if it isn't successful)
do all of the commands up to the next "fi."

      .
fi.
```

There are many tests and commands you can use. The types of tests that you will most often use fall into three categories: tests on strings, tests on numerical values, and tests on files. The following are the most popular, and again, I'm afraid you're back to reading hieroglyphics.

Tests on Strings of Characters, Letters, Numbers, and Punctuation

Strings of letters are either equal (the same) or they're not; or they're of length 0 or they're not. It's as simple as that. If string1 and string2 are being compared, then the following are the possible ways of testing:

✖ string1 == string2   The two strings are exactly equal.

```
If ($1 == $2) then
    echo "They are equal"
else
    echo "They are not equal"
fi
```

Let's put this code in a file called test1 and execute it to see the possible outcome:

```
% test1 roadtrip1 roadtrip3
They are not equal
% test1 roadtrip1 roadtrip1
They are equal
% _
```

✖ string1 != string2   The strings aren't equal.

```
If ( $1 != $2) then
    echo "They are not equal"
else
    echo "They are equal"
fi
```

Let's put this code in a file called test2 and execute it to see the possible outcome:

```
% test2 roadtrip1 roadtrip3
They are not equal
% test2 roadtrip1 roadtrip1
They are equal
% _
```

✖ string1 == ""   This tests to see whether the string is not there (that is, has 0 length).

A typical code looks like the following:

```
if $3=="" then
    echo "You forgot to enter a third filename"
else
```

```
    cat $3
fi
```

Let's put this code in a file called `test3` and execute it to see the possible outcome:

```
% test3
You forgot to enter a third filename
% test3 roadtrip1 roadtrip2 roadtrip3
A journey of a Thousand miles begins, hopefully, with an empty
bladder and all the appliances turned off.
% _
```

In the preceding code example, the `if` statement evaluates the variable `$3` for a zero-length string (that's what `""` means). If `$3` is a zero-length string, it informs the user that he or she forgot to enter the third filename. If the `$3` is not zero but contains a value, then the script executes the command `cat` under the else statement. The `cat` displays the contents of `$3` to the screen.

Tests on Numbers

Numbers are easy, too. We all intuitively know how to compare numbers. The following comparisons can be made between two numbers, `number1` and `number2`:

✖ `number1 < number2`   True, if `number1` is less than `number2`.

```
if ( $1 < $2 ) then
    echo "argument 1 is less than argument 2"
else
    echo "argument 1 is not less than argument 2"
fi
```

Let's put this code in a file called `test4` and execute it to see the possible outcome:

```
% test4 1 2
argument 1 is less than argument 2
% test4 1 1
argument 1 is not less than argument 2
% _
```

✖ `number1 > number2`   True, if `number1` is greater than `number2`.

```
if ( $1 > $2 ) then
    echo "argument 1 is greater than argument 2"
else
    echo "argument 1 is not greater than argument 2"
fi
```

Let's put this code in a file called `test5` and execute it to see the possible outcome:

```
% test5 2 1
argument 1 is greater than argument 2
```

```
% test5 1 1
argument 1 is not greater than argument 2
%
```

✖ number1 == number2   True, if number1 is equal to number2.

```
if ( $1 == $2 ) then
   echo "argument 1 is equal to argument 2"
else
   echo "argument 1 is not equal to argument 2"
fi
```

Let's put this code in a file called test6 and execute it to see the possible outcome:

```
% test6 1 1
argument 1 is equal to argument 2
% test6 2 1
argument 1 is not equal to argument 2
%
```

✖ number1 >= number2   True, if number1 is greater than or equal to number2.

```
if ( $1 >= $2 ) then
   echo "argument 1 is greater than or equal to argument 2"
else
   echo "argument 1 is not greater than or equal to argument 2
fi
```

Let's put this code in a file called test7 and execute it to see the possible outcome:

```
% test7 2 1
argument 1 is greater than or equal to argument 2
% test7 1 1
argument 1 is greater than or equal to argument 2
% test7 1 2
argument 1 is not greater than or equal to argument 2
%
```

✖ number1 <= number2   True, if number1 is less than or equal to number2

```
if ( $1 <= $2 ) then
   echo "argument 1 is less than or equal to argument 2"
else
   echo "argument 1 is not less than equal to argument 2"
fi
```

Let's put this code in a file called test8 and execute it to see the possible outcome:

```
% test8 1 2
argument 1 is less than or equal to argument 2
% test8 1 1
argument 1 is less than or equal to argument 2
% test8 2 1
argument 1 is not less than or equal to argument 2
%
```

✖ `number1 != number2`   True, if `number1` is not equal to `number2`

```
if ( $1 != $2 ) then
    echo "argument 1 is not equal to argument 2"
else
    echo "argument 1 is equal to argument 2"
fi
```

Let's put this code in a file called `test9` and execute it to see the possible outcome:

```
% test9 2 1
argument 1 is not equal to argument 2
% test9 1 1
argument 1 is equal to argument 2
% _
```

Tests on Files

Another type of test involves checking to see if certain things are true about a file. The following are the most common tests:

✖ `-e filename`   Checks that the file exists.

```
if (-e $1) then
    echo "file exists"
else
    echo "no file found"
fi
```

Let's put this code in a file called `test10` and execute it to see the possible outcome:

```
% test10 roadtrip
file exists
% test10 roadtrip2000
no file found
% _
```

✖ `-d filename`   Checks that the file is a directory.

```
if (-d $1) then
    echo "file is a directory"
else
    echo "file is not a directory"
fi
```

Let's put this code in a file called `test11` and execute it to see the possible outcome:

```
% test11 mydir
file is a directory
% test11 roadtrip
file is not a directory
% _
```

✖ -w *filename*   Checks to see if anybody can write to the file.

```
if (-w $1) then
   echo "file is writable"
else
   echo "file is not writable"
fi
```

Let's put this code in a file called `test12` and execute it to see the possible outcome:

```
% test12 roadtrip
file is writable
% chmod o-w roadtrip
% test12 roadtrip
file is not writable
% _
```

✖ -r *filename*   Checks to see if anybody can read the file.

```
if (-r $1) then
   echo "file is readable"
else
   echo "file is not readable"
fi
```

Let's put this code in a file called `test13` and execute it to see the possible outcome:

```
% test13 roadtrip
file is readable
% chmod o-r roadtrip
% test13 roadtrip
file is not readable
% _
```

A Real-Life Example of a Script Using an *if* Statement

I know a programmer who likes to check his mail fairly often. As you know, if you enter the `mail` command with no mail addresses and if you have no mail, then you automatically exit the mail program. What if you want to go into the mail program no matter what, whether you have mail waiting or not? The following shell script does just that:

```
#!/bin/csh

set mail_prog="/usr/ucb/mail"
set mail_path="/var/mail/$USER"

if (! -z $mail_path )  then
   $mail_prog $*
else
   echo No new mail
   $mail_prog -f $*
fi
```

If there isn't anything in the mail file, the system tells the user (echo No new mail) and starts up the mail program with the -f option anyway.

Doing Loops

Say you do a lot of work with files. You probably didn't realize this yet, but UNIX text files use the linefeed character to denote the end of a line, whereas other popular computer systems use the <return> character.

To change between formats, you must enter a line, screen, or word-processing editor and search and replace every single occurrence. It's a pain, so if you could automate the process, you could save some time and aggravation by writing a shell script to do this for you, right?

First, you need to understand that in the following program, instead of letters, numbers are used to represent letters, because everything computers understand must first be converted to numbers in the machine's CPU. When you see numbers instead of letters in the following tr command, it's okay; there are tables that associate the letters of the alphabet, as well as numbers and letters, with numbers. The value for Return is octal \015 and octal \012 for the linefeed character.

Here's a program that does the conversion:

```
#!/bin/csh
set tempfile="temp.$$"
foreach file ($argv[*])
    tr "\015" "\012" <$file>$tempfile
    mv $tempfile $file
end
```

Don't panic. Read it a line at a time. The first line is the standard first line, specifying the shell. The second line defines tempfile, a temporary file where the results of the transformation will be briefly stored. (Remember, you can't redirect or cat a file into itself.) The third line is not like anything you've learned so far. It is a foreach statement; it indicates that you're going to do something with all of the filenames that were in the command line you typed. The general idea of a foreach loop is as follows:

```
foreach value of the variable x in this list of values
    all of the commands until you see the end statement
end
```

The foreach loop is a very useful structure. It helps you perform an action over and over again. In this case, there are two statements in the foreach loop: the line that actually reads from the filename $file, and the line that feeds files a letter at a time to the `tr` command, which changes each `Return` to a linefeed character. The last line, the `end` statement, signals the end of the loop. In this case, it's also at the end of the program. In large programs, that wouldn't necessarily be so; that's why there must be some way to mark when the loop ends and the rest of the program picks up again.

> **NOTE**
>
> You may have noticed a distinctive symbol like $$ as part of `temp.$$` in the preceding program. The $$ is the number of your current process, that is, your current shell process. To see your shell-process identification number, enter `echo $$` at the shell prompt:
>
> ```
> % echo $$
> 1786
> % _
> ```
>
> A process identification number is how the UNIX operating system knows you and your programs. Every program (process) receives a process ID. The tempfile in the preceding shell script is assigned the value `temp.1787`. Why? In your shell program, you execute `#!/bin/csh`; this starts another instance of the shell. For the sake of simplicity, the value $$ in the next instance is `1787`. This would make the tempfile unique.

How would you do the opposite, that is, convert linefeed characters to Return characters wherever you found them in a UNIX file? How would you change the preceding program? What would be different? Certainly not the basic structure. You're still reading a file or a list of files, making a replacement with the `tr` command, and putting the results back into the filename that you originally read in. If you guessed that the only change is the order of the two numbers that you entered, you're right, and you're picking up a valuable skill in the UNIX shell script world: the ability to adapt existing shell scripts to make them be exactly what you want. The following shell script, which is called from UNIX, substitutes linefeed for Returns. Note the parallel structure of the program, which uses the same program structure and almost the same `foreach` loop:

```
#!/bin/csh
set tempfile="temp.$$"
foreach file ($argv[*])
    tr "\012" "\015" <$file>$tempfile
    mv $tempfile $file
end
```

Learning More

You've really learned a lot, and yet there's more to learn. You've basically learned enough of this foreign language to get a table, sit down, understand the menu, and order successfully; but, as you know, learning any foreign language takes years of practice. You may be wondering where you can learn more about UNIX shell scripts and get practice.

Here are some of the everyday tasks that you could automate with C shell scripts:

✖ You could make a script file to automatically create a backup file to a backup directory. Create a file called `vibackup` with following lines:

```
#!/bin/csh
cp $1 $1.bak
vi $1
exit
```

You could create an alias to make calling this program easier.

```
% alias vi vibackup
```

> **NOTE**
>
> Remember to make your shell script executable: `chmod o+x vibackup`

✖ You could search for a friend online. Create a file called `friends` with the following lines:

```
#!/bin/csh
set findfriend = ('who ¦ grep -i $argv[1] )
if ($#findfriend == 0) then
    echo "$argv[1] is not on the system...please try later"
else
    echo "$argv[1] is on the system"
endif
```

Now try the program:

```
% chmod o+x
% friends zachary
zachary is not on the system...please try later
% friends carolyn
carolyn is on the system
% _
```

To learn more, you can consult advanced UNIX texts on shell programming or system administration. Also, shell programming is a hot topic of conversation on many UNIX, programming, and system administration newsgroups, so you can learn something by hanging out there and asking sympathetic, knowledgeable people a few questions at a time.

What You've Learned

In this chapter, you have learned how to create C shell scripts to automate your routine, mundane tasks. You have learned how to pass arguments to shell scripts, `if..else` decision making, and the `foreach` loop.

Rewards

- ✖ You learned that people write shell scripts to automate routine tasks, to do system administration, and to do some simple programming tasks.
- ✖ A shell program is a file of fixed instructions to the shell. These instructions vary in length from a single line to hundreds or thousands of lines. To use these instructions, type the name of the file, and the instructions will be executed.
- ✖ A shell script is a type of shell program that takes shell variables, so that you can vary the input to the shell program at the time you call it.
- ✖ Many of the logical structures that shell programmers use—such as `if`, `for`, and `case` statements—are similar to those of other computer languages such as C, so that learning a little about shell programming can help you if you ever choose to learn a compiled language such as C.
- ✖ You learned about the special shell-script variables: `$#`, argument count; `$*`, which stands for all of the arguments; and `$@`, which stands for the string containing all of the arguments.
- ✖ You learned how to pass variables to shell programs using the command-line arguments.
- ✖ The `if` statements are the way that shell statements handle conditions, such as, "If there were six files in the command line that called the shell script, then do these operations six times."
- ✖ The `for` statement is one way to tell the shell to do something over and over again, for all of the items that fit a particular description or condition.
- ✖ To learn more about shell scripts, you can consult advanced UNIX texts on shell programming or system administration texts. Also, shell programming is a hot topic of conversation on many UNIX, programming, and system administration newsgroups; you can learn something from these resources.

Pitfalls

✖ You can create shell scripts that shouldn't be scripts at all. Instead, try converting a one-line shell script to an alias.

✖ You ruin your information if you run a buggy script. Work in a test directory to be safe.

Appendixes

A

Useful Commands and Switches

```
apropos [ -M path ] [ -m path ] keyword ...
```

Locates commands by keyword lookup.

-M path   Searches *path* instead of $MANPATH.

-m path   Searches *path* in addition to $MANPATH.

```
batch      at (1)
```

Executes commands at a later time.

```
bc [ -cl ] [ file ... ]
```

B Calculator. Provides arbitrary-precision arithmetic.

-c   Compiles the input into dc commands.

-l   Loads the library of scientific functions.

```
biff [ y ¦ n ]
```

Notifies of when mail arrives and whom it is from.

```
cal [ [ mm ] yyyy ]
```

Displays a calendar.

```
calendar      calendar (1)
```

A reminder service.

```
cancel      lp (1)
```

Sends/cancels requests to an LP print service.

Example: The following code shows a file being sent to the printer and then the print job being canceled.

```
% lp status
request id is printer1-345 (1 file)
% cancel printer1-345
```

```
cat        cat (1)
```

Concatenates and displays files.

Example: The following command displays a short text file named
`comfile`.

```
% cat comfile
     You can access various services over the Internet. The
menu-driven interface available through a gopher site often
simplifies the task of locating information.
     For the adventurous, the telnet command can connect to
another computer system as long as you know the computer's
Internet or IP address.
```

`cd [directory]`

Changes working directory.

directory Directory to which current working directory is changed.

Example: The following command displays the current working directory
as /usr/bin and then changes to the user's home directory, /usr/jon:

```
%pwd
/usr/bin
%cd
%pwd
/usr/jon
```
To change to another directory, include the directory name.

```
%cd desktop
%pwd
/usr/jon/desktop
```

`chgrp [ -Rf ] group file ...`

Changes the group ownership of a file.

-R	Recursively descends directory arguments, changing the groups of all files contained therein.
-f	Forces the change and does not display any errors.
group	Group name from /etc/group file.

`chmod [ -Rf ] mode file ...`

Changes the permissions mode of a file.

-R	Recursively descends directory arguments, changing the mode of all files contained therein.
-f	Forces the change and does not display any errors.
mode	Octal number or [ugo][+=-][rwxXst].

```
chown   [ -Rf ] owner[.group] file ...
```

Changes owner of a file.

-R	Recursively descends directory arguments, changing the owner of all files contained therein.
-f	Forces the change and does not display any errors.
owner	User name from /etc/passwd file to change the owner to.
group	Group name from /etc/group file to change the group to.

```
clear
```

Clears the terminal screen.

```
cmp [ -l ] [ -s ] file1 file2 [ skip1 ] [ skip2 ]
```

Compares two files.

-l	Lists the numerical offsets and values differences.
-s	Silent. Prints nothing, sets exit codes only.
skip1	Bytes to skip in file1 before comparing.
skip2	Bytes to skip in file2 before comparing.

```
comm [ -123 ] file1 file2
```

Displays common or different lines from two sorted files.

-1	Suppresses the lines that appear only in file1.
-2	Suppresses the lines that appear only in file2.
-3	Suppresses the lines that appear in both files.
file1	Name of sorted file. A dash (-) indicates standard input.
file2	Name of sorted file. A dash (-) indicates standard input.

```
compress [ -fvc ] [ -b bits ] [ file ... ]
```

Compresses, uncompresses files; or displays expanded files.

-f	Forces compression even if it will not shrink file.

-c	Cat the file to standard output.
-v	Verbose. Prints the percentage reduction of each file.
-b bits	Bits to use for encoding.

```
cp [ -ip ] file1 file2
cp [ -ipr ] file ... directory
```

Copies files.

-i	Inquires whether a file will be overwritten by the copy.
-p	Preserves modes (ignore umask) and modification times.
-r	Recursively copies directories.

Example: This example copies a file named wilbur to the /usr directory. This file will then exist in both the current working directory and the /usr directory.

```
% cp wilbur /usr
```

```
cpio -o[ aBcv ]
cpio -i[ BbcdfmrSstuv6 ] [ patterns]
cpio -p[ adlmruv ] directory
```

Copies into and out from file archives.

-o	Output files listed on "standard in" to an archive format on "standard out."
-i	Input. Extracts files from an archive on standard input.
-p	Pass. Reads standard input for filenames and copies them into directory.
-a	Access times of input files are reset after they are copied.
-B	Block archive 5120 bytes to the record.
-b	Both bytes and half-words are swapped.
-c	Write header information in ASCII character form for portability.
-d	Directories are to be created as needed.
-f	Copy in all files except those in patterns.
-l	Links files rather than copying them.
-m	Modification times are retained on created files.

-r	Renames files interactively.
-S	Swaps half-words.
-s	Swaps bytes.
-t	Table of contents is printed instead of creating files.
-u	Unconditionally copies even if a new file would be replaced.
-v	Verbose. A list of filenames is printed. Makes -t look like ls -1.
-6	6th edition formatted archives are processed.

crontab

User crontab file.

csh

C-shell command interpreter with a C-like syntax.

date

Prints the date.

```
diff [ -biwt ] [ -c [ # ] e ¦ f ¦ h ¦ n ] [ -lrs ] [ -S name ] dir1 dir2
diff [ -biwt ] [ -c [ # ] e ¦ f ¦ h ¦ n ] file1 file2
diff [ -biwt ] [ -D string ]  file1 file2
```

Displays line-by-line differences between pairs of text files.

-l	Long format. Text file diffs are piped through pr to paginate.
-r	Recursively traverses common subdirectories.
-s	Files which are the same are reported.
-S name	Starts the directory diff in the middle with file name.
-c[#]	# Context lines are generated.
-e	ed commands that create file2 from file1 are written to standard out.
-f	Same as -e, except that line numbers don't reflect changes of earlier editing. The line numbers correspond to line in file1.

-h	Half-hearted job diff is done, but works on files of unlimited length.
-n	Numbered changed lines in ed format.
-b	Blank strings are treated as equal, and trailing blanks are ignored,
-i	Ignores the case of letters.
-w	Whitespace is totally ignored.
-t	Tabs are expanded.
-D *str*	Defined merged file with *ifdefs* is created.

dirname *pathname*

Prints the directory portion of a pathname.

echo [-n] [*arg ...*]

Writes value of local or environment variable and strings to standard output.

-n	No newline is printed after the arguments.

ed [-] [-x] [*file*]

Text editor.

-	Suppresses explanatory output.
-x	Extracts and encrypts the file.
file	File to be edited.

edit [-] [-vrlxR] [-t tag] [-w #] [+*command*] *file ...*

Text editor (variant of ex for casual users).

-v	Starts in visual mode.
-r	Recovers lost version.
-l	Lisp and showmatch options are set.
-t tag	Reads tags from file tag.
-w #	Window size is set to #.
-x	Extracts from encrypted file.
-R	Read-only option is set.

275

```
egrep [ -bchilnosvw ] [ -f file ] [ -e ] expr [ files ... ]
```

Searches a file for a pattern using full regular expressions.

-b	Block number is printed before each line.
-c	Count of matches is printed instead of actual lines.
-h	Headers are not printed before each line.
-i	Ignores case in comparisons.
-l	Lists only the filenames that contain a match, once each.
-n	Numbers each line with its line number.
-o	Outputs headers on every line.
-s	Silent mode. Only a status is returned.
-v	All lines except those that match.
-e expr	Expression to use is expr.
-f file	File contains the expression.
files	Files to search in.

```
env
```

Displays or alters environment variables for command execution.

```
ex [ - ] [ -vrlxR ] [ -t tag ] [ -w # ] [ +command ] file ...
```

Text editor.

-v	Starts in visual mode.
-r	Recovers lost version.
-l	Lisp and showmatch options are set.
-t tag	Reads tags from file tag.
-w #	Window size is set to #.
-x	Extract from encrypted file.
-R	Read-only option is set.

```
expand [ -# ] [ -#,#,#,...,# ] [ file ... ]
```

Expands tabs to spaces.

`-#`	Tab stops are set every # characters apart.
`-#,#...`	Tab stops are set at each column numbered.
file	Files to expand.

`fgrep [ -bchilnosvwx ] [ -f file ] [ -e ] expr [ files ... ]`

Searches a file for a character string.

`-b`	Block number is printed before each line.
`-c`	Count of matches is printed instead of actual lines.
`-h`	Headers are not printed before each line.
`-i`	Ignores case in comparisons.
`-l`	Lists only the filenames that contain a match, once each.
`-n`	Numbers each line with its line number.
`-o`	Outputs headers on every line.
`-s`	Silent mode. Only a status is returned.
`-v`	All lines except those that match.
`-x`	Exact matches only.
`-e` *expr*	Expression to use is *expr*.
`-f` *file*	File contains the expression.
files	Files to search in.

`file [ -f list ] file ...`

Determines file type.

`-f list`	File containing a list of types.

`find path ... [ -name fname ] [ -perm onum ] [ -type [bcdfls] ]`
`[ -links n ] [ -user uname ] [ -nouser ] [ -group gname ]`
`[ -atime n ] [ -mtime n ] [ -ctime n ] [ -exec command ]`

Finds files.

path	Start path to begin search.
`-name` *fname*	Filename to find.
`-perm` *onum*	Permission of the file, such as 0555 (read-only).

`-type` *t*	Type of file:
	`b` block
	`c` character
	`d` directory
	`l` link
	`s` symbolic link
`-links` *n*	Number of link to the file.
`-user` *uname*	File owner.
`-nouser`	File is not owned by anyone who is named in `/etc/passwd`.
`-group` *gname*	Group name to which file belongs.
`-atime` *n*	The *n* of days the file was last accessed.
`-mtime` *n*	The *n* of days the file was last modified.
`-ctime` *n*	The *n* of days the file was last changed.
`-exec` *command*	Allows you to put command line arguments to remove, copy, and so on, the files you find with the search criteria. The {} enclosed in quotes represents the found file, and a ; ends the command: `find / -name "core" -exec rm "{}" ";"`

This example removes all the copies of the file named core in the entire file system.

`finger [ -mlqbwfips ] name ...`

Displays information about local and remote users.

`-m`	Matches arguments only on user name.
`-l`	Long output format is forced.
`-q`	Quick output format is forced.
`-b`	Brief output format for specified names.
`-w`	Wide output of location is allowed.
`-f`	Does not display headers.
`-i`	Idle times are displayed.
`-p`	Plan file `.plan` is not printed.
`-s`	Short output format is forced.
name	Name to search for in account, first and last names.

fmt [*goal* [*max*]] [*name* ...]

Simple text formatter.

goal	Goal for line length.
max	Maximum number of characters allowed on a line.

ftp [-vding] [*host*]

File transfer program.

-v	Verbose option is turned on.
-n	No auto-login based on .netrc is attempted.
-i	Interactive prompting during file transfers is turned off.
-d	Debugging is enabled.
host	Machine to connect to.

grep [-bchilnosvw] [-f *file*] [-e] expr [*files* ...]

Searches a file for a pattern.

-b	Block number is printed before each line.
-c	Count of matches is printed instead of actual lines.
-h	Headers are not printed before each line.
-i	Ignores case in comparisons.
-l	Lists only the filenames that contain a match, once each.
-n	Numbers each line with its line number.
-o	Output headers on every line.
-s	Silent mode. Only a status is returned.
-v	All lines except those that match.
-w	Word mode. Expression is searched for as a word.
-e *expr*	Expression to use is *expr*.
files	Files to search in.

Example: The following example searches a file for the pattern telnet and then searches again to display the line number in the file.

```
% grep 'telnet' comfile
For the adventurous, the telnet command can connect to another
% grep -n 'telnet' comfile
```

```
[8] For the adventurous, the telnet command can connect to
another
%
```

groups [*user*]

> Shows group membership of user.
>
> *user*   Name to show group membership for.

kill [*-signal*] pid ...

> Sends a signal to a process.
>
> *-signal*   Signal to send to the processes. SigTERM is default.
>
> pid   Process IDs to send the signal to.

ksh

> Korn shell, a standard interactive shell and scripting language.

last [*-#*] [-f *file*] [-h *host*] [-t *tty*] [*user* ...]

> Displays login and logout information about users and terminals.
>
> *-#*   Maximum # of lines to generate in the report.
>
> -f *file*   File to read log from.
>
> -h *host*   Hostname that the user logged in from.
>
> -t *tty*   *tty* to limit the report to.
>
> *user*   User to limit the report to.

leave [*hhmm*]

> Tells you when you have to leave, at appropriate time.
>
> *hhmm*   Hour and minute you want to leave.

ln [-s] *filename* [*linkname*]

> Makes a link to a file.
>
> -s   Symbolic link will be made.
>
> *filename*   Filename to link to.
>
> *linkname*   Name of the link.

`look [ -df ] string [ file ]`

> Find words in the system dictionary or lines in a sorted list.
>
> `-d`   Dictionary order. Only letters, digits, and blanks are compared.
>
> `-f`   Fold uppercase letters equal to lowercase letters.

`lp`

> Send/cancel requests to an LP print service.
>
> Example: The following command sends the `sales` file to the printer. The request ID is `printer1-345`, which is usable with `cancel` or `lpstat` commands.
>
> ```
> %lp sales
> request id is printer1-345 (1file)
> %
> ```

`lpq-Pprinter`

> Shows what is printing on the printers.
>
> `-Pprinter`   `printer` is the name of printer for which print jobs are displayed.

`lpr -Pprinter`

> Prints files.
>
> `-Pprinter`   Specifies which printer to print to.

`lprm -Pprinter job`

> Removes jobs from the line-printer spooling queue.
>
> `-Pprinter`   Specifies from which printer to remove jobs.
>
> `job`   Specifies which printer job or jobs to remove. Separate jobs by a space.

`lpstat`

> Prints information about the status of the LP print service.

```
ls [ -acdfgilqrstu1MR ] name ...
```

Lists contents of directory.

-M	Lists in Macintosh format.
-l	Lists in long format.
-g	Includes the group of the file in a long output.
-t	Sorts by time modified.
-a	Lists all entries.
-s	Gives size in kilobytes of each file.
-d	If argument is a directory, lists only its name.
-r	Reverses the order of sort.
-u	Uses time of last access.
-c	Uses time when file status was modified.
-i	For each file, prints the inode.
-f	Forces each argument to be interpreted as a directory.
-F	Causes directories to be marked with a trailing /, sockets with a trailing =, symbolic links with a trailing @, and executable files with a trailing *.
-R	Recursively lists subdirectories encountered.
-1	Forces one entry-per-line output format.
-C	Forces multicolumn output.
-q	Forces printing of nongraphic characters in filenames as the character ?.

Example: The following command displays the contents of the current working directory:

```
% ls
Mail            dead.article    jonsnews        resume
News            dead.letter     k12             test
```

With the -l option, the ls command displays more detailed information about the directory contents:

```
% ls -l
total 888
drwx------  2 jleer  jleer      512 Feb 22 11:36 Mail
drwxr-x---  2 jleer  jleer      512 Nov 19 15:51 News
-rw-r-----  1 jleer  jleer      384 Dec  9 12:01 dead.article
-rw-------  1 jleer  jleer      945 Apr 22 10:00 dead.letter
-rw-r-----  1 jleer  jleer   418501 May 17 10:44 jonsnews
-rw-r-----  1 jleer  jleer    12344 May 13 13:03 k12
-rw-r-----  1 jleer  jleer     1792 Nov 24 10:15 resume
-rw-r-----  1 jleer  jleer      301 May 17 15:17 test
```

To display all files in the directory, including hidden files, include the -a option:

```
% ls -a
.              .gopherrc    .new2         .pnewsexpert  dead.article
..             .gopherrc~   .newsrc       .rnlast       dead.letter
.article       .login       .newsrc.bak   .rnsoft       jonsnews
.article2      .logout      .nn           .signature    k12
.article3      .mailrc      .oldnewsrc    Mail          resume
.cshrc         .msgsrc      .pinerc       News          test
```

mail

>   Reads mail or sends mail to users.

```
man -k [ -M path ] [ -m path ] keyword ...
man [ -acw ] [ -M path ] [ -m path ] [ section ] name ...
```

>   Finds and displays reference manual pages.

-a	All of the manual pages are displayed instead of only the first one.
-c	Copies the manual page to standard out instead of using more.
-w	Which manual pages would display are listed.
-k	Keyword lookup of description lines (same as apropos command).
-M path	Search path instead of $MANPATH.
-m path	Search path in addition to $MANPATH.

Example: The following command accesses the man page for the trn command. Because this is a long entry, you are prompted to type any key to continue.

```
% man trn
```

```
TRN(1)                                                              TRN(1)


NAME
       trn - threaded read news program

SYNOPSIS
       trn [options] [newsgroups]

DESCRIPTION
       Trn  is  a  threaded version of rn, which is a replacement
       for the readnews(1) program. Being "threaded" means  that
       the articles are interconnected in reply order. Each dis-
       cussion thread is a tree of articles where all  the  reply
       (child)  articles  branch off from their respective
```

```
                 originating (parent) articles. A representation of  this  tree
                 (or a portion of it) is displayed in the article header as
                 you are reading news. This gives you a  better  feel  for
                 how all the articles are related, and even lets you see at
         --More--
```

mkdir *dirname* ...

Makes directories.

dirname   Name of the directories to create.

Example: To create a new directory named exe, you would enter this command: % **mkdir exe**

more [-cdflMsu] [-#] [+#] [+/*pat*] [*name* ...]

Browses or pages through a text file.

-c   Clears the screen before displaying each page.

-d   Displays user-friendly messages.

-f   Folding is not done on lines.

-l   ^L (form-feed) is not treated as an end of screen.

-s   Squeezes multiple blank lines into one blank line.

-u   Underlining is suppressed.

-#   Number of lines per page.

+#   Start displaying # lines into the file.

+/*pat*   Starts displaying two lines before the pattern *pat* is found.

name   Name of the file to display.

Example: This command displays a file and pipes it through more to display a screen at a time.

```
         % cat comfile ¦ more
         You can access various services over the Internet. The
         menu-driven interface available through a gopher site often
         simplifies the task of locating information.

         For the adventurous, the telnet command can connect to another
         computer system as long as you know the computer's Internet or IP
         address.

         -more-

         Of course, by using telnet requires that you be aware of a valid user
         name and password at the host computer to which you are connecting.
```

```
            More
            importantly, you may have some difficulty finding your way around
            once
            you are connected unless the remote computer has a friendly user
            interface.
            % _
```

```
mv [ -if ] file1 file2
mv [ -if ] file ... directory
```

Moves (renames) `file1` to `file2` and removes any existing `file2`. The second form moves multiple files into a directory.

-i	Inquires whether `file2` should be removed if one already exists.
-f	Forces the move without question.
file1	Name of the file to rename.
file2	Name of the new file.

Example: This command renames a file from `kroger` to `mitschnel`:

`% mv kroger mitschnel`

```
nice [ -# ] command [ arguments ]
```

Runs a command at lower priority.

-#	Number by which to increment the priority. Max is 20, default is 10.

```
od [ -abcdfhilo ] [ -s[#] ] [ file ] [ [+]offset[.][b] [label] ]
```

Displays an octal, decimal, hex, or ASCII dump of a file.

-a	ASCII character names are displayed for each byte.
-b	Bytes are displayed as unsigned octal.
-c	Characters are displayed for each byte with \ names.
-d	Decimal unsigned values are displayed for each short word.
-f	Floating point values are displayed for each long word.
-h	Hexadecimal unsigned values are displayed for each short word.
-i	Integer signed values are displayed for each short word.

-l	Long words are displayed as signed decimal values.
-o	Octal unsigned values are displayed for each short word.
-v	Verbose: shows all data, including identical lines.
-x	Hexadecimal values are printed for each short word.
-s [#]	Strings of minimum length # that are null terminated are searched for.
-w [#]	Width (in bytes) to display in each line.

page

Same as more. Same parameters and switches as more.

passwd [*user*]

Changes login password for yourself or a given user (root only).

printenv [*varname*]

Prints out environment variables.

ps

Shows your running processes. Switches vary greatly.

pwd

Prints working directory pathname.

rcp [-p] *file1 file2*
rcp [-pr] *file ... directory*

Remote file copy.

-p	Preserves modes (ignore umask) and modification times.
-r	Recursively copies directories.

```
rm [ -efri- ] file ...
```

Removes (unlinks) files.

`-e`	Echoes the name of each file as it is removed.
`-f`	Forces the file to be removed without question.
`-r`	Recursively removes directories.
`-i`	Inquires whether each file should be removed.
`-`	None of the rest are switches; useful if a filename starts with a dash (-).

```
rmdir directory ...
```

Removes directories if they are empty.

```
rsh
```

Remote shell.

```
script
```

Creates a file of everything you type in your current UNIX session.

```
sed
```

A stream editor. See Appendix C, "Commonly Used Editor Commands."

```
sh
```

Bourne shell, the standard shell command interpreter.

```
sort
```

Sorts and/or merges files.

```
spell
```

Finds spelling errors.

`stty`

Sets the options for a terminal.

`su`

Substitutes user id temporarily.

```
tail [-f] [-bcklmn[+/-num]] file
tail [-f] [+/-num[bcklmn]] file
```

Shows the last *n* lines of `file`.

`-f`	Called the *follow* option. You can use the option to follow the file as it grows. As new data is added to `file`, it is displayed to the screen. You can use this to watch data go into a file from another program.
`-num`	Displays the last *num* lines in a file. `-50` would display the last 50 line in the file.
`+num`	Displays all the lines from *num* to the end of the file. If a file was 200 lines long, `+50` would skip the first 50 line, then, starting with line 51, would display all the lines to the end of file.
`+num1` or `-num1`	either of these two follow by unit specifiers b, c, k, l, m, n:

b	blocks
c	characters
k	kilobytes
l	lines (default)
m	megabytes
n	lines (default)

`talk` *person*

Talk to another user.

person	To whom you want to talk.

`tar`

Tape archiver, and add or extract files.

`tee`

Replicate the standard output for pipe fitting.

`telnet host`

User interface to a remote system using the TELNET protocol.

`host`	Remote host to connect to.

`test expression`

Condition evaluation command. Expressions include these:

`-e file`	True if `file` exists.
`-r file`	True if `file` permission is readable.
`-w file`	True if `file` permission is writeable.
`-d file`	True if `file` is d directory.
`-x file`	True if `file` permission is executable.
`string`	True if `string` is not empty.
`string1=string2`	True if `string1` is equal to `string2`.
`string1!=string2`	True if `string1` is not equal to `string2`.
`num1 .eq num2`	True if `num1` is equal to `num2`.
`num1 .ne num2`	True if `num1` is not equal to `num2`.
`num1 .ge num2`	True if `num1` is greater or equal to `num2`.
`num1 .gt num2`	True if `num1` is greater than to `num2`.
`num1 .le num2`	True if `num1` is less or equal to `num2`.
`num1 .lt num2`	True if `num1` is less than to `num2`.
`expr1 -a expr2`	Logical AND `expr1` and `expr2`.
`expr1 -o expr2`	Logical OR `expr1` and `expr2`.
`! expr1`	Negate `expr1`.
`(expr1)`	`Group expr1`. Used to group a number of expressions together with other operators.

`time`

Times a command.

`tr`

> Translates characters.

`tty`

> Gets the name of the controlling terminal.

`uname`

> Prints name of current system.

`users`

> Provides a compact list of users who are on the system.

`vi`

> Calls up a screen-oriented (visual) display editor based on ex.

`view`

> Calls up a screen-oriented (visual) display editor based on ex.

`w`

> Shows who is logged in, and what each is doing.

`wait`

> Waits for a process to finish.

`wc`

> Displays a count of lines, words, and characters in a file.

whatis *command*

> Displays a one-line summary about a keyword.
>
> *command*   Command for which the summary is displayed.

which *command*

> Locates a command; displays its pathname or alias.
>
> *command*   The command for which path or alias is shown.

who

> Shows who is on the system.

whoami

> Prints your current user id.

whois

> Internet user name directory service.

B

Commonly Used Newsreader Commands

This appendix lists the basic commands for using the rn, nn, and trn newsreader programs to read various newsgroups.

Commands for *rn*—The Read News Program

The command-line syntax for rn is as follows:

```
rn [options] [newsgroups]
```

The rn program operates on three levels: newsgroup selection, article selection, and paging. Each level has its own set of commands and its own help menu.

Commands for Newsgroup-Selection Level

y,SP	Do this newsgroup now.
.command	Do this newsgroup now, but execute command before displaying anything. The command is interpreted as if given on the article-selection level.
=	Do this newsgroup now, but list subjects before displaying articles.
n	Go to the next newsgroup with unread news.
N	Go to the next newsgroup.
p	Go to the previous newsgroup with unread news. If there is none, stay at the current newsgroup.
P	Go to the previous newsgroup.
-	Go to the previously displayed newsgroup (regardless of whether that one is before or after the current one in the list).
1	Go to the first newsgroup.
^	Go to the first newsgroup with unread news.
$	Go to the end of the newsgroup list.
g newsgroup	Go to newsgroup.
/pattern	Scan forward for a newsgroup matching pattern.

`?pattern`	Same as /, but search backward.
`u`	Unsubscribe from current newsgroup.
`l string`	List newsgroups not subscribed to which contain the `string` specified.
`L`	Lists the current state of the `.newsrc`, along with status information.
`m name`	Move the named newsgroup somewhere else in the `.newsrc`.
`c`	Catch up—mark as read all unread articles in this newsgroup.
`o pattern`	Display only those newsgroups whose name matches `pattern`.
`a pattern`	Add new newsgroups matching `pattern`.
`&`	Print out the current status of command-line switches and any newsgroup restrictions.
`&switch {switch}`	Set additional command-line switches.
`&&`	Print out the current macro definitions.
`&&keys commands`	Define additional macros.
`!command`	Escape to a subshell.
`q`	Quit.
`x`	Quit.
Control+K	Edit the global KILL file.

Commands for Article-Selection Level

n,SP	Scan forward for next unread article.
N	Go to the next article.
^N	Scan forward for the next article with the same subject, and make ^N default (subject search mode).

295

p	Scan backward for previous unread article. If there is none, stay at the current article.
P	Go to the previous article.
-	Go to the previously displayed article.
Control+P	Scan backward for the previous article with the same subject.
Control+R	Restart the current article.
v	Restart the current article verbosely, displaying the entire header.
Control+L	Refresh the screen.
Control+X	Restart the current article.
X	Refresh the screen.
b	Back up one page.
q	Quit this newsgroup and go back to the newsgroup selection level.
^	Go to the first unread article.
$	Go to the last article.
num	Go to the specified article number.
range{,*range*} *command*{:*command*}	Apply a set of commands to a set of articles.
j	Junk the current article—mark it as read.
m	Mark the current article as still unread.
M	Mark the current article as still unread, but not until the newsgroup is exited.
/*pattern*	Scan forward for article containing *pattern* in the subject.
/*pattern*/h	Scan forward for article containing *pattern* in the header.

/pattern/a	Scan forward for article containing pattern anywhere in article.
/pattern/r	Scan read articles also.
/pattern/c	Make search case-sensitive.
/pattern/modifiers:command{:command}	Apply the commands listed to articles matching the search command (possibly with h, a, or r modifiers).
?pattern	Scan backward for article containing pattern in the subject.
k	Mark as read all articles with the same subject as the current article.
K	Do the same as the k command, but also add a line to the local KILL file for this newsgroup to kill this subject every time the newsgroup is started.
Control+K	Edit the local KILL file for this newsgroup.
r	Reply through net mail.
R	Reply, including the current article in the header file generated.
f	Submit a follow-up article.
F	Submit a follow-up article, and include the old article, with lines prefixed either by > or by the argument to an -F switch.
c	Cancel the current article (but only if you are the contributor or superuser).
z	Supersede the current article (but only if you are the contributor).

c	Catch up in this newsgroup—mark all articles as read.
u	Unsubscribe to this newsgroup.
s *destination*	Save to a filename or pipe using sh.
S *destination*	Save to a filename or pipe using a preferred shell, such as csh.
¦ *command*	Shorthand for s ¦ *command*.
w *destination*	The same as s *destination*, but saves without the header.
W *destination*	The same as S *destination*, but saves without the header.
e *directory*	Extract a shell archive or uuencoded binary to the designated directory.
e *directory*¦*command*	Extract other data formats than .shar or uuencoded files, or use to override the decisions made by the automatic-extraction selection.

NOTE

The .shar is a packed Bourne shell script in executable format. The preceding command will do extractions for you, but to unpack to a shell script, do this: sh filename.shar.

The Internet doesn't allow you directly to send executable or binary files through e-mail or newsgroups. Instead, you can encode the binary files with UNIX-to-UNIX encode, abbreviated uuencode. The uuencode basically takes a binary, which is in 8-bit format, and encodes it as the 6-bit format known as ASCII. You can then attach this encoded file to a message and mail it. At the destination, the reader simply detaches the file and decodes it with uudecode. To encode a binary, here is the syntax:

uuencode *in-filename* *out-filename* > *in-filename*.uue

The *in-filename* is the file you want to encode. The *out-filename* is the name the file receives when it is decoded. The > is for "redirect output to," and *in-filename*.uue is the name of the encode file. To decode, use this: uudecode in-filename.uue.

E	End any multipart uuencoded file extraction that you began, but are unable (or unwilling) to complete.
&	Print out the current status of command-line switches.
&*switch* {*switch*}	Set additional command-line switches.
&&	Print out current macro definitions.
&&*keys commands*	Define an additional macro.
!*command*	Escape to a subshell.
=	List subjects of unread articles.
#	Print last article number.

Commands for the Pager Level

At the pager level (within an article), the prompt looks like this:

`--MORE--(17%)`

You can use a number of commands.

SP	Display next page.
x	Display next page.
d, Control+D	Display a half-page more.
CR	Display one more line.
q	Go to the end of the current article (don't mark it as either read or unread). Leaves you at the What next? prompt.
j	Junk the current article. Mark it as read and go to the end of the article.
Control+L	Refresh the screen.
X	Refresh the screen and decrypt as a rot13 message.
b, Control+B	Back up one page.
g*pattern*	Go to (search forward for) *pattern* within current article.
G	Search for g*pattern* again.
Control+G	Skip articles in a digest.
TAB	Skip inclusions of older articles.
!*command*	Escape to a subshell.

Options for *rn* Commands

On the command line, these options can be set by the RNINIT environment variable, or by a file pointed to by the RNINIT variable, or from within rn by the & command. Options can generally be unset by typing +switch. Options include the following:

-c	Checks for news without reading news.
-C<*number*>	Tells rn how often to checkpoint the .newsrc, in articles read.
-d<*directory name*>	Sets the default save directory to something other than ~/News.
-D<*flags*>	Enables debugging output.
-e	Causes each page within an article to be started at the top of the screen, not just the first page.
-E<*name*>=<*val*>	Sets the environment variable <*name*> to the value specified.
-F<*string*>	Sets the prefix string for the F follow-up command to use in prefixing each line of the quoted article.
-g<*line*>	Specifies the line on the screen to search for strings when you search with the g command within an article.
-h<*string*>	Hides (disables the printing of) all header lines beginning with *string*.
-H<*string*>	Sets the magic flag for the header line beginning with *string*.
-i=<*number*>	Specifies how long (in lines) to consider the initial page of an article.
-l	Disables the clearing of the screen at the beginning of each article.
-L	Leaves information on the screen as long as possible.
-m=<*mode*>	Enables the marking of the last line of the previous page printed.
-M	Forces mailbox format in creating new save files.
-N	Forces normal (non-mailbox) format in creating new save files.

-q	Bypasses the automatic check for new newsgroups when starting rn.
-r	Causes rn to restart in the last newsgroup read during a previous session with rn.
-s	Suppresses the initial listing of newsgroups with unread news.
-S<number>	Causes rn to enter subject search mode (^N) automatically whenever a newsgroup is started up with <number> unread articles or more.
-t	Starts terse mode.
-T	Enables you to type ahead of rn.
-v	Sets verification mode for commands.
-/	Sets SAVEDIR to %p/%c and SAVENAME to %a.

Commands for *nn*: No News is Good News

This is the command syntax for nn:

```
nn [ options ] [ newsgroup ¦ +folder ¦ file ]...
nn -g [ -r ]
nn -a0 [ newsgroup ]...
```

Select (Toggle)

a-z0-9	Specified article.
x-y	Range x to y.
x*	Same subject as x.
.	Current article.
@ ~	Reverse/undo all selections.
=regexp	Matching subjects (=. selects all).
L/JJJJ	Leave/change attributes.

Movement Keys

,	Next menu line.
/	Previous menu line.
Space	Next menu page (if any).

301

< >	Previous/next menu page.
^ $	First/last menu page.

Show Selected Groups

Space	Show (only when on last menu page).
z	Show now, and return to this group afterwards.
X	Show now, and continue with next group.

Go to Other Groups

X	Update current group, skip to next.
N P	Go to next/previous group.
G	Go to named group or open a folder.
B A	Go back/forward in groups already read.
Y	Group overview.
~/.nn/init:	Defines group presentation sequence.

Miscellaneous

U C	Unsubscribe/cancel.
:man	Online manual.
F R M	Follow-up/Reply/Mail.
:help	More online help.
S O W	Save articles.
!	Shell escape.
:post	Post new article.
"	Change menu layout.
:unshar :decode :patch	Unpack articles.
Q	Quit nn.

Frequently Used Options

-a0	Catch up on unread articles and groups.
-g	Prompt for the name of a newsgroup or folder to be entered (with completion).
-r	Used with -g to prompt repeatedly for groups to enter.

-1*N*	Print only the first *N* lines of the first page of each article before prompting to continue. This is useful on slow terminals and modem lines if you want to see the first few lines of longer articles.
-s*WORD*	Collect only articles that contain the string *WORD* in their subject (case is ignored). This is normally combined with the -x and -m options to find all articles on a specific subject.
-s/*regexp*	Collect only articles whose subject matches the regular expression *regexp*. This is normally combined with the -x and -m options to find all articles on a specific subject.
-n*WORD* or -n/*regexp*	Same as -s, except that it matches the sender's name instead of the article's subject. This is normally combined with the -x and -m options to find all articles from a specific author. It cannot be mixed with the -s option!
-i	Normally, searches with -n and -s are case independent. Using this option, the case becomes significant.
-m	Merge all articles into one "meta group," instead of showing them one group at a time. This is normally used with the -x and -s options to get all the articles on a specific subject presented on a single menu (when you don't care about the group to which they belong). When -m is used, no articles are marked as read.
-x[*N*]	Present (or scan) all (or the last *N*) unread as well as read articles. When this option is used, nn will not mark unread articles as read (that is, .newsrc is not updated).
-X	Read/scan unsubscribed groups also. Most useful when looking for a specific subject in all groups, read or unread, for example, nn -mxX -s*Subject*. If none of these arguments is given, only subscribed newsgroups will be

used. Otherwise, only the specified newsgroups and files will be collected and presented. In specifying newsgroups, the following "meta notation" can be used: if the newsgroup ends with a period (or with .all)—for example, comp.sources.—all subgroups of the newsgroup will be collected. If a newsgroup starts with a period (or all.)—for example, .sources.unix—all the matching subgroups will be collected. The argument all identifies all (subscribed) newsgroups.

The following commands work in both selection mode and reading mode.

?	Help. Gives a one-page overview of the commands available in the current mode.
Control+L	Redraw screen.
Control+R	Redraw screen (same as ^L).
Control+P	Repeat the last message shown on the message line. The command can be repeated to shown successively previous messages (the maximum number of saved messages is controlled by the message-history variable.)
!	Shell escape. The user is prompted for a command, which is executed by your favorite shell (see the shell variable).
Q	Quit nn. When you use this command, you lose neither unread articles in the current group nor the selections you might have made (unless the articles are expired in the meantime).
V	Print release and version information.
:command	Execute the command by name. This form can be used to invoke any of nn's commands, including those that cannot be bound to a key (such as :coredump) or those that are not bound to a key by default (such as post and unshar). Related and basic variables are these: backup, backup-suffix, confirm-auto-quit, expert, mail, message-history, new-group-action, newsrc, and quick-count.

The Threaded Read News Program, *trn*

Here is the trn command synopsis:

```
trn [options] [newsgroups]
```

Article Selection Commands

n,SP	Find next unread article (follows discussion-tree in threaded groups).
N	Go to next article.
Control+N	Scan forward for next unread article with same subject in date order.
p, P, Control+P	Same as n, N, ^N, only going backward.
_N, _P	Go to the next/previous article numerically.
-	Go to previously displayed article.
<, >	Browse the previous/next selected thread. If no threads are selected, all threads that had unread news upon entry to the group are considered selected for browsing. Entering an empty group browses all threads.
[,]	Go to article's parent/child (try left-arrow and right-arrow also).
(,)	Go to article's previous/next sibling (try up-arrow or down-arrow also).
{, }	Go to tree's root/leaf.
t	Display the entire article tree and all its subjects.
num	Go to specified article number.
range{,range}:command{:command}	Apply one or more commands to one or more ranges of articles.

	Ranges are of the form: `number ¦ number-number`. You may use `.` for the current article, and `$` for the last article. Valid commands are `e`, `j`, `m`, `M`, `s`, `S`, `t`, `T`, `¦`, `+`, `++`, `-`, and `--`.
`:cmd`	Perform a command on all the selected articles.
`/pattern/modifiers`	Scan forward for article containing pattern in the subject line. (Use `?pat?` to scan backward; append `f` to scan from lines, `h` to scan whole headers, `a` to scan entire articles, `r` to scan read articles, `c` to make case-sensitive.)
`/pattern/modifiers:command{:command}`	Apply one or more commands to the set of articles matching *pattern*. Use a `K` modifier to save entire command to the KILL file for this newsgroup. Commands `m` and `M`, if first, imply an `r` modifier. Valid commands are the same as for the range command.
`f,F`	Submit a follow-up article (`F` means "include this article").
`r,R`	Reply through net mail (`R` means "include this article").
`e dir{¦command}`	Extract to directory using `/bin/sh`, `uudecode`, `unship`, or *command*.
`s ...`	Save to file or pipe by `sh`.
`S ...`	Save by preferred shell.
`w,W`	Like `s` and `S` but save without the header.
`¦ ...`	Same as `s¦....`.
`c`	Cancel this article, if yours.
`Control+R,v`	Restart article (`v` is verbose).

Control+X	Restart article, rot13 mode.
c	Catch up (mark all articles as read).
b	Back up one page.
Control+L	Refresh the screen (you can get back to the pager with this).
X	Refresh screen in rot13 mode.
^	Go to first unread article. Disables subject search mode.
$	Go to end of newsgroup. Disables subject search mode.
#	Print last article number.
&	Print current values of command-line switches.
&switch {switch}	Set or unset more switches.
&&	Print current macro definitions.
&&def	Define a new macro.
j	Junk this article (mark it read). Stays at end of article.
m	Mark article as still unread.
M	Mark article as read but to-return on group exit or Y command.
Y	Yank back articles marked as to-return by the M command.
k	Kill current subject (mark articles as read).
,	Mark current article and its replies as read.
J	Junk entire thread (mark all subjects as read in this thread).
A	Add current subject to memorized commands (selection or killing).
T	Add current thread or subthread to memorized

	commands (selection or killing).
K	Mark current subject as read and save command in KILL file.
Control+K	Edit local KILL file (the one for this newsgroup).
=	List subjects of unread articles.
+	Start the selector in whatever mode it was last in.
_a	Start the article selector.
_s	Start the subject selector.
_t	Start the thread selector.
_T	Start the thread selector if threaded (otherwise, the subject selector).
U	Unread some news—prompts for thread, subthread, all, or select.
u	Unsubscribe from this newsgroup.
q	Quit newsgroup.

Commonly Used Editor Commands

This appendix lists the commonly used commands for the vi, sed, and Emacs editors.

vi Editor Commands

The vi editor is a screen editor. After you access the editor, you can use the following commands. The ^ represents the Control key; for example, ^B means press the Control key while you press B. Remember that vi is case-sensitive, so B is different from b.

^B	Page up by one screen.
^D	Page down by half screens (setting count).
^E	Put one more line at the bottom of screen.
^F	Page down by one screen.
^G	File status.
^H	Move left by one character or backspace in insert mode.
^J	Move down by one line.
^L	Redraw screen.
^M	Move down by one line and insert line (to first nonblank).
^N	Move down by one line.
^P	Move up by one line.
^R	Redraw screen.
^T	Indent text.
^U	Page up by half screens (setting count).
^V	Input a literal character (insert mode only).
^W	Go to beginning of word (insert mode only).
^Y	Put one more line at the top of screen.
^[<Escape>	Leave input mode, return to command mode.
^^	Switch to previous file.
<space>	Move right by columns.
!	Filter through command to motion.
$	Move to end of line.
(	Move back a sentence.
)	Move forward a sentence.
+	Move to first character on next line.
, (comma)	Repeat and reverse last F, f, T, or t search.

-		Move to first character of previous line.
. (period)		Repeat the last command.
/		Search forward.
0		Move the beginning of the line.
: (colon)		Ex command.
; (semicolon)		Repeat last F, f, T, or t search.
?		Search backward.
A		Append to the end of line.
B		Move back one word.
C		Change to end-of-line.
D		Delete to end-of-line.
E		Move to end of word.
G		Go to specific line.
H		Move to top of screen.
I		Insert at beginning of line.
J		Join lines.
L		Move to bottom of screen.
M		Move to midpoint of screen.
N		Search in reverse direction.
O		Insert new line above current line.
P		Paste buffer before cursor.
Q		Quit vi and switch to ex mode.
R		Replace characters.
S		Change and replace whole line.
T		Find search before character in current line.
U		Restore the current line.
W		Move to beginning of next word.
X		Delete character before cursor.
Y		Yank a copy of current line into buffer.
ZZ		Save file and exit.
[[		Move back a section.
]]		Move forward a section.
^		Move to first character (nonblank) of current line.

a	Append text after cursor.
b	Move back one word.
c	Allow change to text.
d	Allow delete of text.
e	Move to end of word.
f	Find next search on current line.
h	Move left by one character.
i	Insert text before cursor.
j	Move down by one line.
k	Move up by one line.
l	Move right by one character.
n	Repeat last search.
o	Insert new line below current line.
p	Paste text after cursor.
r	Replace current character.
s	Substitute current character.
t	Find search before character in current line.
u	Undo last change.
w	Move to beginning of next word.
x	Delete current character.
y	Copy text into buffer.
z	Redraw window.
{	Move to beginning of previous paragraph.
n¦	Move to *n*th column.
}	Move to beginning on next paragraph.
~	Reverse case.

sed Editor Commands

The sed editor is a stream editor; sed commands are entered at the shell prompt to process one or more lines in one or more files.

SYNOPSIS

```
sed [-an] command [file ...]
sed [-an] [-e command] [-f command_file] [file ...]
```

The following command options are available:

-a	The files listed as parameters for the "w" functions are created or truncated before any processing begins, by default. The -a option causes sed to delay opening each file until a command containing the related "w" function is applied to a line of input.
-e *command*	Append the editing commands specified by the command argument to the list of commands.
-f *command_file*	Append the editing commands found in the file *command_file* to the list of commands. The editing commands should each be listed on a separate line.
-n	By default, each line of input is echoed to the standard output after all of the commands have been applied to it. The -n option suppresses this behavior.

The form of a sed command is as follows:

```
[address[,address]]function[arguments]
```

sed Command Summary

```
[2addr] function-list
```

Execute *function-list* only when the pattern space is selected.

```
[1addr]a\
text
```

Write text to standard output immediately before each attempt to read a line of input, whether by executing the "N" function or by beginning a new cycle.

```
[2addr]b[label]
```

Branch to the ":" function with the specified label. If the label is not specified, branch to the end of the script.

```
[2addr]c\
text
```

Delete the pattern space. With 0 or 1 address or at the end of a 2-address range, text is written to the standard output.

`[2addr]d`

Delete the pattern space and start the next cycle.

`[2addr]D`

Delete the initial segment of the pattern space through the first newline character and start the next cycle.

`[2addr]g`

Replace the contents of the pattern space with the contents of the hold space.

`[2addr]G`

Append a newline character, followed by the contents of the hold space, to the pattern space.

`[2addr]h`

Replace the contents of the hold space with the contents of the pattern space.

`[2addr]H`

Append a newline character, followed by the contents of the pattern space, to the hold space.

```
[1addr]i\
text
```

Write text to the standard output.

`[2addr]l`

Write the pattern space to the standard output in a visually unambiguous form. This form is as follows:

backslash	\
alert	\a
form-feed	\f

newline	\n
carriage-return	\r
tab	\t
vertical tab	\v

`[2addr]n`

Write the pattern space to the standard output if the output has not been suppressed, and replace the pattern space with the next line of input.

`[2addr]N`

Append the next line of input to the pattern space, using an embedded newline character to separate the appended material from the original contents. Note that the current line number changes.

`[2addr]p`

Write the pattern space to standard output.

`[2addr]P`

Write the pattern space, up to the first newline character to the standard output.

`[1addr]q`

Branch to the end of the script and quit without starting a new cycle.

`[1addr]r file`

Copy the contents of `file` to the standard output immediately before the next attempt to read a line of input. If `file` cannot be read for any reason, it is silently ignored and no error condition is set.

`[2addr]s/regular expression/replacement/flags`

Substitute the replacement string for the first instance of the regular expression in the pattern space. Any character other than backslash or newline can be used instead of a slash to delimit the regular expression and the replacement. Within the regular expression and the replacement, the regular expression delimiter itself can be used as a literal character if it is preceded by a backslash. The optional flags are as follows:

`0 ... 9`	Make the substitution only for the *n*th occurrence of the regular expression in the pattern space.
`g`	Make the substitution for all non-overlapping matches of the regular expression, not just the first one.
`p`	Write the pattern space to standard output if a replacement was made. If the replacement string is identical to that which it replaces, it is still considered to have been a replacement.
`file`	Append the pattern space to file if a replacement was made. If the replacement string is identical to that which it replaces, it is still considered to have been a replacement.

`[2addr]t [label]`

Branch to the *label: function* bearing the label if any substitutions have been made since the most recent reading of an input line or execution of a "t" function. If no label is specified, branch to the end of the script.

`[2addr]w file`

Append the pattern space to the file.

`[2addr]x`

Swap the contents of the pattern and hold spaces.

`[2addr]y/string1/string2/`

Replace all occurrences of characters in *string1* in the pattern space with the corresponding characters from *string2*. Any character other than a backslash or newline can be used instead of a slash to delimit the strings. Within *string1* and *string2*, the delimiter itself can be used as a literal character if it is preceded by a backslash.

```
[2addr]!function
[2addr]!function-list
```

Apply the *function* or *function-list* only to the lines that are not selected by the addresses.

```
[0addr]:label
```

This function does nothing; it bears a label to which the b and t commands may branch.

```
[1addr]=
```

Write the line number to the standard output, followed by a newline character.

```
[0addr]
```

Empty lines are ignored.

```
[0addr]#
```

The # and the remainder of the line are ignored (treated as a comment), with the single exception that if the first two characters in the file are #n, the default output is suppressed. This is the same as specifying the -n option on the command line.

Emacs Editor Commands

Emacs is a screen-oriented editor. Emacs commands often require use of the Esc key. If your keyboard doesn't have an Esc key, try the Alt key instead.

Basic Cursor and Screen Control Commands

Ctrl+v	Move forward one screen.
Esc+v	Move backward one screen.
Ctrl+l	Clear screen and redisplay everything.
Esc+f	Move forward a word.
Esc+b	Move backward a word.
Esc+<	Move to the beginning of the file.
Esc+>	Move to the end of the file.

Ctrl+f	Move forward a character.
Ctrl+b	Move backward a character.
Ctrl+n	Move to next line.
Ctrl+p	Move to previous line.
Ctrl+a	Move to beginning of line.
Ctrl+e	Move to end of line.
Esc+a	Move back to beginning of sentence.
Esc+e	Move forward to end of sentence.
Esc+<	Go to beginning of file.
Esc+>	Go to end of file.
Esc+r	Move cursor to the line in the middle of window.
Esc+f	Move cursor forward one word.
Esc+b	Move backward one word.
Ctrl+u<number> <command>	Repeat what follows a specific number of times.
Ctrl+g	Stop an active operation, or erase a numeric argument or the beginning of a command.
Ctrl+x 1	Retain one window (kill all other windows).
Ctrl+x Ctrl+c	Exit Emacs editor.
Ctrl+z	Temporarily exit to shell.
Ctrl+x <n>	Split screen into <n> windows.
Ctrl+X o	Switch between the windows.
Ctrl+h a	Access the apropos help system.
Ctrl+x k	Remove help text.

Major Mode Commands

Esc+x fundamental	Activates fundamental mode.
Esc+x text-mode	Activates text mode.
Ctrl+h m	Access help on current major mode.

Minor Mode Commands

Esc+x auto-fill-mode	Toggle autofill on or off.
Esc+x auto-save-mode	Toggle autosave on or off.
Esc+x	Toggle overwrite mode on or off.

Editing Commands

Ctrl+d	Delete the character to the right of the point.
Delete key	Erase the character to the left of the point.
Esc+d	Kill the word to the right of the point.
Esc+Delete	Kill the word to the left of the point.
Esc+k	Kill the whole sentence to the right of the point.
Ctrl+k	Kill from the cursor to the end of the line.
Ctrl+x u	Undo the most recent change.
Ctrl+y	Yank back killed text.
Ctrl+x Ctrl+b	List buffers.
Ctrl+x l	Get rid of buffer list.
Ctrl+x s	Save some buffers.
Ctrl+x Ctrl+s	Save file.

Search and Replace Commands

Ctrl+s+Esc+Ctrl+w	Search for text in the forward direction.
Ctrl+r Esc Ctrl+w	Search for text in the backward direction.
Esc+x	Replace-string prompt for text to find and replacement text.
Esc+%	Search for text and prompt for replace.
Ctrl+h or ?	Display a list of all of the possible responses.
space bar or y	Perform the replacement.
Delete or n	Skip this occurrence.
<Esc>	Exit without replacing any more text.
Ctrl+x Ctrl+f	Find file and read it into buffer.
Ctrl+s	Search forward.
Esc+v	Move back.

Control Letters: When and Why to Use Each

To use these control letters, hold down the Control key and press the appropriate letter.

Control+\   quit

Use this command to terminate a currently running program and to generate a "core dump" or image of the process when it is quit.

> **NOTE**
>
> The term *core dump* means that the operating system is copying what is in memory to a file to read by a programmer to figure out what went wrong.

Control+c   delete

Use this command to interrupt and terminate a process that is currently running. Unlike the Control+\ command, this sequence does not generate a core dump of the process.

Control+d   EOF or logout

Use this command when you are editing a file and must include an end-of-file character.

Also, use this command at the shell prompt to quit the shell program and subsequently log out of UNIX.

Control+g   ring bell

Use this command when you want to insert a "ring bell" command in a file to be processed later by UNIX. The ringing of the system bell can alert you that a specific event has occurred (for example, a file has been printed).

Control+h   backspace

Use this command to erase the preceding character in your input line. This is useful when the Backspace key is not recognized by the currently running program.

Control+i   tab

Use this command to generate a tab character. This performs the same function as the Tab key on your keyboard.

Control+m   return

Use this command to perform the same function as the Enter key on your keyboard.

Control+q	resume output
	Use this command to resume output to the terminal when output has been previously suspended by entering Control+s.
Control+s	stop output
	Use this command to temporarily suspend output to the terminal. This can be useful when output is being displayed rapidly across your monitor. See also Control+q.
Control+u	line kill
	Use this command to erase the entire command line.
Control+z	switch to a shell level
	Use this command to switch between multiple interactive shells started with the shl command. This is useful when you need to run several tasks concurrently. Each shell is started with the shl program; you can then switch between tasks with the Control+z command sequence.

Glossary

absolute pathname The full filename, also called *basename* of a UNIX file, that locates exactly where the file can be found in the UNIX directory-tree structure. This name starts at the root directory and proceeds through each subdirectory to the filename itself. See also *relative pathname*.

account name The name of a legitimate user on the UNIX system. This name is necessary to log in to UNIX. Each account name is associated with an account password.

alias A synonym for a program or a string of programs. Used to assign long, tedious commands to a short symbol name.

anonymous ftp A file transfer method that allows access to Internet sites established for public information access. Users log in as anonymous and use the UNIX `ftp` program to retrieve files.

append Add information to the end. Using `>> filename` in a command line appends the command output to the end of the specified file. If you are editing a file, an append command adds what you type after the current cursor position.

application A program created to perform a specific task.

argument A value or option passed to a program that is to be acted upon or that causes changes in the way the program executes.

bang Among UNIX users, a common expression for the exclamation (!) mark. A bang functions as an automatic shell parameter, identifying the process identification number, or PID, of the last background command invoked. With some applications, such as the vi editor and mail, the exclamation mark used with a UNIX command as in *!command* escapes to the shell. ! is used as the not operator in logical expressions.

buffer A temporary storage area for data being processed by an application.

central processing unit The "brain" of the computer. It manages all other activity. See *CPU*.

command interpreter A program that interprets and processes each command line that you enter at the prompt (usually called a shell). Several shells are available, including the Bourne, C, and Korn shells. See *shell*.

command line A line of text that you send to the computer as a command. The line of text includes a command name and associated arguments and is terminated by pressing the Enter key.

command mode One of two modes that can be active while the vi editor is used. While this mode is active, keystrokes are interpreted as commands rather than text to be inserted in the file (for example, input mode). When vi is invoked, this is the initial mode.

computing environment See *environment*.

control characters A character sequence, typically entered by pressing simultaneously the Control (Ctrl) key and another letter on the keyboard, that controls input and output at the terminal. For example, Ctrl+m is the same as typing Enter. Ctrl+d identifies the end of input to a program.

CPU The computer's central processing unit, or "brain," which manages all activity in the computer.

current working directory The directory in which current work is performed. This is the first place that UNIX looks before searching the PATH shell parameter for performing all command processing and file manipulation.

directory A branch in the UNIX tree-structured file system where subordinate files and subdirectories are stored. See also *root directory, home directory,* and *current working directory*.

downsizing Reducing an organization's computing dependency on mainframes, at the same time enhancing the use of networked PCs and workstations. Euphemistically called *rightsizing*.

e-mail Electronic mail. E-mail consists of messages and embedded files sent from one computer to another either on the same network or across multiple networks. The basic UNIX e-mail command is mail.

editor An application used to create and modify the contents of a UNIX file. UNIX editors include Emacs, sed, and vi. An editor differs from a word processor in that an editor is typically used for manipulating text and data contained in a file; a word processor, on the other hand, also encompasses document-production resources.

environment   The shell configuration that is currently active. The environment is set up when you log in to UNIX and is defined by a table of variables. These variables control such characteristics as the prompt, the type of terminal being used, the home directory, and the search paths for commands.

environment variable   A shell parameter that defines the current operating environment.

escape sequence   A sequence of characters that turns off or "escapes" normal processing. Often, it is used to turn off a delimiter or special character so that those characters are interpreted as literal characters. In other cases, the sequence escapes to the shell for processing a UNIX command.

executable file   A program that can be run by simply entering the command name along with any associated command arguments.

execute permission   A permission assigned to a file that allows the file to be executed by the current user, owner of the file, or group of users.

file mode   The permission assignments for a file or directory.

global change   An editing transaction that modifies all occurrences within a file. Typically, this is accom-plished by a find-and-replace sequence on a specific character string.

gopher client   The user interface to services managed by a Gopher site (server). Typically, you select server options from a menu-driven interface, and the server processes the requested transactions.

gopherspace   Represents the linking of all the gophers running on computers connected to the Internet.

graphical-user interface   A shell to the operating system aimed at giving the user a iconic point-and-click way of executing programs, moving files, and so on. OSF/Motif, X Windows, and Microsoft Windows are examples of graphical user interfaces.

GUI   See *graphical-user interface.*

header   One of two basic components of an e-mail message, the other being the *body* of the message. The header contains such information as `Date:`, `cc:`, `From:`, and `Subject:`.

history   A listing of the most recent commands entered at the keyboard. This is useful for troubleshooting.

home directory   The current working directory at login. When you change the directory with the `cd` command without an argument, the current working directory becomes the home directory.

icon   A symbolic representation of a program or process.

input redirection symbol The less-than (<) character that is used to redirect standard input. In this instance, the command line retrieves input from what follows this symbol (for example, a file) instead of from the keyboard.

insert When editing a file, the insert command places all keystrokes in the current line without deleting characters already in the line.

Internet The growing global communication network consisting of thousands of educational, commercial, and government networks and connections.

kernel A set of programs that manage UNIX resources. Users interact with the kernel through the command-line interpreter.

keyboard The typewriter-like device that enables you to enter input into the computer. What you type is displayed on the computer monitor.

line editor An editor that is line oriented. Line-oriented implies that each line is the focus of the editor.

local variable A variable defined by the user for use by the shell. Local or personal variables supplement the standard shell variables and are available only to the shell in which they were created.

login name A valid account name for logging into UNIX.

login shell The shell that is started at login, according to the environment.

machine The computer on which UNIX is running.

mail A program for sending and retrieving e-mail. See *electronic mail*.

mainframe A multiprocessor computer capable of processing a high volume of transactions simultaneously.

major mode Character mapping used with the Emacs UNIX editor for interpreting keystrokes entered at the keyboard. Only one major mode can be used at a time. The default major mode is the "fundamental" mode. Others can be accessed for processing documentation or programming.

manual (man) page An online manual page describing the syntax and use of a UNIX command. Enter man *command* to see a man page.

metacharacters Characters with special properties, such as character matching, redirection of input or output, or return value of a shell variable. To process one of these characters as a literal, it should be preceded by a backslash or contained within single quotes. See *escape sequence*.

minor mode An editing mode for use with the Emacs UNIX editor. A minor mode is similar to a major mode, but with a smaller scope. Multiple minor modes can be active simultaneously. Common modes include auto-fill, auto-save, overwrite, and read-only mode.

monitor The computer display on which appear the keyboard sequences you type and the corresponding computer responses.

multitasking The capability of an operating system to perform several tasks simultaneously.

multiuser The capability of an operating system to allow several users to be logged in and executing processes simultaneously.

newsgroup An electronic magazine for a specific topic where publicly distributed e-mail is posted. Subscribers to the newsgroup read current messages and post new messages using one of the available newsreaders, such as `rn`, `trn`, and `tin`.

operating system A collection of programs that manage the operation of computer hardware and software. UNIX is an operating system.

parameters See *arguments*.

pathname The name of a UNIX file that locates exactly where the file can be found in the UNIX directory-tree structure. Refer to *absolute, full,* and *relative pathnames* in this glossary.

permission changes Modifications to the file mode of a file or directory. Permissions can be changed using the `chmod`, `chown`, or `chgrp` commands.

permissions The access rights for reading, writing, or executing a file. For each file, permissions are assigned for the owner of the file, users associated with the file's group, and all remaining users.

port A hardware port identifies a connector on a computer for cabling computer peripherals and resources such as the keyboard, monitor, printer, and modem. On the Internet, a port is an identifier for a service running on a remote computer.

postings Messages sent by users to a publicly accessible newsgroup.

power switch The switch on your computer that turns power on and off. In most configurations, it is important to perform a shutdown prior to turning power off to prevent corrupting the file system.

process An instance of a program that is currently running. Each time a program is executed, UNIX assigns a process identifier, or PID. It is possible for multiple copies of the same program to be running, each with its own PID.

program An executable file that, when invoked, processes a specific procedure.

prompt A system response displayed on your monitor indicating that the system is waiting for further input. The UNIX command line is preceded by the shell prompt.

read permission One of the three access privileges (read, write, execute) defined in a file's file mode and assigned to the file owner, user group, and remaining users. This permission allows the file to be read.

redirection operator   A symbol that is included in a UNIX command to change the source of command input or output. The greater-than symbol (>) causes output to be sent to another location, such as a file, instead of to the screen. The less-than symbol (<) retrieves command input from another source, such a file, instead of from the keyboard.

redirection symbol   See *redirection operator*.

regular expression   A character sequence specified as a pattern recognized by UNIX commands. Typically, the pattern is used for character matching. A regular expression may include literal characters as well as special symbols to indicate how the character sequence should be interpreted.

relative pathname   The pathname of a file identifying the location of the file in relation to the current working directory.

rn   A newsreader for reading messages posted to a newsgroup. There are many other newsreaders available, including trn and tin.

root account   The login account with superuser privileges. See *superuser*.

root directory   The directory at the base of the UNIX file system's directory-tree structure.

root password   The password to the special login account root. The root account carries superuser privileges.

script   See *shell script*.

sed   A standard UNIX stream editor. This editor retrieves input from a list of files or from the keyboard, batch processes each line according to the specified editing options, and outputs the results to the screen, unless output is redirected to a file. Because of its versatility, sed is often included in shell scripts.

shell   A program that serves as an interface between the user and the UNIX kernel. Several shells are available, including the Bourne shell (sh), the C shell (csh), and the Korn shell (ksh). Each shell has its unique features for using UNIX.

shell script   A sequence of shell and UNIX commands corresponding to a specific procedure. Typically, the script is stored in a file for later use.

shell variables   Parameters whose values define the environment in which the shell processes user commands. Default values are defined when you log in.

standard input   The default source for command input. Typically, the standard input is from the keyboard. When a redirection symbol is used, input can be accessed by another source, such as a file.

standard output   The default destination for command output. Typically, the standard output is to the monitor. When the redirection symbol is used, output can be sent to another destination, a file for example.

subscriber   A user who requests access to a specific newsgroup. A subscriber can read all postings to the newsgroup and send e-mail to the entire newsgroup or to individuals who have posted news.

superuser   A user who is not restricted by file permissions, for example, the root account. Superuser privileges are often restricted to users who administer the UNIX system.

switch   A command option.

system administrator   A user who maintains the UNIX system, assigning user accounts and privileges and managing the system configuration.

terminal   An input (keyboard) and output (monitor) device attached to a computer.

threads   Links between e-mail messages that allow you to read all the messages in a conversational form about a particular subject. Much like a telephone conversation, but each person communicates with e-mail messages. You will find these posted to newsgroups. Threaded newsreaders enable you to follow a conversation before moving to the next topic.

unsubscribe   Remove enrollment in a specific newsgroup or mailing list.

usergroups   Different classes of users. This is useful for organizational classification as well as for implementing a file-protection strategy.

variable   See *shell variables*.

veronica   An indexing service for the many gopher-site menus. This is particularly useful for performing broad searches for information across *gopherspace*.

vi text editor   A standard UNIX screen editor. This editor differs from line and stream editors in that you can move freely through the file, inserting and editing its textual contents.

wildcard   Special characters that represent actual letters or numbers. See *metacharacter*.

word processor   An application that allows you to create and edit a file using a screen editor and to lay out file contents as a document for publication.

workgroups   See *usergroups*.

workstation   A single-user computer running UNIX.

write permission   One of the three access privileges (read, write, execute) defined in a file's file mode and assigned to the file owner, user group, and remaining users. This permission allows the file to be modified.

Index

I

Symbols

A

W

X–Y–Z

GO AHEAD. PLUG YOURSELF INTO
MACMILLAN COMPUTER PUBLISHING.

Introducing the Macmillan Computer Publishing Forum on CompuServe®

Yes, it's true. Now, you can have CompuServe access to the same professional, friendly folks who have made computers easier for years. On the Macmillan Computer Publishing Forum, you'll find additional information on the topics covered by every Macmillan Computer Publishing imprint—including Que, Sams Publishing, New Riders Publishing, Alpha Books, Brady Books, Hayden Books, and Adobe Press. In addition, you'll be able to receive technical support and disk updates for the software produced by Que Software and Paramount Interactive, a division of the Paramount Technology Group. It's a great way to supplement the best information in the business.

WHAT CAN YOU DO ON THE MACMILLAN COMPUTER PUBLISHING FORUM?

Play an important role in the publishing process—and make our books better while you make your work easier:

- Leave messages and ask questions about Macmillan Computer Publishing books and software—you're guaranteed a response within 24 hours
- Download helpful tips and software to help you get the most out of your computer
- Contact authors of your favorite Macmillan Computer Publishing books through electronic mail
- Present your own book ideas
- Keep up to date on all the latest books available from each of Macmillan Computer Publishing's exciting imprints

JOIN NOW AND GET A FREE COMPUSERVE STARTER KIT!

To receive your free CompuServe Introductory Membership, call toll-free, **1-800-848-8199** and ask for representative **#597**. The Starter Kit Includes:

- Personal ID number and password
- $15 credit on the system
- Subscription to CompuServe Magazine

HERE'S HOW TO PLUG INTO MACMILLAN COMPUTER PUBLISHING:

Once on the CompuServe System, type any of these phrases to access the Macmillan Computer Publishing Forum:

GO MACMILLAN **GO BRADY**
GO QUEBOOKS **GO HAYDEN**
GO SAMS **GO QUESOFT**
GO NEWRIDERS **GO ALPHA**

Once you're on the CompuServe Information Service, be sure to take advantage of all of CompuServe's resources. CompuServe is home to more than 1,700 products and services—plus it has over 1.5 million members worldwide. You'll find valuable online reference materials, travel and investor services, electronic mail, weather updates, leisure-time games and hassle-free shopping (no jam-packed parking lots or crowded stores).

Seek out the hundreds of other forums that populate CompuServe. Covering diverse topics such as pet care, rock music, cooking, and political issues, you're sure to find others with the same concerns as you—and expand your knowledge at the same time.

Add to Your Sams Library Today with the Best Books for Programming, Operating Systems, and New Technologies

The easiest way to order is to pick up the phone and call

1-800-428-5331

between 9:00 a.m. and 5:00 p.m. EST.
For faster service, please have your credit card available.

ISBN	Quantity	Description of Item	Unit Cost	Total Cost
0-672-30326-4		Absolute Beginner's Guide to Networking	$19.95	
0-672-48440-4		UNIX Networking	$29.95	
0-672-48448-X		UNIX Shell Programming, Revised Edition	$29.95	
0-672-48513-3		UNIX Desktop Guide to the Korn Shell	$27.95	
0-672-30402-3		UNIX Unleashed (Book/CD)	$49.99	
0-672-22836-X		UNIX Desktop Guide to X/Motif	$27.95	
0-672-30171-7		UNIX Desktop Guide to EMACS	$27.95	
0-672-30466-X		Internet Unleashed (Book/Disk)	$39.95	
0-672-30485-6		Navigating the Internet, Deluxe Edition	$29.95	
0-672-30023-0		UNIX Desktop Guide to Open Look	$27.95	
		Shipping and Handling: See information below.		
		TOTAL		

Shipping and Handling: $4.00 for the first book, and $1.75 for each additional book. Floppy disk: add $1.75 for shipping and handling. If you need to have it NOW, we can ship product to you in 24 hours for an additional charge of approximately $18.00, and you will receive your item overnight or in two days. Overseas shipping and handling adds $2.00 per book and $8.00 for up to three disks. Prices are subject to change. Call for availability and pricing information on latest editions.

201 W. 103rd Street, Indianapolis, Indiana 46290

1-800-428-5331 — Orders   1-800-835-3202 — FAX   1-800-858-7674 — Customer Service

❑ 3 ½" Disk

❑ 5 ¼" Disk

Book ISBN 0-672-30460-0